FOR MEN AND ELDERS

For Men and Elders

Change in the Relations of Generations and of Men and Women among the Nyakyusa-Ngonde People 1875–1971

BY

MONICA WILSON

AFRICANA PUBLISHING COMPANY

New York

FOR THE INTERNATIONAL AFRICAN INSTITUTE

First published in the United States of America 1977 by
Africana Publishing Company
a division of
Holmes & Meier Publishers, Inc.
101 Fifth Avenue
New York, New York 10003

Library of Congress Cataloging in Publication Data
1. Wilson, Monica Hunter.
   For men and elders.

   Bibliography: p.
   Incudes index.
   1. Nyakyusa (African tribe)—Social life and customs.
2. Ngonde (African tribe)—Social life and customs.
3. Acculturation. 1. Title.
DT443.W52 1977   301.29'678   77-4203

ISBN 0-8419-0313-1

3-12-79

Printed in Great Britain

CONTENTS

MAPS

All the maps were drawn by W. O. West, Department of Geography, Rhodes University, to whom my thanks are due

TABLES

CASES

ACKNOWLEDGEMENT

For leisure to write this book I am indebted to the University of Cape Town for research leave; to the Center for Advanced Study in the Behavioral Sciences in California for a Fellowship, and to Girton College, Cambridge, for the Helen Cam Visiting Research Fellowship. The field-work on which the study is based was supported by the Rockefeller Foundation, the International African Institute, and the Carnegie Corporation of New York. Publication has been made possible by a most generous grant from the Ernest Oppenheimer Memorial Trust.

Helpful criticism of draft chapters was liberally given by four anthropologists who were Fellows at the Behavioral Sciences Center in 1971–2: W. H. Davenport, James Fox, Max Gluckman, and Robert A. LeVine; by colleagues in the School of African Studies, University of Cape Town: W. R. Huntington, Martin West, and Michael Whisson; by three historians, Robin Hallett, Christopher Saunders, and Leonard Thompson; by two economists, D. Hobart Houghton and Francis Wilson; and by Audrey Richards. I am most grateful for their patient reading and commentaries.

My great debt to the Nyakyusa and Ngonde people, and to other social scientists who have worked among them, is noted throughout the book. I thank the Director of the Afrika-Studiecentrum, Leiden, for permission to quote from the invaluable Leiden reports.

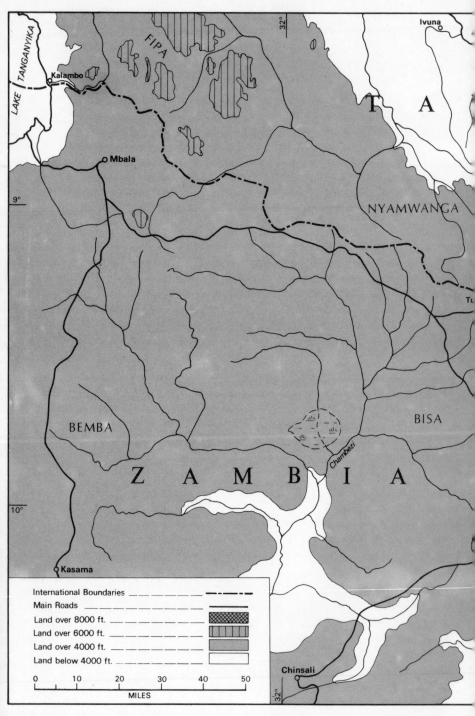

Map 1: The Ma

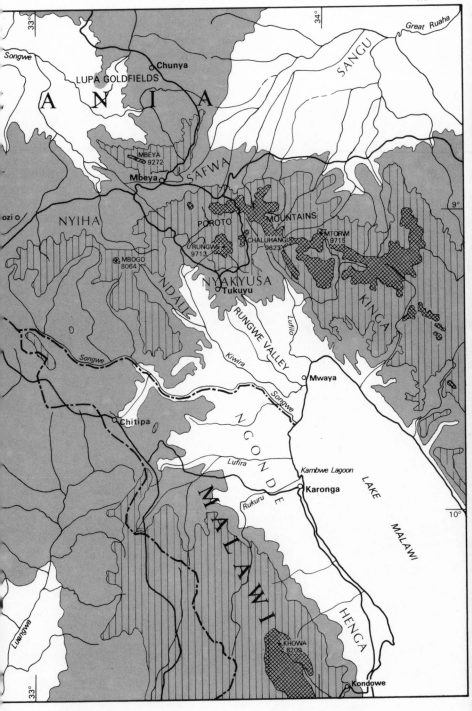

MAP 1

...anyika Corridor

Chapter 1

INTRODUCTION

The changing structure of Nyakyusa–Ngonde society

THIS book is about the Nyakyusa people of Tanzania and the Ngonde of Malawi, who live on opposite sides of the Songwe river and who speak one language. It is concerned with how marriage relationships and relations between generations have changed between 1875, when written records began, and 1971, when a new marriage law for Tanzania was promulgated. Chapter 1 contains an outline of Nyakyusa–Ngonde society when first observed by professional anthropologists in 1934–8, together with an account of remembered history, archaeological evidence, and the written record. A chronological table is given in Appendix I. The significance of diversity as a key to the study of change, and the sources of evidence are discussed in chapter 2.

The Nyakyusa and Ngonde were a people distinguished by the fact that they lived in age-villages. In 1934 every boy moved out of his father's village and built with his age-mates when he reached the age of ten or eleven, or rather older if leopards were troublesome: it was considered improper that a boy approaching puberty should continue to sleep at home. Boys built on land allocated by their fathers, at one side of the men's village, but they were not necessarily sons of one village only; they might be joined by contemporaries from other villages with whom they were friendly. Some continued to help in herding their fathers' cattle, and each boy hoed for his father in his own mother's fields, and perhaps those of his father's other wives, and he went home to his own mother for meals, or to any other 'mother' for whom he had hoed. But though bachelors ate at their parents' homes they still usually ate in the company of their own friends: a group of bachelors living in the same boys' quarter went round together, eating at the house of each one's mother in turn.

The boys' quarter grew as younger boys joined it, but when the eldest were perhaps seventeen or eighteen the quarter was closed and younger brothers were told to build elsewhere. Then, in their late twenties, the young men began to marry. They brought their wives to the age-quarter, built larger houses, and hoed fields there, so the settlement expanded and adjacent pasture land was brought under cultivation. Once he was married a man no longer went to his father's homestead for food, but was cooked for by his wife; however friends continued to eat together regularly. In 1935, Mwaisumo, himself a clerk, explained: 'A man eats with friends of other homesteads; it is the custom. Three men, each with his own homestead, may eat together. The custom is beginning to diminish now because poisoning [the English word was used] has become common. Some people do not wish to eat with others on that account, and clerks may refuse to eat together on account of differences in rank. Clerks are always poisoning their fellows: there have been many cases.' Day by day we saw small groups of men eating together, and perhaps their wives eating in a women's group, but more often a mother ate alone with her young children.

A number of villages of men and boys formed a chiefdom under a hereditary chief, and once in a generation power was handed over from fathers to sons. This occurred when the senior members of the sons' generation were in their late thirties, and their fathers ranged from about forty to seventy. At that time the two senior sons of the chief took office, dividing the old chiefdom between them and often extending its boundaries, and the age-quarters were rebuilt as villages of the ruling generation.[1] There was a redistribution of land in the whole chiefdom, presided over by the retiring chief and his village headmen. It was they, also, who selected headmen for each of the young men's villages now being legally established. They chose two senior headmen for each young chief and a number of others—usually between four and ten—depending upon the population of the chiefdom. In traditional law village headmen were commoners, and the office was not hereditary; both the son of a chief and the son of a retiring village headman were excluded from office, with the proviso that a headman who died might be replaced by his heir, to hold office for the generation in which the original headman would have held office, and no longer. The retiring chief and headmen selected young commoners who came from families of substance with the wealth necessary to provide hospitality; but character and ability in judging cases, summed up as wisdom (amahala), was an essential qualification. Until the early colonial period, courage in war was also necessary, for the village headman led his men in defence and attack.

During the great 'coming out' ritual the young men were expected to seize some of their fathers' cattle, and the land allocated to their villages impinged on that occupied by their fathers. The old men were required to 'move aside' to make room for their sons, and the land-marks of old villages show that they did so. Only one type of land was excluded from the new deal and that was the very fertile land in old craters: these fields (which could be cultivated during the dry season) were inherited like cattle within patrilineages. Land within a village was allocated by the headman, but since land was plentiful such allocation was rarely subject to acute competition (G. Wilson 1938). Cultivation was fixed, not shifting. Crop-rotation, green-manuring, and periodic fallow during which fields reverted to pasture were practised, and only for millet, cow-peas, and pumpkins was a seed-bed of ash prepared. Then it was weeds and grass which were burnt: there was no chitemene (pollarding trees and burning the branches) as among neighbouring peoples. In 1934 there were still unoccupied belts of fertile land between some chiefdoms which were not even used for pasture, and it has been shown that villages of up to seven successive generations remained within three miles of one another (M. Wilson 1959: 88–92, 101).

The ritual of 'coming out', involving the movement of some men, continued in at least one chiefdom until 1953 (M. Wilson 1959: 49–57, 100,

Pls 6, 7). It was dropped in Ngonde after 1913, and in some Nyakyusa chiefdoms by 1934, but the separation of fathers and sons in different age-quarters continued. The distinction between a village of young men legally established on its own land at a 'coming out', and an age-quarter occupied by boys or young men who had not yet come out, grew in importance as land became scarce.

A village was defined not only by recognized territorial boundaries and land rights, but by legal and ritual obligations between members. Fellow villagers were held jointly responsible for a member's torts; a litigant in a chief's court was invariably accompanied by his village headman; and in war or in defence of cattle and fields against dangerous animals, fellow villagers fought as a unit, relying one upon the other. Certain rituals to ensure productivity in the fields were led by the village headman and his wife on behalf of the members of the village (M. Wilson 1957a: 2–3).

From 1891, German missionaries north of the Songwe bought land and settled their followers on it as tenants of the mission, secure in tenure if they conformed to church rules, but liable to eviction if they became polygynists, or left the church for some other reason. By 1934 many Nyakyusa christians preferred to move off mission land but still to build together with fellow christians in a section of a village of their own contemporaries. Christian boys often built around the school they attended in their own christian age-quarter, and adherents of newly formed churches, such as the Watch Tower, built together in separate village sections or quarters (M. Wilson 1951a: 41–3, 48–9, 131; see map 5). Dr J. H. Konter noted that still, in the 1965–9 period, many Nyakyusa christians preferred to live with fellow believers.[2] In Ngonde such a separation never took root, for the Scottish missionaries advised their converts to remain in their own homes and convert their neighbours (M. Wilson 1959:166).

In the christian villages on mission land that were so important to the first generation of Nyakyusa christians, the leaders were elders of the church; until 1914 they were independent of control of the chief and even after 1925, under the system of Indirect Rule, though paying taxes and taking cases to chiefs, they retained a measure of independence. In the christian sections of pagan villages the leader was again an elder, if one lived there, sometimes a teacher, sometimes a respected fellow christian not holding any church office. Whoever he was, such a section leader was subordinate to the village headman established at the 'coming out' and looked to him for decisions in land disputes, or representation at the chief's court.

So long as the old chief lived there was, traditionally, a somewhat uneasy division of power between generations, but the old chief was expected to 'die soon' and, indeed, up to the colonial period he had been smothered by his senior headmen and priests if he were ailing, for the fertility of women, cattle and fields, and the welfare of the country as a whole were believed to be bound up with the health and vitality of the chief. He must die 'with the breath in his body' that the country might live (M. Wilson 1959: 63–5). His senior village headmen became priests serving the grove in which he was buried, and the villages of their generation shrank as the old men died and their heirs chose

not to move to their homesteads. The chiefdom split into two independent
chiefdoms, expanding into unoccupied land, each under a young chief, and
. the generation of sons who had 'come out' exercised full power, each chief
with his village headmen controlling his own court and the poison ordeal. The
leaders in war were the senior village-headmen of the ruling generation;
young men and boys from the age-quarters that had not yet 'come out' fought
as units, each under the leadership of the headman of the fathers' village to
which it was attached. Fighting was mostly for cattle and women: one chief
might seize another's cattle and retire, or he might drive his neighbour out of
his country, incorporating some of his men into one larger chiefdom. The
Nyakyusa–Ngonde structure was unique in that age-mates were expected to
live together through life, but the underlying principle was common: age-
villages were but one elaboration of a system, widespread in eastern Africa, in
which political and military power was vested in corporate age groups.

Change in this system took place piecemeal, and the date of change varied
with the degree of isolation: Ngonde which was most accessible to the outside
world changed first, and Selya which lay in the centre of the Rungwe valley,
cut off by rivers and mountains, changed last. The geography of the area is
important in understanding degrees of isolation and the pace of change. Lake
Malawi lies in the Rift Valley, walled in east and west by mountains, and
blocked to the north by Rungwe volcano which rises from the Rift to nearly
10,000 feet. The Nyakyusa occupy the valley tumbling down from this
mountain to the Lake, living in 1934 up to 6,000 feet, but up to 8,000 in 1971.
They spread out on the hot, malaria-ridden plain, barely over 1,200 feet in
altitude, which borders the nothern end of the lake, separated from Ngonde,
the western portion of the plain, by a great marsh, still sparsely occupied in
1937. The whole area is divided by rivers which are difficult to cross. In 1955 I
walked across the raging Kiwira on a traditional foot-bridge, made by felling
great trees on opposite banks and binding the tallest branches where they met
with bamboos, three slippery bamboos laid side by side spanning the chasm. I
watched with astonishment as a young man slung his bicycle on one shoulder
and followed me across. The main pass to the north lay at 8,000 feet, and cases
had been known of men dying of exposure as they sought to cross. A road had
been made before 1914, but until 1938 vehicles were constantly bogged in the
mud and post might come by runner. Ngonde is more accessible by water
than the northern tip of the lake, which lies between mountains and is subject
to squalls so violent as to sink a lake steamer in 1946. Ngonde means primarily
the Malawi plain, south of the Songwe river, but by extension includes the hill
area once forming part of the kingdom of the Kyungu. The name Rungwe is
used for the peak, the valley extending to the lake, the administrative district
embracing this valley and hills to the west, and the first Moravian mission
station built on the slope of the peak in 1891 (maps 1, 3, 5).

Though 'coming out' rituals were not celebrated in Ngonde after 1913,
they continued for a generation in some Nyakyusa chiefdoms: in 1935
Godfrey Wilson attended the 'coming out' of the 'sons of Mwangoka' of the
Kukwe line, north of Tukuyu, and in 1953 the 'coming out' of Mwanyilu
(177) 'grandson' of Mwaipopo (116) was celebrated in Selya.[3] By 1934 old

chiefs no longer 'died soon' after the 'coming out' of their sons: in Selya, Mwaipopo (116) and Mwaihojo (147) were elderly and retained power, but this was recognized as a constitutional change. According to local gossip: 'in former times Mwaipopo would not have survived his last illness; the priests would have smothered him'. As late as 1924 a Scottish mission doctor, working in Selya, reported a case in which he believed an ailing chief had been killed (quoted by Charsley 1969: 89-90).

In 1934 in Selya the obligation of old men to 'move aside' at the 'coming out' was taken for granted, but where coffee had been planted or substantial houses built men were unwilling to move, and by 1955 old men moved in few chiefdoms (M. Wilson 1959:206). In early accounts of age-villages it was noted that the system was dependent upon a redistribution of land in each generation and was unlikely to survive (M. Wilson 1951a:39-40). By 1958 Philip Gulliver (1958:29) was speaking of the 'break down in the essential age-basis' of village organization, and by 1971 J. H. Konter (who worked in villages which had never 'come out') was questioning whether the old men had ever, in fact, really moved to make way for the next generation. These differences in observation reflect both rapid change in social structure and the modification of oral tradition to fit the new system. The change has primarily affected the legal structure of villages and land rights. Age-quarters in which boys built together still survived in 1969, but the establishment of a young men's village as a corporate group on its own land no longer continued. As land became scarce rights of inheritance expanded to cover not only the precious fields in old craters, but increasingly valuable coffee, rice, tea, and vegetable land elsewhere.

Relations between generations thus changed radically. By 1955 young men had no certainty of acquiring political power, land, and cattle when the older members of their generation were in their late thirties, as they had fifty years earlier, and the separation of fathers and sons, which had been thought of as the basis of morality, was much modified. These shifts are one of the themes of this book.

Women played no part in the traditional age-based organization[4] except in so far as the senior wives of chiefs and village headmen participated in rituals the leaders performed, and the position of women in 1934 was far more subservient than it was in many other African societies, notably the nearby Bemba. But the position of women changed fast as missionaries proclaimed new values: the first Nyakyusa convert baptised was a woman and Moravians, following their custom at Herrnhut, appointed women as well as men as elders of the church. Courts in the colonial period supported a woman who refused to enter into a marriage distasteful to her, and they refused to recognize marriages contracted before puberty and later repudiated. Moreover, from the moment foreign families arrived, new patterns of relationships between men and women were observed. 'Kagile [M.W.], you do not know what being a woman is like. You *eat* with your husband!' This comment was volunteered in 1936 by a plain woman, a junior wife in a large household, who could aspire neither to being the *unkasikulu*, the senior wife whose son would be heir to his father, nor the *unkondwe*, the beloved. It epitomized the attitude of many Nyakyusa women to differences they noted between Europeans and themselves. Godfrey and Monica Wilson were living in a Nyakyusa village in a house like those of the neighbours, eating often in the open, and the subject of interested enquiry, much as the villagers were to them.

By 1934 marriage among the Nyakyusa was exclusively virilocal and descent patrilineal, and a legal union was dependent upon the transfer of cattle from the groom's lineage to that of the bride. There was a lively tradition of an alternative form of marriage-by-service with matrilineal descent but, although many cases were quoted in which such marriages had occurred, no such marriage in existence was recorded. Marriage-by-service was referred to as 'cock marriage', 'because chickens follow the hen'; it was regarded as a poor man's expedient which condemned him to an inferior status. Since, by 1934, cattle could be earned through labour on the Lupa gold-fields, self-respecting men no longer married in that fashion, but every man continued to hoe for some years for his in-laws, or pay a substitute to hoe for him; such service was an essential part of the marriage contract.

Polygyny was approved by pagan men and widely practised by the middle-aged and wealthy. The preferred form was for a wife to 'bring out' (*ukusakula*) a younger sister or brother's daughter to join her as a co-wife. Inheritance was usually fraternal within a 'house' of full-brothers, failing that it went to a half-brother who was linked through the practice of *ukukamanila*, 'milking-one-another's-cows'. This implied exchanging cattle between 'houses', and between the sons of brothers, at marriages and funerals. Cattle came in for daughters when they married and went out for sons, and cattle were required for funerals, so full-brothers, half-brothers, and parallel cousins assisted one another when cattle were needed, and returned the debt when cattle came in, obligations being honoured from one generation to the next. 'Milking-one-another's-cows' was spoken of as one of the means of holding a lineage-segment together.

Before colonial rule was effective, kinsmen were required to meet the debts of a son, brother, half-brother, or parallel cousin who had committed some crime such as theft, seduction, or murder, and was fined by the chief's court. Fellow members of an age-village were also corporately responsible for members of their village, but their obligation was less than that of kinsmen, for if one of their number were killed in revenge for the action of an age-mate who had fled, or their cattle were seized, they might legally recoup themselves by suing the kinsmen of the wrong-doer. In 1938 cattle given in marriage were still being attached for debts, which led to divorce: court messengers would actually seize cattle from a father-in-law to meet a fine owed by a son-in-law. Cattle belonging to a father, or the senior full-brother who had inherited from him, might also be seized, but not the cattle of a half-brother or parallel cousin. By 1965–9 the range of responsibility had been restricted still further. Konter (1974a:19) notes that court messengers might take a debtor to his father-in-law to seek cattle owing, and the father-in-law might 'ask his daughter to return home' temporarily, but this was not regarded as a divorce. As men began to earn cattle for themselves they sought to leave their property to their sons, rather than to a younger brother, and therefore some would refuse to accept family property from an older brother. Such a choice of filial, rather than fraternal inheritance had existed in exceptionally rich families before whites came but it increased greatly during the colonial period and by 1969 was the accepted practice. It reflected a further diminution of the solidarity of lineage-segments.

Lineages were not named nor were their boundaries precisely defined by a rule of exogamy (as in an Nguni clan): the range of recognized kinship was demonstrated most clearly by exchange of cattle, by avoidance of direct contact between father- and daughter-in-law and those identified with them, and by participation in common rituals. Such participation was not only a matter of convention or good manners; kinsmen were thought to be 'members one of another' in the sense that failure to attend a ritual might lead to sickness. Since the rituals were directed to the shades, a man could celebrate only at a homestead of his own lineage, or that of a maternal grandfather or his heir, never at the homestead of in-laws; but a woman was a member of two lineages: at marriage she joined that of her husband, but she retained ritual links with that of her father, and her children, though belonging to her husband's lineage, shared her links with her father (M. Wilson 1957a: 190–202, 222–6). The bond between two lineages established by the exchange of a woman for cattle was ideally permanent, a wife or husband who died being replaced by a kinswoman or kinsman, but practice and ideal diverged.

Lineages were dispersed since full-brothers, differing in age, mostly joined different villages. In the 1934–55 period many men moved from their home village either for fear of witchcraft or in pursuit of profit, but they were not precluded from celebrating rituals with kin. The closest kinship bonds were between parents and children, and between full siblings: the anger of a father or senior brother who was his heir, and therefore 'father', was thought to bring illness, sterility, and misfortune on a son or daughter, on the son's wives, and on the children of both son and daughter; and, reciprocally, neglect of obligations to his wards by an heir was thought to endanger his health. Kinship obligations were thus firmly supported by mystical sanctions (M. Wilson 1957a: 214–21, 226–8).

Nyakyusa themselves maintained in 1934–8, and again in 1955, that they chose to build in a village on account of the company of contemporaries, personal friendship, or economic opportunity, not on account of kinship ties, and a census of two villages supported this (M. Wilson 1959: 224–5), but it has been demonstrated that, once land grew scarce, many men were compelled to build near their fathers or senior brothers in order to obtain land (Gulliver 1958: 20–3, 32; Konter 1972: 43). Already in 1938, a few go-ahead men in Porokoto's chiefdom were building far apart on 'farms' which they planted with coffee, and a married son sometimes built on a corner of the 'farm'. It is likely that movement between villages *increased* as security in a foreign chiefdom grew, and the means of dealing with supposed witches through the poison ordeal diminished, but that movement decreased again as land became scarce (Konter 1974b).

Remembered history and archaeological evidence

The Nyakyusa–Ngonde people live in the Corridor between two great lakes on the edge of a watershed which has been an ancient crossroads in African history (see map 1). Iron-working had begun by the fourth century at Kalambo and iron tools dating from the third century have been found on the Ngonde plain (Clark 1974: II, 57; Robinson and Sandelowsky 1968; Fagan 1969: 160). Cattle-bones unearthed at Ivuna near Lake Rukwa have been dated to the thirteenth century (Fagan and Yellen 1968).

According to a consistent oral tradition, supported by genealogies, the chiefs (*abanyafyale*) came from the mountains to the east—BuKinga—and spread through a valley and over a plain sparsely occupied by small groups of hunters and cultivators who had no chiefs, no cattle, no iron, and, the myth goes, no fire. The chiefs thought of themselves as benefactors who had brought civilization—fire, cattle, iron—and commoner leaders, village headmen, related the same story: 'We ate our food raw'. The village headmen at each 'coming out' shared in the re-enactment of the myth as old fires were extinguished and new fires lighted and distributed from that kindled by the chief and senior village headman twirling the firesticks in a trough together. 'Eating meat raw' was associated with witches, and with the mystical power of commoners vis-à-vis chiefs; fire symbolized lordship (M. Wilson 1959: 7–99, 111). There is no word in Nyakyusa tradition of chiefs having fought their way in; only on Mbande hill in Ngonde was a former leader ousted. Elsewhere, it seems as if chiefs were welcomed as sources of wealth, of mystical power to create fertility and rain, and of authority to settle disputes, much as they were welcomed within historical times among the Alur (Southall 1953: 12–18, 92–6, 181–6).

Chiefs married commoner women and a balance of power was established between chiefs on the one hand and commoner headmen on the other. The spread of the chiefs and their followers can be traced in detailed local traditions and sacred groves which mark former villages of certain chiefs named in the genealogies (M. Wilson 1959: 87–92). From about 1925–41 a similar spread of Nyakyusa settlers, often led by the younger son of a chief, was continuing north of the Poroto mountains and one historian has supposed this to be an innovation (Wright 1971: 24), whereas in fact only the area of occupation was new, the process was ancient.

North of the Songwe river chiefdoms split each generation, and though small chiefdoms were sometimes absorbed by stronger neighbours no kingdom developed: indeed, the chiefdoms remained so small, numbering 100 to 3000 adult men in 1934, that S. R. Charsley (1969) and Marcia Wright (1971), following early German writers,[5] deny to traditional Nyakyusa *abanyafyale* the respect of the title *chief*. Charsley (1974: 422) states 'Nyakyusa society in the late 19th century has to be regarded as acephalous', but for such beheading no evidence is provided (M. Wilson 1975). In the Rungwe valley chiefs were connected by kinship ties, most deriving from two royal lineages. Groups of chiefdoms, such as those of Selya, Saku, Kukwe, and others, acknowledged a common origin and shared common rituals, but no political structure united them. Selya chiefs joined with Kinga (who spoke another language but to whom they believed themselves related by kinship) to make offerings at a hill shrine, Lubaga, to their founding hero and divine king, Lwembe. Certain other chiefs joined them at Lubaga, exactly who depending upon the occasion. However, no political structure united Selya or any other group of chiefs north of the Songwe.

South of the Songwe a kingdom did develop under another divine king, the Kyungu. The emergence of this kingdom was connected with the growth of a trade in ivory, exchanged for cloth. According to a precise oral tradition, collected in 1937 from Peter (the Kyungu then in office) and his hereditary nobles (*amakambara*), and others, the trade of ivory for cloth began with the first Kyungu, and the trade route went north over the Ndali hills until the time of about the tenth Kyungu, when it began to go south east across the lake. No ivory trade developed north of the Songwe, probably because of the geographical barriers. Here oral tradition is confirmed by the observation of Giraud in 1883 that the Nyakyusa were the only people he had come across in Africa among whom the chiefs did not claim a tusk of every animal killed (1890: 186). There was plenty of ivory: in 1882 elephant were 'the plague of the country' and fifteen were shot in one day near the mouth of the Mbashi (Moir 1923: 90, 109), but a trade in ivory from the Nyakyusa plain was only just beginning (Thomson 1881:1,269-74). Thomson also described the absence of cloth in Mwamakula's (106) chiefdom in 1879. Moreover, there was no tradition of Lwembe, the Nyakyusa divine king comparable to the Kyungu, distributing cloth as successive Kyungus had done. What did circulate from Lubaga, the grove of Lwembe, were iron hoes and salt, brought by priests from BuKinga, both to Lubaga and to a lesser shrine at Likyala (PaliKyala). The collection of hoes for Lubaga in BuKinga is described by Park (1966: 229-37).

The office of divine king was perpetual; when a Lwembe or Kyungu died he was replaced with a living representative. This continued in Selya until about 1913 (M. Wilson 1959: 18, 28, 93) when the last Lwembe died, and still continues in Ngonde, though by 1937 the nature of the office had greatly changed (G. Wilson 1939:76-85). The office of priest, whether royal or commoner, was also perpetual, but chiefs did not hold perpetual titles. If a chief died young he was replaced, like any commoner, by a brother or half-brother who took his name and social personality, but after the 'coming out' the old chief must 'die soon' and he was succeeded by his sons who represented their own generation.

The chiefs *probably* reached the Rungwe valley and the Ngonde plain in the late fifteenth or early sixteenth century. The genealogies of Nyakyusa chiefs provide a guide to the number of generations since forty-six lines are co-ordinated and a 'coming out' (which included the coronation) was celebrated only once in a generation in each chiefdom. Should a chief die young, his heir replaced him and no coronation was celebrated (M. Wilson 1958:12). Only for the divine kings, the Kyungu and the Lwembe, was installation not coordinated with generation. A change in pottery type on Mbande hill which was occupied by the first Kyungu was dated by

radiocarbon to 1410 ± 80 (Robinson and Sandelowsky 1968; Fagan 1969:161;
see M. Wilson 1972a: 136–47); but much more archaeological work will be
necessary before any certain dating of the arrival of the Kyungu and the
Nyakyusa chiefs can be given.

Slavery existed as an institution in Ngonde but not among the Nyakyusa.
Slaves were of two categories: war captives and the kin of those convicted of
treason against the Kyungu; however it appears that few slaves were sold
outside Ngonde until the late nineteenth century. The Lungwani traders who
came across the lake brought cloth and wire waist-rings (*amanyeta*) and took
back ivory. Perhaps they used slaves from elsewhere as porters to the coast (for
ivory without carriers was worthless) but there is no evidence in Ngonde
tradition of any regular export of slaves, not even those who were war
captives, before the arrival of the notorious Mlozi about 1875 (G. Wilson
1939: 39, 41, 49, 62). He exported slaves from Ngonde and by 1881 Arabs
were intervening in a dispute between Nyakyusa chiefdoms and seizing slaves
from the Nyakyusa plain (Fotheringham 1891; Moir 1923:132–51;
Macmillan 1972: 263–82). At the same time the Sangu chief, Merere, from
his stronghold in Utengule, north of the Poroto mountains, began raiding the
Rungwe valley and seizing slaves (Wright 1971:36–9). There was no
evidence in oral tradition of earlier slave-raiding in the isolated valley.

Ivory, cloth and white porcelain were repeatedly mentioned as the articles
of trade in Ngonde from the time of the first Kyungu; waist-rings made of
copper or brass wire are said to have come later from across the lake, and
waist-rings reached the Nyakyusa valley from Ngonde. But three other
commodities were important in trade for four centuries at least before the
colonial period: these were iron, pots, and salt. No iron-ore was known in the
Rungwe valley but it was smelted in the Kinga mountains to the east and by
the Nyiha to the west. Hoes and spears came from one side or the other (Elton
1879: 321; M. Wilson 1959: 97; 1958: 32). Quantities of pots were made from
a seam of clay with minimal shrinkage which lay along the north east shore of
the lake. This was exploited by local Kisi who, confined on a narrow ledge
between the lake and the Livingstone escarpment, made a living by selling
pots for their fill in grain. The pot-market at Pupangandu (map 5, page 31)
was in full swing when Joseph Thomson, the first traveller to leave a written
record of the north-east shore, passed that way in 1879 (Thomson 1881: I,
260–3) and clay of some pots found by archaeologists in Ngonde and dated to
the fifteenth century, resembles the Pupangandu clay. According to oral
tradition, salt came to the Rungwe valley with iron through BuKinga, from
Ubena, though archaeological evidence shows that the main centre for salt
production was Ivuna, north west of Rungwe. It is likely that the Kinga, who
in the period 1934–8 had a great reputation as porters, had long acted as
middlemen in a salt trade. By 1934 salt was one of the staples in every tiny
shop in the Rungwe valley, and small packets circulated as gifts.

In the 1934–8 period pots were traded by canoe round the northern shore of
the lake, and by carriers (often Kinga) through the Rungwe valley and across
to Mbeya and the Lupa gold-fields. Nyakyusa women also walked up to
twenty miles to buy pots for themselves at the market. It was said then that the

trade extended further than it had done in the pre-colonial period, but that trade in pots along the northern shore of the lake and some way inland over the plain was ancient. During the war of 1939–45 the trade increased, and extended further than in 1938, because imported goods were scarce.

These are but tantalizing glimpses of a long-continuing process of change. What is relevant to the discussion of relationships between men and women, and between generations, is that the Nyakyusa and Ngonde had had chiefs

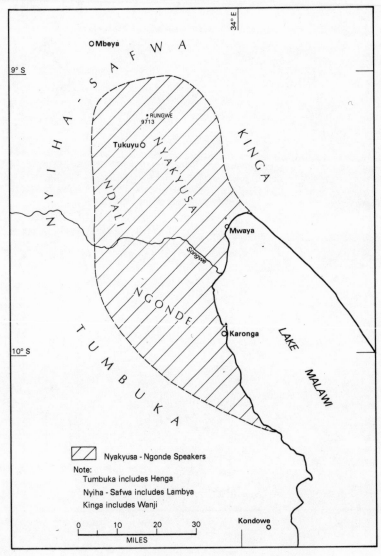

Map 2: Area of Common Language, 1934–8

12

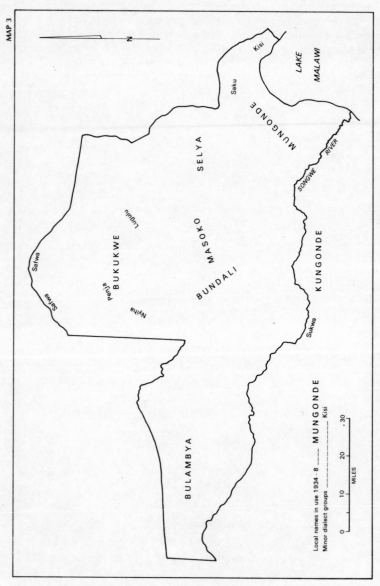

Map 3: Local Names, Rungwe District, 1934–8

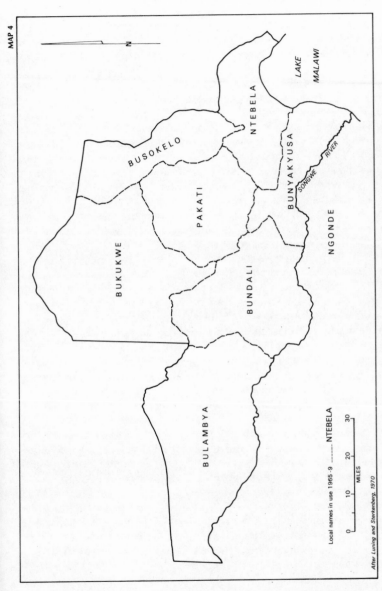

Map 4: Local Names, Rungwe District, 1955. After Luning and Sterkenburg 1970

and cattle for perhaps four centuries before the century of revolution we are to examine began; that domestic slavery had existed in Ngonde but was absent among the Nyakyusa; that the Rungwe valley remained so isolated that not even ivory was exported in any quantity before 1875, whereas the Ngonde plain was less isolated and the ivory trade dated from the arrival of the first Kyungu. Differences between localities in degree of isolation remained conspicuous right through the colonial period, and form a continuing thread in this book.

Neither the territorial boundary established in 1891 on the Songwe, nor the district boundaries of 'Neu Langenburg', or Rungwe, and 'North Nyasa' co-incided with language boundaries. Within Rungwe district in the 1934-8 period, and still in 1955, Safwa speakers predominated along the Poroto range, though there were Nyakyusa immigrants among them, and Nyiha and Lambya occupied the high Malila plateau and the hill country to the west, stretching across the Songwe, again with Nyakyusa speakers (particularly Ndali) as immigrants among them. Safwa, Nyiha, and Lambya spoke dialects of one language, here called Nyiha-Safwa (M. Wilson 1958: 28-32, 40-3; Harwood 1970: 1). In North Nyasa district, south of the Songwe, there were Henga and other smaller groups of Tumbuka speakers, and in the hills, Nyiha speakers (M. Wilson 1958: 39-40).

Within the valley spilling down from Rungwe volcano to the lake the terms used for localities changed through time (see maps 3 and 4). The term 'Nyakyusa' applied primarily to chiefs of the lake plain north of the Songwe, and those around Masoko, but by 1938 it frequently included Selya, and in many contexts was already extended in everyday conversation to include the Kukwe of the hills. A Kukwe man working on the Lupa gold-fields would call himself a Nyakyusa, though in Tukuyu he might call himself a Kukwe. Such extension of a local name has, of course, repeatedly taken place as the range of relationships has extended, the more inclusive name being used at a distance, the more particular name locally. The terms 'Nyakyusa' and 'Ngonde' are used in this book, as in previous publications, in an extended sense (G. Wilson 1936:254-5; M. Wilson 1951a:2). 'Nyakyusa' is used to include Selya, Kukwe, Ndali, Sukwa, and the small groups of Penja, Lugulu, Nyiha, and Kisi which they absorbed, as well as the people of Masoko and the lakeshore plain who are distinguished as 'Nyakyusa proper';[6] Ngonde is used to include Sukwa and others absorbed into the kingdom of Ngonde.

Between 1891 and 1963 terms for the states in which Ngonde and Nyakyusa were incorporated also changed. South of the Songwe 'Nyasaland Protectorate' was succeeded by 'Malawi'; north of the Songwe 'German East Africa' by 'Tanganyika' and then 'Tanzania'. To avoid confusion, I use a geographical term when possible, otherwise the name of the state as it was at the relevant period.

The written record

Contact with the outside world expanded rapidly from the late nineteenth century. Within eighty years colonial rule began and ended, and the independent states of Tanganyika (later Tanzania) and Malawi were established. The first whites to live in the area were Scottish missionaries and traders of the African Lakes Corporation, a company formed in response to the insistence of Livingstone on the need to establish 'legitimate trade' on the lake as a means of ousting slavers. In 1875, a party from the Livingstonia mission (then established at the south end of the lake) circumnavigated the lake in the mission steamer. They sighted the north shore and landed in Ngonde, where they attempted to buy rights to a harbour at Kambwe lagoon (Young 1877: 230–1). The following year James Stewart and Robert Laws, missionaries from Livingstonia, took Frederick Elton, British Consul in Zanzibar, and his party to the north end of the lake. Elton travelled through the Rungwe valley and over the Poroto watershed, reaching the Sangu chief Merere's stronghold, but he died on the journey back to the coast (Stewart 1879: 289–304; Elton 1879: 345, 385). Merere was then trading slaves to the coast and raiding the Rungwe valley to secure them, and Mlozi, an Arab from the coast, established himself in Ngonde and sent caravans of slaves across the lake. The nucleus of a British trading station was established at Kambwe lagoon in 1879, then moved north of the Songwe to a site near the mouth of the Mbaka, where Mwaya now stands. John and Fred Moir were the first managers of the African Lakes Corporation and the name Mwaya derives from Moir (Moir 1923: 191). The station shifted south again to Karonga in 1882 (Macmillan 1972: 265; Fotheringham 1891: 12) and Moir began building in 1884. Scottish missionaries started work at Kararamuka, near the present Kyimbila, in 1888, but in 1891 Moravian and Berlin Society missionaries arrived from Germany, and the Scots withdrew south of the Songwe. A war dragged on at Karonga between the slavers and the men of Ngonde supported by Nyakyusa, 150 Lakeside Tonga, and a handful of Scots from the African Lakes Corporation and Livingstonia mission under Captain F. D. Lugard (Lugard 1893: I, 51–167). Harry Johnston arrived in 1895 with more men and arms, and finally Mlozi was defeated and executed. From 1891, when the Songwe river became the boundary between a British Protectorate in Nyasaland and a German Colony in East Africa, differences between the manner of life of Ngonde and Nyakyusa increased.

The war between Britain and Germany which broke out in 1914 was fought in East Africa as well as in Europe, and the Nyakyusa endured a campaign which swept through their valley and involved many of them as porters, working under compulsion. After the peace settlement, when Tanganyika became a British Mandated Territory some differences between British and German rule disappeared, but policies in Nyasaland, which was a Protectorate, and Tanganyika which was held under Mandate, remained considerably different. Mission policies also continued to be different, though the Scottish mission administered the German stations north of the Songwe from 1920–25. The Livingstonia mission concentrated on education and, at Kondowe (Overtoun), established a school which produced the best educated Africans in Central Africa who, between 1920 and 1940, filled clerical posts not only in Nyasaland, but also throughout Southern Rhodesia, Northern Rhodesia, Tanganyika, and even the Belgian Congo. Among the Nyakyusa, education lagged behind, for many of the German missionaries were not

convinced that education was their function (see Wright 1971: *passim*), and
their central school at Rungwe mission was a matter of controversy among
them. But under the Mandate, agriculture developed among the Nyakyusa,
and coffee and rice were established as peasant crops for export, in a way they
were not south of the Songwe. Cotton flourished for a short time in Ngonde,
but this was the furthermost part of Nyasaland's 'dead north', and little
sustained economic development took place.

Under the system of 'Indirect Rule' in Tanganyika, the power of Nyakyusa
chiefs vis-à-vis commoners increased, and courts were created which heard
cases from groups of chiefdoms. A titular 'paramount chief' existed for a short
period but never exercised power. In 1955 it was suggested in Rungwe district
that a real paramount chief, such as had been appointed among the Chagga,
would be useful to speak on behalf of the Nyakyusa, and possible candidates
were mentioned, among them Peter the Kyungu of Ngonde, for, it was
thought, all those who spoke one language should be united. However, no
support for a paramountcy came from the British administration, and after
Independence the office of chief was abolished throughout Tanzania. It was
not abolished in Malawi, and Peter, the Kyungu who held office from 1927,
first as Regent, later as Kyungu in his own right, was a man of great personal
force. In 1953 he was succeeded by a son who died within the year, and Peter
returned to office, continuing in it until his own death in 1966.

Population increased during the colonial period, the Nyakyusa population
nearly doubling between 1931 and 1967, and the sparser population of
Ngonde increasing still faster. The increase was due to a higher birth rate and
the survival of more children and, in Ngonde, to immigration.

Since 1925, there has not only been an increase in population north of the
Songwe but a rapid growth of farming for a market, with the result that land,
once plentiful, has become scarce, and there is competition for it both between
generations and between men and women. In 1934 all the villages we knew
sought to attract new members, for the prestige of the village as a whole
turned on a large membership, and since, until the previous generation, its
success in war had also depended upon membership, size and prosperity were
linked in men's minds. The welcoming attitude to recruits was reflected in
everyday conversation, in hospitality, and in rituals celebrated. This did not
preclude competition for the *best* land, such as fields in old craters, but
adequate arable and grazing land was readily available, indeed, great strips
were still unoccupied, the haunt of buffalo and lion. By 1955, in two rice-
growing chiefdoms, only 17%–25% of the young men had paddy land of their
own. 'On the other hand, so deeply engrained is the notion of the prestige and
power which accrues to a village by virtue of the number of its inhabitants,
that headmen and villagers alike remain most reluctant to refuse to accept
newcomers . . .' (Gulliver 1958:25). By 1965–9 land had become family
rather than village property. 'Nowadays land belongs to and is used by
members of a nuclear family. In Buloma, a village on the Nyakyusa plain,
57·5% of the acreage had been allocated to the holder by a relative . . . (and)
in the most densely populated area . . . many people do not possess sufficient
land for sharing with their brothers. Consequently a large group of landless

people tend to come into existence' (Konter 1971 : 24–8).

Cattle were a resource comparable to land, but the number of cattle in proportion to population fluctuated. It fell dramatically with the rinderpest epidemic of 1892–3, rose again until perhaps 1940, but has since fallen. Control of cattle for marriage was, and still is, a matter of acute competition between men. The difference in status between chiefs and commoners was reflected in the number of cattle given at marriage for their wives and daughters, and in fines for adultery or seduction; other differences between rich lineages controlling many cattle and poor ones lacking cattle are discussed in chapter 4. Even within one family, father and sons were in competition for a scarce commodity. In 1934–8 the chief Mwaipopo (116), over 70 years of age and very wealthy by the standards of his place and period, was marrying young wives, while his sons in their thirties were still bachelors, unable to marry for lack of cattle. A son was required to hoe for his father, and cattle with which to marry were explicitly regarded as the reward for dilegence. But there were alternative means of acquiring cattle. In the pre-colonial period raiding offered a quick method whereby a bold man might enrich himself and marry:[7] after the 'coming out' a young chief was expected to lead his men on a raid in a neighbouring chiefdom, and at the same ritual they might legally seize some cattle from their fathers. No doubt most young men married at that point. After the 'pacification' under colonial rule raiding ceased, but employment for wages began, and many men earned the wherewithal to marry, often handing over their earnings to their fathers and receiving cattle in return, but sometimes buying cattle directly for themselves. Opportunity for employment and the balance between the number of cattle demanded at marriage, their cost, and wages earned were all important to young men. How this has changed through time is discussed in chapter 4.

The marriage age of both men and girls fluctuated, that of girls falling when wealth increased and the demand for brides, both by young men and older polygynists, was great. But it rose under the pressure of new ideas. The incidence of polygyny also fluctuated, first rising and then falling, and divorce increased (pp. 41–55, 111–17, 140–1, 189–92).

Employment for wages began on a small scale with the arrival of whites and their demand for carriers to transport their goods, as well as men to help them build and cultivate, cut firewood, draw water, clean and cook. It developed with the great demand for labour on the gold mines of South Africa during the first decade of the twentieth century (van der Horst 1942; F. Wilson 1972 : 4), and the demand for labour on coastal plantations in German East Africa during the same period. As already noted, many Nyakyusa were compelled to serve as carriers either for the German or British armies during the 1914–18 war, and after it there was a little local employment on coffee estates and one tea garden. 26,000 acres of land was alienated in the Rungwe district and a very small area in Ngonde, but already by 1934–8, any grant of land to whites was viewed as a threat. Plantation wages were very low and most men preferred to walk to the Lupa gold-fields, fifty miles from the Rungwe valley. There about sixty miners were at work in 1925 (MacKenzie 1925: 25) and by 1937 there were 7,000 Nyakyusa, as well as a large number of men from

Ngonde. In 1937 about 25% of the able-bodied Nyakyusa men were working outside Rungwe district, but seven out of eight of them were on the Lupa and working for short periods (M. Wilson 1951a: 16). From the northern district of Nyasaland (including Ngonde) 'probably 50%' of the adult men were away in 1935, many of them also on the Lupa (Nyasaland Protectorate 1936: 36; Read 1942). In the 1940s and 1950s large numbers of men from both sides of the Songwe went south to the gold mines of South Africa, to the coal mines of Southern Rhodesia, and to the copper mines of Northern Rhodesia (Gulliver 1957), Nyakyusa walked across the Tanganyika–Nyasaland boundary to sign on at Chitipa, whence they were flown south to the gold mines. From Rungwe district 14,000 men (25% of the total adult males) were absent and 90% of these were in the south in 1954. In 1955 wages and working conditions on the Copperbelt were considered better than in South Africa or Southern Rhodesia, but a man had to make his own way to the Copperbelt, whereas air transport to South Africa was provided from Chitipa. In 1963, after Tanganyika became independent, migrant labour to Southern Rhodesia and South Africa was prohibited; labour on the Copperbelt was being stabilized and, for the Nyakyusa, the opportunities of earning cash diminished abruptly. In contrast, men from Ngonde continued to work in South African mines and Malawians began to outnumber Tanzanians on the Copperbelt.[8]

By 1937 the wives of educated Ngonde men already took it for granted that their husbands would travel for work, and they were prepared to accompany them, but Nyakyusa women, other than prostitutes, or wives of settlers moving across the watershed to Mbeya district, rarely travelled: indeed for a man to insist on his wife accompanying him abroad was regarded by Nyakyusa women almost as a ground for divorce. By 1955 a great change had occurred: a bus service plied twice daily between Mbeya and Tukuyu and women, as well as men, travelled to and fro visiting kin, attending church meetings, shopping: KiNyakyusa was constantly spoken in Mbeya market. A few Nyakyusa girls attended secondary school outside Rungwe District and one had gone to Makerere University. Women began to accompany their husbands to the Copperbelt, and joked with me about how fearful they had been of travel twenty years earlier.

One effect of the employment of men as migrant labourers and the growing of cash crops, combined with population increase and pressure on land, was a fall in the food available per person. This was conspicuous in the Nyakyusa valley in 1955 when the food supply was compared with that in 1934–8, and such a fall has been widespread in Africa as labour was expended for purposes other than food production, and pressure on land increased. Shortage of food and the entry into the cash economy also eroded old values, and competitiveness which, with its stress on individual 'initiative' began to escape traditional restraints, has increased the difficulty of establishing economic cooperation in *ujamaa* villages. The rise in potential consumption, the increasing gap between income and wants, and the weakening of obligations to distribute wealth are continuing trends through the period.

Migrant labour directly affected the age-village organization in that young married men feared to leave their wives unsupervised, and began to place them in the care of their (the husbands') mothers, building for them to one side of the parental homestead 'in the bananas'. This was a direct negation of the traditional value of totally separating father-in-law and daughter-in-law.

As school education began and men learnt new skills, earnings varied with the type of employment, and access to education became of great importance in determining earnings. It also affected the balance between generations since it was mostly *young* men who became literate, and learnt a second language, and they knew more about the outside world than their fathers. With a few exceptions in Ngonde, education beyond the bare literacy required for baptism was pursued only by men for two generations after schools began, but suddenly, after the 1939–45 war, Nyakyusa women took to education as their sisters in Ngonde had begun to do rather earlier. The demand for educated wives began to change the attitude of Nyakyusa girls to education which, up to 1938, had been one of supreme indifference. In education as in other matters Ngonde women were the 'beginners'.

The effects of employment for wages and of literacy are to draw men and women away from village preoccupations and engage them in the ideas and activities of a wider world. The shift in this regard, already conspicuous for men in 1934, was apparent also for women by 1955. And a further effect of outside contacts is that the old order is no longer taken for granted: the hierarchy of age and sex is questioned. The shift from a society organized 'for men and elders' to one whose ideal is 'African socialism' is explicit in Tanzania, though not in Malawi, but in Malawi also the yeast of new ideas is fermenting in family relationships. With Independence many young men came into power. Whether young men will remain in power, or whether the revolutionaries, growing old, will generally claim a traditional African respect for age such as is already claimed by President Banda of Malawi, remains to be seen. What balance will be struck between men and women also remains uncertain, but the Tanzania marriage law of 1971, and the proposals of TANU put forward before the law was promulgated, are suggestive.

Increase in the range of relationships did not stop short with the colonial period, but has visibly extended as close relationships have been established with powers other than Britain and more people travel abroad. The influence of China, Holland, Scandinavia, Germany, and the USA is conspicuous in technical assistance, in education, and in investment. The Tanzam railway passed Mbeya and a branch through Rungwe district was begun in 1974. Local diversities within Tanzania and Malawi diminished, fostered in Tanzania by the use of Swahili in all schools, but national differences between Tanzania and Malawi increased. So also did diversity between rich and poor, urban and rural, educated and uneducated, conservative and radical.

NOTES

[1] The need for terms distinguishing legally established *villages* with their own land, and *boys' quarters* dependent upon their fathers for land became clear to me in 1969, during discussions with the Leiden team which had worked in Rungwe, and my suggestion of *age-quarter* in place of 'boys' village' was acceptable to them. I am indebted to the Leiden team for clarifying my ideas on this

and other points as well as for their great body of evidence on the 1965–9 period which has been used in this book.

[2] I am much indebted to Dr Konter for the gift of a copy of his unpublished Ph.D. thesis (1974b) and for permission to refer to it. In a few instances a fuller, earlier draft is quoted.

[3] A number after a name refers to the genealogy of the 'sons of Lwembe' reprinted in Appendix IIa, and a number preceded by K to the genealogy of Kukwe chiefs in Appendix IIb.

[4] A girl Ijonga (114) went through the 'coming out' ritual in Selya as a stand-in for an infant brother, just because she could have no claim to chieftainship.

[5] Alexander Merensky, upon whom both largely depend, had worked first in South Africa, where he had taken an active part in tribal politics. He viewed chieftainship in terms of the Pedi chief, Sekhukhuni, then creating a kingdom and defending his country against Afrikaner, Swazi, and Ndebele (see Wangemann, 1957).

[6] I have been scolded by Dr Wright (1972: 157) for extending 'Nyakyusa proper' to include Selya, as so many informants did. Here, to meet her criticism, I revert to the narrower usage.

[7] In South Africa in 1835, the opposition of whites to *lobola* (giving cattle in marriage) was due partly to the conviction that it led to cattle raiding (M. Wilson and Thompson 1969–71: 1,266). In 1972 President Idi Amin attributed raiding in northeastern Uganda to the fact that between 60 and 70 cattle were demanded in marriage among the Karamajong.

[8] The effects of long-term circulatory labour on communities in Southern Africa convince me that, though immediately inconvenient, the prohibition of migration was in the long-term interests of the Nyakyusa.

Chapter 2

A MODEL THAT MOVES

Change and diversity

MOST anthropologists are agreed that models of society which leave out time are inadequate: they are too far from reality to be illuminating theoretically, and of limited use in planning development. Our concern is not whether to study change in society but *how* to study it. Two problems beset us: the first is to find precise material on the changes that have taken place; the second to select relevant facts from the mass of happenings.

Most changes in a society begin as a divergence in the behaviour of one person, who is then followed by others. As the number following the innovator increases, the new pattern becomes the norm for a sub-group in the society, as when missionaries first established a school in BuNyakyusa in 1894 very few people attended, but gradually the number increased and schools multiplied, though still in 1971 to stay away from school was hardly peculiar. Personal eccentricities which never catch on have to be distinguished from diversities which become accepted. For example, one of the first converts at Rungwe, following the advice of Moravian missionaries, agreed to the marriage of his sister without receiving cattle from her husband (p. 148) but the christian community, as it grew, decided that the marriage bond should continue to be marked by the transfer of cattle as among pagans, and Fibombe's lead was rarely followed. In this regard Fibombe remained an eccentric, a crank. 'A man with a new idea', Mark Twain said, 'is a crank until the idea succeeds.' New ideas, values, customs, tools frequently come from outside contacts, and sometimes social change is imposed upon a community by an external power, but social change does not occur until the new idea, custom, law, or object is incorporated into the society. The process of change is experimentation with new forms (whether borrowed freely or under compulsion or invented) by innovators—'the beginners'—and the recruitment of others to accept these forms. A static society is also a homogeneous society: it is poor in cranks.

If a paradox can be swallowed, change is diversity, and diversity is a cross-section of change. Viewed in a moment of time, change is a divergence between the behaviour of two men, A and B, and social change gathers momentum as more and more people act as B does and abandon the behaviour of A. This paradox is unhelpful to some who cannot conceive of a 'moment of change' and see change only as a succession of events, but time in itself is a construct.

Since change is reflected in diversity (G. and M. Wilson 1945: 12, 48, 84) we find the innovators by studying the deviants (Parsons 1952: 253), although not all deviations are sustained as innovations. And it will be realized that the change with which we are here concerned is not the developmental cycle within family, village or chiefdom, which has been so well documented for a number of peoples, but change in the structure of society, of groups and categories of persons and the relationships between them.

Proceeding from these premises, the anthropologist analysing what happened between 1875 and 1971 among the Nyakyusa–Ngonde people is concerned not only with the succession of events, though this is relevant, but with diversity—local, economic, religious, legal, conventional—within the community of common language and custom; and with the connections between generation and sex relationships and the changing economy, political structure, law, and religion. So many threads are interwoven he may well despair of achieving order and clarity, and suspect that the historian's lucid account of events is achieved partly at the expense of ignoring the complexity of reality.

Diversity among the Nyakyusa–Ngonde people was studied by Godfrey and Monica Wilson between 1934 and 1938. At that period there were marked local differences, most conspicuous between Ngonde south of the Songwe and Nyakyusa on the plain north of the Songwe, and among the Selya in the lower hill country, the Kukwe in the higher hills, the Saku to the east, the Ndali and Sukwa to the west (see map 3). Some scholars now writing and a number of their predecessors have been blinkered by the political boundary on the Songwe which dates as a rigid line of state demarcation only from 1891 and which, for seventy years thereafter, was largely disregarded by villagers. But all these peoples spoke a language which was mutually intelligible though with differences in accent, and minor differences in vocabulary and grammar. Nyakyusa–Ngonde were clearly distinct in language and custom from the neighbouring Kinga, Safwa, Nyiha, and Henga (see map 2) though the Nyakyusa–Ngonde chiefs had come from BuKinga, and some common rituals were celebrated by Nyakyusa and Kinga. The area of common language and the dialect differences recorded in 1934–8, and again by Monica Wilson in 1955, matched exactly with those defined by a Scottish mission doctor, Kerr-Cross, in 1888 (Kerr-Cross 1890: 281–93).

Awareness of diversity is closely linked to the increase in scale which is the most fundametal change that has taken place in Africa during the last hundred years (G. and M. Wilson 1945:24–41). People became more conscious of dialect and language boundaries as travel increased. At the same time, dialect differences began to be eroded as more and more people moved from one part of the area to another, seeking land for cash crops, or seeking employment. Old men in Ngonde pointed out in 1937 that their sons, who went to work on the Lupa gold-fields and mingled there with Nyakyusa, spoke more like Nyakyusa of the lakeshore plain than they did. An administrative officer commented in 1934 on the fact that there were many minor differences in law in Rungwe District: panels of assessors from different areas judged differently, though each panel was unanimous. One of the visible changes going on was the co-ordination of law throughout the Rungwe valley by the establishment of one Appeal Court in 1936, and the appointment of a paid professional bench in 1954.

Contact with outsiders, which was the main source of new diversities, had a local dimension, and new differences began to emerge due to the proximity of a main road or market; suitability of soil and climate for a cash crop; the siting and quality of a school; the character of a particular missionary and his interaction with local leaders. The differences in policy of Scots Presbyterians working south of the Songwe, and German Moravians and Lutherans north of it had visible effects. In Ngonde, partly because whites had been allies of the people against Mlozi,[1] and partly because of the quality of the school at Kondowe (south of Ngonde), mission work developed fast. In 1937 the proportion of converts was considerably higher than in BuNyakyusa[2] and the pattern of relationships between generations, and between men and women, was already similar to that which developed in BuNyakyusa twenty years later. In Karonga, in 1937, more girls attended school for longer periods than in BuNyakyusa; the marriage age was higher; women had begun hoeing; money was used to replace marriage cattle, and some women were refusing to marry polygynists. At that time the *Hausfrau* ideal was dominant in German mission families, and education of women, or activity of married women outside the home, was suspect. With one notable German exception, the wives of Scottish missionaries took a much greater part in mission work than did the German wives.

Throughout the colonial period the Songwe boundary was crossed and recrossed by ordinary villagers; in 1937 a canoe lay ready by the main path to ferry people across the river (M. Wilson 1964, Pl. 11). Intermarriage took place and, when the movement of cattle was prohibited, the Kyungu arranged for transactions to be made through his father-in-law, chief Mwakyembe, on the Tanganyika side of the Songwe. Cattle were taken to the bank of the river by those negotiating, for those of the other party to see, and, if agreement were reached, they were lodged with the Kyungu or Mwakembe and credited on the opposite side of the river. Kisi pots were traded to Karonga as (it seems) they had been for centuries, and the cheap manufactured goods which entered the Mandated Territory, Tanganyika, came south also. Ngonde rice and cattle returned. A good housewife shopped on whichever side of the river goods were cheapest, regardless of customs regulations. And since education in Karonga was regarded by many Nyakyusa as superior to that available to them locally, some crossed the Songwe and enrolled as pupils in Karonga. In the 1934–8 period the flow of labour was from Malawi to Tanganyika, the unskilled going to work on the Lupa gold-fields, the educated seeking jobs as clerks or teachers in Tanganyika, where education had lagged; but as the copper mines of Northern Rhodesia developed, and an air-lift for labourers for the South African gold mines was opened at Chitipa, the flow turned the other way, many Nyakyusa crossing the western hills to make their way to the Copperbelt or sign on for the gold mines. Occasionally the boundary was exploited as a barrier, as when a Nyakyusa man who had eloped with a married women fled to Ngonde because there, before 1935, he was outside the jurisdiction of Tanganyikan courts. But common ties predominated; common genealogies and tales of battles continued to be related; Nyakyusa warriors had indeed played a crucial part as allies of Ngonde in the war against Mlozi. The sense of unity was vividly reflected in the 1955 gossip in Nyakyusa villages that the Kyungu might best represent all Nyakyusa–Ngonde speakers. If understanding of the process of change is indeed rooted in the study of diversity within a wider unity, comparison of the communities on both sides of the Songwe provides essential evidence: in our enquiry into how particular changes began the answer was repeatedly found in Ngonde.

Differences between chiefs and commoners were much less defined among Nyakyusa–Ngonde than in a stratified society such as Rwanda, nevertheless there were distinctions in status acknowledged in marriage law and in ritual. Equality within an age-village was constantly stressed, but within the family—between father and son, elder and younger brother, father and daughter, husband and wife—inequality was taken for granted until the war of 1939–1945. The pattern of inequality in the family extended to the chiefdom with the recognition of villages of 'fathers' and of 'sons'; of 'elder brothers' and 'younger brothers'; and the expression used by a male priest in addressing the shade he served: 'I am your wife'. One of the observable changes is the questioning of such traditional differentiation.

By 1934 there were marked differences in the manner of life of pagans and christians; there were differences, too, between the customs and ideas of elderly pagans and those of their pagan sons; still greater differences between the ideas of elderly women living in remote parts of the country which could be reached only on foot, and those of young women living near Karonga. Law and custom were changing fast but experience of life in pre-colonial times was part of the furniture of men's minds. Constant reference was made to the period when war was endemic; when to spear an adulterer was right and proper; when poor men married without handing over cattle but hoed for their fathers-in-law. By 1955 the balance between conservative and radical had notably shifted and men spoke rather of 'before the war' and after it.

Muslims have played a much smaller part among the Nyakyusa–Ngonde than elsewhere in eastern Africa. Mlozi the slaver was a muslim; his followers did not remain after his defeat and the Ngonde had no inclination to accept his religion. In an address to Fred Moir (of the African Lakes Corporation) in 1921 the men of Karonga declared: 'The people of this country look on you as their saviours who liberated them from the Arabs ... We are glad we are free now and the country is free from the slave trade' (Moir 1923:195). The leading muslim north of the Songwe was the Sangu chief, Merere, also a slaver who raided the Rungwe valley. Rev. Mr Meyer of Rungwe wrote in 1892: 'The name Merere is hated and feared here. Our station is part of a village that has been laid waste by him' (quoted in Wright 1971: 48). The Sangu were still spoken of as enemies by some Kukwe in 1934–8 (M. Wilson 1957b: 111–2). By that time there was a small community of muslim traders in Tukuyu but it was not conspicuously wealthy: the leading family of traders were Goans, Portuguese in surname and christian in faith. Few Nyakyusa became converts to islam.

Every society includes some awareness of time, for a moment cannot be analysed without reference to the previous moment which conditioned it; but the measure of time admitted in observation varies. Similarly, no society is wholly homogeneous, but the degree to which diversity is admitted in generalization varies. Every scientific study makes generalizations and must do so if it is to illumine facts. This implies that some diversities are ignored, others admitted. The student selects 'significant' or 'relevant' differences, seeking a generalization that defines the regularities which contain the minor differences. For example, kinship terms are themselves generalizations, for all kinship systems classify kin (not only those called 'classificatory') and the terms are short-hand for the categories. Diversities are treated as relevant in this book in so far as they constitute variations within a framework of common language and custom and modify social relationships. There was no modification of social relationships if Nyakyusa women chose to wear blue cloths rather than yellow, but there was a modification when they chose to wear imported cotton cloth rather than home-made bark-cloth. And the differences between Nyakyusa–Ngonde and their neighbours who spoke other languages (Safwa–Nyiha, Sangu, Kinga, Tumbuka–Henga) are so wide that comparison becomes too general to illuminate our theme. In Chapter 7 an attempt is made to press home the range of diversity observed within one language area, and its significance as reflecting the process of change.

Social change demonstrably occurred in Nyakyusa–Ngonde country before 1875, but we know little about its pace. Archaeologists have shown that tool kits may remain almost unchanged over five thousand years; even a wooden hoe from Egypt, dated in the British Museum to 1400 BC, is exactly like a Nyakyusa hoe in use in 1934–8. Nyakyusa tradition states that once a new world was created when chiefs came with fire, cattle, and iron, then time stood still; Ngonde tradition admits of continuing change connected both with a continuing flow of immigrants and external trade. However it is likely that, even in Ngonde, the pace was slow by contrast with the century of revolution. Royal lineages and the traditions associated with the 'coming out' ritual proved illuminating, particularly since chiefly lineages were collated by those who recited them with the 'coming out' of a generation, not the life-span of an individual. Godfrey Wilson was able to tap the oral traditions of Ngonde at a moment in time before they began to be forgotten and while outstanding men from all over the plain were prepared to spend days relating them. These men included commoners, nobles, and Peter the Kyungu himself. But the need to consider oral tradition critically struck home in 1935, before we went to Ngonde, when Kinga elders ascribed to the Ngoni a place of origin in the Kinga mountains! (cf. Hunter 1934).

Returning to BuNyakyusa in 1955 after leaving in 1938, I was astonished not by certain radical changes which had occurred, but by the fact that the former pattern was all but forgotten. Two examples must suffice. Until 1938 the plain north of the Songwe was normally spoken of by Nyakyusa as Mungonde, in contrast to Kungonde, south of the Songwe (see map 3); the central area was spoken of as Selya east of the Mbaka river and Masoko in the valley itself and westward. The hill country was Kumwamba ('in the hills') but, since much of it was dominated by chiefs of the Kukwe lineage and the meaning of Kumwamba varied with the position of the speaker, it was also called BuKukwe. These terms are reflected in texts written by Nyakyusa speakers; they were used in the earliest mission records and certainly dated from pre-colonial times (Kerr–Cross 1890).

By 1955 only the name BuKukwe was still in everyday use (see map 4). The central area was Pakati, not coinciding exactly with the old Masoko or Selya for it straddled the Mbaka river, and an area to the east which had been part of the old Selya was included in a new division in the Lufilio valley, called Busokelo. The plain was Ntebela. But not only had names changed: I was assured by a number of people that these new names (introduced by the Administration in 1949, with later modifications) (Kingdon 1951:190) had 'always been used'. The different names are given in Maps 3 and 4, for to use the 1955 names when speaking of the 1934–8 period would be as much an anachronism as to speak of the Tanganyika and Nyasaland of that time as Tanzania and Malawi.

The second example is more profound. Up until 1938 most pagan women wore only bark-cloth: their covering was exiguous but they were as fussy about it as a Victorian woman about her crinoline, and what should be covered must not be exposed. Nakedness was indecent but the definition of 'naked' was narrow. The women who wore cloth were christians, muslims, and the wives of a few sophisticated men who, while not christian or muslim, preferred their wives to be covered. Most pagan women did not possess cloths but those who did were likely to wear them folded for display, not for covering. By 1955 all this had changed, and I was told it had changed suddenly, when Nyakyusa men who had served in the army returned, and felt it indecent to see their wives and mothers uncovered. So they insisted on their wearing cloth, but at the same time they did not all wish to pay for the cloth, so it was said that women must grow millet, brew beer, and buy themselves cloth with which to cover their nakedness. This had implications for the relationships of men and women, and access to land, as we shall see (p. 131), but an astonishing and significant fact was the speed with which ideas of 'decency' changed. I was affronted by the sniggers of teen-age boys looking at photographs in *Good Company*, photographs which, when taken, were perfectly 'decent' and conventional, but which by 1955 were no longer so. A third example related to the content of the word *Kyala* (Lord, God) which changed radically. The evidence on this has already been published (M. Wilson 1959: 156–9).

Words indeed present great difficulties: for example, the word 'pagan' is felt by some to have a derogatory implication. Any word used by an in-group for 'outsiders' may gain such an implication, whether 'unbeliever', 'gentile', 'jew', 'muslim', 'christian' — as used in the first century AD (I Peter, 4, 14–16) and sometimes in the twentieth — 'marxist', 'communist', 'atheist', 'immigrant', 'settler', 'white'. Dr Magubane's objection (1973: 1709) to the use of a number of the words he lists in South Africa are well justified and derogatory implications are not confined to one language in South Africa. In 1931 *umlungu* (white) as used in Xhosa in the Transkei had sometimes the implication of 'whitey' in the American usage of 1971. Nevertheless, in any social analysis, some distinctions between groups must be made and words found to do this. In a study of change among the Nyakyusa it is essential to compare those who embraced christian teaching and became members of churches, and those who held fast to traditional beliefs and rituals. In KiNyakyusa those following traditional ways were referred to as *abankaja*, 'people of the homesteads'. 'Pagan', in its original Latin sense of 'villager', 'rustic' (and so used by Augustine the African) is the closest translation we could find. It is not here used with any derogatory overtones.

The argument of this book is that analysis of diversity in space and time provides a model that moves. The focus is on change in the relationships of men and women, and between generations. As the period in time advances, contradictions in Nyakyusa society become more and more apparent, for example, the contradiction between the men's assumption of a legal and ritual inequality between men and women and the questioning of this by some women; contradiction between close co-operation in the age-village and individual economic advancement; contradiction between polygyny and monopoly of wealth by older men, and the desire of young men to marry. There can be no doubt that in all three examples the tension has increased since 1934, and all the evidence indicates that the coherence of Nyakyusa–Ngonde society was high in 1934, higher than it was by 1955. But even in 1955 it was infinitely greater than in other areas with which I have been familiar: Hala (Auckland) in the Ciskei in 1931, East London or Grahamstown in 1932, Kabwe (Broken Hill) in 1939–40, or Langa in 1955–62 (Hunter 1934:335–8, 340; 1936:434–504; G. Wilson 1941–2; M. Wilson and Mafeje 1963). Degrees of conflict are very difficult to measure, but wide differences in degree do strike a field worker. Were there no coherence, no regularities, in a society it could not be described for no generalization about it could be true; where conflict is acute there is scarcely any 'custom', but diverse behaviour in similar situations.

Sources and limitations of evidence

Material on change through time is drawn: (1) from field work by Godfrey Wilson, 1934–8, and Monica Wilson, 1935–8 and 1955; (2) from oral tradition recorded by Godfrey or Monica Wilson 1934–8; (3) from written records by eye witnesses, beginning with E. D. Young who circumnavigated the lake in 1875, the Scottish missionaries, James Stewart and Robert Laws, and the travellers Frederick Elton and Joseph Thomson, through the much fuller reports of later missionaries, both German and Scottish, traders, travellers, and administrators; (4) from other social scientists, notably Philip Gulliver (field work 1954–5) and J. H. Konter, P. M. van Hekken, K. de Jonge, and J. J. Sterkenburg from Leiden University (1965–9) who have worked among the Nyakyusa.[3] Mr N. K. Mwangoka, Field Officer of the Ministry of Agriculture and himself a Nyakyusa, worked with the Leiden team, making an invaluable contribution. Professor Gulliver provided solid material on labour migration and the changes in law and custom arising from pressure on land in 1954–5. The Leiden team collected statistical evidence which was lacking in my own studies, and which is essential to understanding an increasingly diverse society. I am particularly indebted to Dr J. H. Konter and Mrs Maggie Konter (herself a Nyakyusa), and Mr R. M. Mwansasu of Lusungo and Mbeya for personal help on various points relating to the period 1960–71. My debt to innumerable Nyakyusa and Ngonde men and women for friendship, and the education of a stranger, is enormous. I learnt from them far more about life and about good and evil than appears here.

Mission and government archives have been used by historians—notably John Iliffe, Marcia Wright, John McCracken, H. W. Macmillan, and an anthropologist, S. R. Charsley. I have drawn on their findings. Archaeological evidence now being systematically assembled by Desmond Clark, K. R. Robinson, Brian Fagan, and others is relevant to the economic and social history of the area, especially since it may enable us to date the introduction of cattle and the arrival of chiefs.

Evidence on relationships between men and women and between generations is tenuous for the period covered only by oral tradition and travellers accounts; it is fuller from the time missionaries and traders established themselves, and is fairly detailed from 1934 onwards; but it will be apparent to readers that precise information on many points is lacking. For example, we have no adequate statistics on change in the incidence of divorce through time, though informants had definite ideas about changes which they believed had taken place (pp. 190–2). Nor do we know the proportion of men who married by 'cock marriage', without giving cattle, before the rinderpest epidemic of 1892–3 and after it, or the cattle holdings in relation to population at these dates. Even the accuracy of the 1931 census (and of cattle holdings) is doubtful. Nevertheless, certain trends are perfectly clear, notably increase in the security of life and property, increase in population, pressure on land, the disappearance of age-villages, greater familiarity between fathers and sons, and questioning of the traditional place of women. Our knowledge of how changes in social relationships were initiated, and why some were accepted and others rejected is meagre. Attention is therefore directed to such evidence on process as could be assembled. William Blake (1804) spoke of 'the holiness' of 'Minute Particulars'. This book is full of minute particulars for only in them is social process manifest.

The wider relevance

In much historical writing, and also now in the writing of some anthropologists, the idea is implicit that political structure and the actions of political leaders are more important than anything else. Family relationships are treated as peripheral.[4] The view taken here is that revolution in kinship relationships is as far-reaching as revolution in the form of government. The changes described among the Nyakyusa–Ngonde people are not peculiar to them: similar changes are proceeding in other parts of Africa, in Europe, the Americas, and Asia.[5] The time and pace vary, but the general direction of change from subservence of women and sons towards a greater equality with husbands and fathers is moderately consistent. It will be shown that, for the Nyakyusa, change is not wholly consistent but zig-zags in one general direction, and this pattern of waves advancing and retreating in a tide that is flowing in one direction is widespread.

The Tanzanian marriage law of 1971 recalls both legal changes in marriage law in Britain during the past century, and the Chinese marriage law of 1950. It is often forgotten that the property rights of a Victorian woman were less than those of a Nyakyusa–Ngonde woman in 1934, or that marriage for love was far from universal in England until recently—in 1650 Dorothy Osborne thought it would be self-indulgent to marry for love rather than for family interest (Moore Smith 1928: xxxvi; cf. Trevelyan 1942:64–70). In China, Chairman Mao's *Thoughts* turn on persuading parents that a woman should have free choice in marriage, as well as on transferring land to the tiller. Sons in England in the nineteenth century, and in China in the twentieth, were required to show a degree of filial respect unknown in Europe or North America today, and obligations were supported by both religious and economic sanctions.

Change in the relationship between generations turns on access to education, and the opportunity of employment or production independently of the wealth or goodwill of fathers. Change in the relationships of men and women likewise turns on access by women to education, to land—a right preoccupying, for example, Chinese women (Hinton 1966: 396)—to other capital, and to employment. But the greatest change in the lives of women comes with health and family planning services which mean, eventually, a limitation in the number of pregnancies desired or endured. Technical changes which eliminate the back-breaking tasks of hoeing, cutting and carrying firewood, and drawing water make the elderly less dependent upon the able-bodied, and increase the importance of skill as compared with physical strength. So change in kinship relationships are inextricably bound up with changes in the economy and values.

NOTES

[1] Rev. Mr Faulds, Scottish missionary in Karonga in 1937, told me that he believed this alliance had been of great importance to the success of the mission, cf. p. 24.

[2] In BuNyakyusa 16% and in Ngonde 40% of the population were professing christians in 1937. Congregations in the Karonga area included Henga as well as Ngonde and it was not possible to discover the proportion of Ngonde only who were christian.

[3] Some of the Leiden reports covered Rungwe District which includes BuLambya and Malila, not Nyakyusa-speaking areas. I am indebted to Dr Thoden van Velzen who worked in BuLambya for stimulating ideas, but only material covering Nyakyusa-speaking villages is used here.

[4] A number of French and English historians rejected this view a generation ago. In 1942 G. M. Trevelyan wrote (1942: vii), 'Without social history economic history is barren and political history unintelligible.' The Cambridge Group for the History of Population and Social Structure is now making notable contributions to English kinship studies.

[5] In the large literature, see particularly: Hunter 1933; Richards 1940; 1966; Ariès 1960; Goode 1963; Yang 1965; Perlman 1966; 1969; Simons 1968; Goody 1969:120–46; Douglas 1969:121–35; Colson 1971; Laslett and Wall 1972; Little 1973.

Chapter 3

'KINSHIP IS CATTLE'

Establishing a marriage

'UBUKAMU *syo ngombe*' (kinship is cattle) was how an intelligent Nyakyusa discussing marriage and family relationships in 1936 summed up the situation. At that time cattle passed between lineages in exchange for women, and it was their passage which gave a husband exclusive uxorial rights, possession of children born of his wife, and control over her labour. A bride, for whom cattle were given, moved to another lineage. As Kalunda, a middle-aged commoner, explained: 'she moves from us, she is just a person (an outsider) to her "fathers" now, *those* are her relatives.' Her lineage ancestors were notified, her father offering the ritual cut of a bull slaughtered in his banana grove, and calling upon his shades to 'move aside a little' that she might conceive at her husband's. If cattle did not pass the bride was no *nkamu*, no kinswoman, of her husband. A young chief confirmed this: 'If I marry a girl and take no cows to her father then she is not my kinswoman, she is not of my lineage (*ikikolo*), but if I take cows then she becomes one, and if I take no cows her father is no kin to me, but if I take cows he rejoices and says "this man is my kinsman."' And he added: 'Since you Europeans don't give marriage cattle where does kinship come from? If you beget children with your wife whose are they? Do the children really belong to the husband even though he does not give the father of the girl anything? With us love is small, it comes from cattle, we look very much to property . . .' After cattle had passed, a first wife washed her hands with her husband in water to which a powder, representing 'the blood of the lineage' (*his* lineage) had been added, and this too symbolized kinship. 'It means that she is of my lineage (*ikikolo*) now . . . They will bury my wife as they bury me'—that is, the form of ritual will follow that of her husband's lineage, not her father's. But washing together could not stand alone; it was a confirmation of, not a substitute for, the passage of cattle.

Cattle also circulated *within* a lineage and in so doing maintained bonds created by birth and inheritance. Exchange of gifts of food was a mark of friendship; exchange of cattle was proof of kinship; and it was *ukukamanila* 'milking-one-another's-cows', i.e. cows received by a father from the marriage of a daughter and passed on to his kinsmen, that held a lineage together. Cows were received at marriages of daughters of a lineage, and expended for the marriages of sons. They were slaughtered at funerals of members of the lineage and their wives, and of parents of wives of the lineage. Friends coming to mourn brought cloth, kinsmen and affines brought cattle. The sources and distribution of cattle for particular marriages, and the reciprocity through generations, reflect lineage structure.

The time depth of a lineage within which cattle were given and received was three generations: men said that 'the descendants of a common grandfather milk-one-another's-cows', but often it was only the descendants of *one* of the grandfather's wives who did this, because full-brothers (or brothers whose mothers were kin) co-operated more closely than did half-

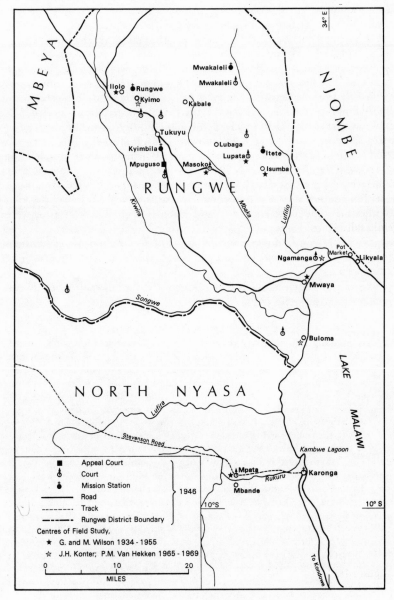

Map 5: Rungwe and North Nyasa, 1934–69

brothers. Since such exchanges disappear in a money economy (in BuNyakyusa and elsewhere) and some now question whether they ever in fact occurred, or whether accounts of them are merely statements of an ideal, details of the complicated exchanges in three wealthy lineages recorded in 1934–6 are given in appendix III. The fact that such exchanges actually took place implied a degree of co-operation in a group, wider than the elementary family, which was difficult to achieve a generation later.

Exchange of cattle within and between lineages established a network of obligation and reciprocity which could be enforced by conventional and moral pressure, and by appeal to the courts. The network included both living and dead. The heir was obliged to kill at a funeral for 'did not the dead leave cattle and property in women? Had he not the right to be buried with a cow? Would he not cause sickness if the heir neglected his obligation?' If a man, owning cattle, failed to take a cow to his mother-in-law's funeral he was shamed; his wife was shamed; his father-in-law was insulted; he feared lest his child fall ill or his wife fail to conceive again. If he had not yet completed the marriage payment due, his father-in-law might press for a cow in court. Similarly, if his eldest daughter married and he failed to give his father or elder full-brother at least one cow he lost prestige, he feared illness either in his own person or that of his children, and a law-suit might follow. A father whose son insulted him might publicly disinherit him, and brothers who quarrelled irreconcilably might 'divorce one another' (ukulekana) in court, counting up the claims in cattle each had on the other, the debtor handing over the balance due.

The mutual claims made by half-brothers and the implications of 'divorce' between them are reflected in case 1:[1]

CASE 1 : A SPENDTHRIFT HALF-BROTHER

Ngemela's younger half-brother A went off [from Selya] to Mungonde, with his mother p, for whom Ngemela had first built, but who had left him. Then Ngemela's half-sister q, by the same mother as A, who was at first married 'from Ngemela's place' to a man of Masoko B, left her husband B and followed her full-brother A to Mungonde. She had been betrothed as a child, during the lifetime of her father, before Ngemela inherited their father's homestead. Ngemela received all the five cows given for q, but later he paid four of them in adultery fines for her full-brother A. When in August 1935 B, the husband of q, came to Ngemela demanding either his wife or his cattle, Ngemela sent him to Mungonde saying: 'All of them have moved to their own place, follow them there.' B went to A in Mungonde for his cattle. A replied: 'No! It is true that q is to be married by others but those cattle will be mine; since we [Ngemela and I] have divorced (tulekene) let Ngemela pay back all five cattle. When his full-sister was married I received no cattle from her, so I should receive the cattle from my sister.' So Ngemela went himself with B to have the case heard before chief Mwakyembe.

Previously A had run off with a wife of chief Mwandosya (123), and Ngemela paid two cows as fine for him. Again he seduced two women, wives of commoners, and Ngemela paid one cow in each case saying 'he is my child.' So Ngemela argues: 'It is true that I gave him no cattle from my own sister, but then I paid four cows as fines, which must be taken into account. Later Ngemela gave A two cows inherited from their father, to marry with, so that all together he had paid out six cows for A.

When his father died Ngemela built for his own mother s[1] (an old woman) but his mother's sister s^2, whom she had fetched as a junior wife for her husband (*asakwile*) was still young, and Ngemela gave her to C, a junior half-brother of his father, 'his little father' (*ugwise unandi*). Ngemela inherited the mother of A, with whom he was now disputing. He had not given his mother's sister s^2, his 'little mother' (*unna unandi*), to A because he said: 'It is not right to exchange our mothers: that would look as if we were both adult men (*abanyambala*), whereas I am his father.' But by 1935 when this case flared up Ngemela was saying: 'I was wrong to give the woman [s^2] to my little father [C], because he and my father did not milk each other's cows, each milked his own cows. So I was giving away my property. I should have sent her home to her father and taken the cows when she married again.'

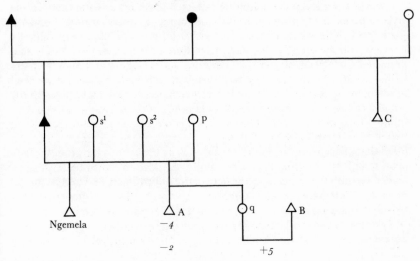

Key to all case diagrams

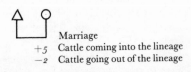

△ Man alive
▲ Man dead
○ Woman alive
● Woman dead

Marriage
+5 Cattle coming into the lineage
−2 Cattle going out of the lineage

As it was, A went and 'stole' s^2 from C, seducing her, but C refused to make a case and left it to Ngemela, saying: 'Really she is yours, you claim, and any cattle paid shall be yours.' So Ngemela made a case and claimed two cows from A 'for seducing my mother'. Later he reduced the claim to one cow, which he received. Then A brought him a bull 'to enter and make friends' saying: 'Indeed, I wronged you, my father.' But Ngemela said: 'Well, if you wish to make friends again you must also bring a cow for the village to eat, so that all shall know that I have forgiven you.' A agreed and brought a heifer calf which was eaten by the village. Now A is claiming that these cattle should be taken into account, but Ngemela says: 'No, they were to discipline you when you ran off with my mother.'

Later A went off to Mungonde taking his own mother p and now his sister q. If the case is just tried that is not divorce. Only if one of the half-brothers wishes to divorce the other and says 'count all the cows' will there be a divorce. In such an event, Ngemela would claim all the cows from q which he has returned and one extra, and the five cows which their father had given for p, since, Ngemela argues: 'You [A] have taken away your mother whom I inherited . . . The cows you [A] paid after running away with my mother [s²] don't count: I disciplined you according to the custom of childhood, as you were my child.' [So far as we heard, neither half-brother sought a divorce.]

Honouring obligations and showing generosity provided security, for once a cow had been given one might be expected to return at some time. In the 1934–8 period a cattle-owner in BuNyakyusa was always afraid of losing his stock through disease or confiscation, either for a case of his own or that of a kinsman and, before 1893, he had feared losing them to raiders. A rich man preferred to disperse his herd, placing out one cow here and another there with a client, who was required to return both cow and progeny when called upon to do so, but who could use the milk meantime, and might hope for the gift of a calf sometime. Giving cattle to kinsmen of the lineage and to in-laws, fulfilled the same function. The cattle, whether kept or killed for a funeral, had to be returned later on. This was so clearly understood that the heir at a funeral might refuse to accept some of the cattle brought by sons-in-law of the dead to kill, on the ground that he could not afford to return them. A stock owner's wealth therefore lay in the network of obligation to him and he spread his risks. This network of obligation was the Nyakyusa equivalent of a personal following living in a rich man's village among the Bemba.

Reciprocity and inheritance followed well-known rules enforceable in court, but there was always the possibility of manipulating kinship relations by asking politely for help *now*, by persuading a senior kinsman or in-law who owned cattle that he should be generous and help one out. In 1935 we watched Kititu, a young son of the chief Mwaipopo (116) doing this. Mwaipopo was very slow to provide cattle for his sons to marry and Kititu, like several of his elder half-brothers, had run off with a girl whom he longed to marry. He left her with a friend on the lake plain thirty miles away and came back to Selya to attempt to collect cattle. He owed two cows as fine for she was already married, and six more cattle to marry her. Her father would be angry for he would have to pay one cow as a fine. Mwaipopo gave Kititu one cow towards his fine and told him to find the other. Kititu visited his mother's brother and asked for a cow. Failing there, he tried the husbands of his sisters, but failed again. So he went off to the Lupa gold-fields to earn one cow and three years' tax.

Whenever a man was in need of a cow or bull to pay a fine, or tax money, he pressed one or another of his kinsmen or affines on whom he had some claim. In 1937 Kasitile was selling us milk to gain his tax money, and he found himself short of milk in his own household, so he sent off his son to claim a cow from one of his sons-in-law. Cases 7, 12 and 27 illustrate both successful and unsuccessful claims of this sort. From those on whom he had a claim a man might also expect assistance in cultivation and the provision of food for feasts (pp. 100–03).

Death, replacement, and inheritance

The ideal of Nyakyusa marriage in 1934–8 was a perpetual affinity between lineages. If a wife died she should be replaced by a sister or brother's daughter; if a husband died he was replaced by his heir, a younger full-brother, or a son by another wife. If a dead wife was not replaced her husband claimed for return of all the cattle given: if a widow refused the heir he (the heir) claimed for the cattle originally given. The individuals concerned, the *ulupagasa* who replaced a dead wife and the widower, or the widow and heir who inherited her, celebrated rituals to mark the new sex unions, and notified the shades of both lineages (M. Wilson 1957a:42–85), but the relationship between lineages remained constant. In traditional law further marriage cattle were not claimed for a sister who replaced the dead 'but now in European times, if she has born children, men claim another set of marriage cattle (*ingwela*).' In practice the sororate was not frequent and by the period 1934–8 two or three cattle were given for a second sister, though not a full *ingwela*.

A substitute wife was also due if a woman proved barren: her father was expected to provide another 'daughter' to live with her and bear children who inherited as if they were hers; just as children of a leviratic union inherited as if they had been the children of the deceased. Sometimes it happened that if no girl was available a boy was sent temporarily as surety. Angombwike (aged about 27) explained in 1936: 'When my elder sister died I went as the substitute (*ulupagasa*) and lived with her in-laws. Later, when another girl was sent, the in-laws gave me a cow to say "thank you". If the "fathers" of the wife who has died are poor and say there is no girl to send as replacement the husband claims all the cattle and progeny. He claims strongly saying: "Do you wish to divorce? Then give us our cattle." Formerly we gave two cows as marriage cattle but perhaps there were twenty calves and people were pacified' [i.e. they could not afford to divorce]. So long as a wife remained with the husband's lineage the cattle given remained with her father's lineage, but if no wife remained (or only one who was barren) the cattle given were reclaimed. Until 1935 both the original marriage cattle and progeny were claimed and the chief, Mwaipopo (whose experience in court dated from before whites came), held that traditionally no cattle were left to balance the children born. 'We said: "Did you beget them? They are my blood, my children, your child has died, I want my cattle."'

Mwafula, a village headman near Rungwe mission, who was already married when missionaries arrived in 1891, elaborated on differing circumstances:

If my wife dies after bearing children and my father-in-law does not like me, and does not replace her with another wife, then I claim my cattle and progeny, but I do not claim strongly for everything. Those calves which have died I do not claim back, and the hoe and spear which were given I do not claim, but I claim all the cattle which are living. I claim in kinship, because the woman left children who visit their grandparents, and they and I attend each other's funerals, though without taking cattle for burial. But if one of my children asks for a cow from his grandfather then his grandfather swears at him saying: 'Why? Your father has claimed them all.' My son cannot claim the cow of the mother's brother. If my wife died without bearing children, and her father did not like me and refused to replace her, then, long ago, I claimed all the cattle and progeny, even those which had died, and my hoe and spear. It was as if she had run away. Then we divorced one another and did not attend each others funerals: there was enmity, they were just people.

This explanation of Mwafula's fitted with the view of one or two informants, expressed in 1935, that if children had been born one calf (or even one calf for each child) was left to maintain the relationship. But when no child had been born even dead animals had to be returned or replaced. 'Formerly, if a calf from the marriage cows died, they carried it to me. If the woman had not borne a child I ate it all. They feared to eat because the woman had not borne a child; they said to themselves: "If she dies and we have eaten this calf they will claim another from us." If she has borne a child and they bring me a dead calf I give them two legs and I eat two.' After 1935, when the courts ruled that progeny would no longer be returned, all the marriage cattle were claimed and all the calves left, irrespective of children.

CASE 2: A SUBSTITUTE WIFE (SORORATE)

Some years ago Mbetwa married the daughter of Mwalwingi, who bore one daughter. Mbetwa gave one cow which bore four calves at Mwalwingi's, but Mbetwa took back all these. Another daughter was born and Mwalwingi came to claim cows from Mbetwa. 'Give me another cow, see all those you took back!' So Mbetwa gave Mwalwingi two more cows. Then Mbetwa died and Mwalwingi brought one cow to bury him. The son of Mbetwa went and hoed for Mwalwingi, who gave him two cows with which to marry. Then Mbetwa's wife died. Mbetwa's younger brother, Mbetwa

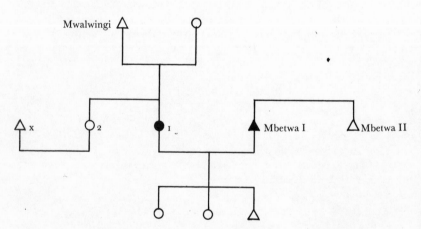

II, had built for her but had not yet inherited her. He brought a hen to Mwalwingi and said: 'She has died, give me another wife in her place (ulupagasa).' Mwalwingi agreed saying: 'I will give you this woman but you must give me a cow.' A little girl was allocated as wife of Mbetwa II, but he refused to bring a cow, so the girl lived for a long time at her father's, about five years. She was approaching puberty, and someone else married her. Then Mbetwa II brought a summons against Mwalwingi. 'Since you refuse to give me a girl, though you told me to bring a cow, and others have married her, give me cows. There are three at your place.' Mwalwingi said he had no cows of Mbetwa's. He had returned three; one for the funeral and two for the marriage of a grandson. Mbetwa II admitted: 'You received my child. Let us hear from him. If he received two cows from you I accept that.' [A message was sent to the son, and the case was pending in chief Porokoto's court in September 1937.]

When the senior of a set of kinswomen married to one man died, a ritual was celebrated to maintain the relationship, and it was repeated when all the children of these sisters and their mother's brother had died, to reassert the relationship between cross-cousins. Its overt purpose was to perpetuate kinship, to assert that though a generation had died the bond between lineages remained (M. Wilson 1957a 44–5). The ritual also reflected the fact that an affinal relationship in one generation became a mother's brother relationship with a sister's son in the next, for a man who inherited from his father took over the obligation of mother's brother to his father's sister's children; and thus the man who by birth was cross-cousin (*untani*) became mother's brother (*umwipwa*) by inheritance; but a son, even though his father's heir, never became 'husband' to his own mother, so he remained 'sister's son' (*umwipwa*) to his mother's brother, and that man's heir.

In the period 1934–8 replacement of a dead wife was considered right and proper by most *men*. Sometimes it was the children of the dead woman who took the initiative and went to their mother's father or his heir to ask for 'another mother to look after us.' A woman could be claimed each time a wife died, even though a younger sister or brother's daughter had already been married as a junior wife and remained with her husband, a representative of the dead wife's lineage. But the legal and ritual provisions for terminating the relationship show that it had not always continued in the manner approved, even before colonial times.

Inheritance in Nyakyusa society was traditionally fraternal, passing from elder to junior brother within a group of full-brothers, and then to the senior son of the eldest. If all of a group of full-brothers died before the son of any was adult then it passed either to the senior half-brother or a junior half-brother linked by cattle, until the senior son of the original 'house' grew up. Two well-known cases of inheritance by a senior son were recorded in the royal lineage.

CASE 3: A SENIOR HALF-BROTHER HOLDS PROPERTY FOR A MINOR

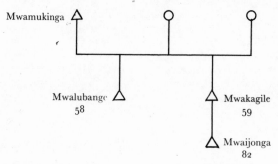

The chief Mwakagile had no younger full-brothers, and when he died his senior half-brother Mwalubange inherited, but when Mwakagile's son, Mwaijonga, grew up then Mwalubange removed to his own place and built there, leaving Mwaijonga to occupy his father's homestead. Had there been a younger full brother of Mwakagile, Mwalubange could not have claimed the inheritance.

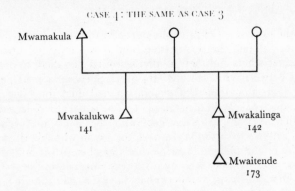

CASE 4: THE SAME AS CASE 3

[Similarly,] when Mwakalinga died, his senior half-brother Mwakalukwa inherited, but when Mwakalinga's son Mwaitende grew up then Mwakalukwa moved to his own place.

The property inherited included cattle, wives, and homestead, and in the period 1934–8 the obligation on a widow to accept the heir designated was strong. As one father put it to his reluctant daughter: 'See, he also is a husband who married you.' If a widow refused to be inherited by any kinsman of her husband the case was treated as a divorce, all the cattle given for her (and until 1935 their progeny) were reclaimed and she lost all rights over her children. But the inheritance of widows was modified by the rule that no man could inherit his own mother or her kinswoman: they must go to some other possible heir, such as a junior half-brother of the deceased or a son by another house. A second modification was the practice observed in some large estates, but not in all, of giving widows a right of choice within the group of potential heirs. This was noted particularly in lineages of chiefs who had so many wives that no one heir was capable of celebrating the ritual with all of them (M. Wilson 1957a 42–3, 54).

CASE 5: A WIDOW'S CHOICE

Makimbula, widow of the chief Mwaijonga (82) was inherited by Mwaipopo I (115) and, when he died, she refused his younger full-brother and heir, Mwaipopo II (116) but chose to be built for by a junior brother of another house, Mwakilusisye. At his place she bore a child but, when Mwakilusisye also died, Mwaipopo II inherited her. 'Yes,' they agreed when she said: 'I am going to Mwakilusisye.' [Is this an old custom?] Yes, see, when Mwamakula (106) died in Mungonde his wives scattered to different kinsmen.

The heir killed the funeral cows and this act established a re-sponsibility for dependants of the dead. 'If my younger brother comes claiming a cow for marriage and I refuse he reminds me: "You are the senior, you killed the cattle," and I agree. Or if my sister's husband brings a cow when my father dies and I kill it, then later her son comes to me and says: "Give me the cow of mother's brothership (*ubipwa*) you are my superior (*uli mpala gwangu*)." If I refuse he reminds me that I killed the cow, and I give him a cow.' If the deceased had several wives and his sons were grown up, the senior of each house who inherited the property of that house killed separately. Sometimes the father had given instructions before his death precisely which cattle were to be killed for his funeral. The obligations of an heir were enforced by mystical sanctions: 'If I neglect my dead brother's children he and my father will be very angry; they will not come to meet me when I die. I shall wander a long time on the way to the country of the shades, because I shall have no relatives to show me the path. When I get there they will drive me away from them, and I shall live alone, separately.' 'The living also murmur (*ukwibunesya*) saying I am senior to them all at home, I, the man, I the father of all. And my neighbours should feast that they may know that I am the owner of the homestead now.' 'Murmuring' is thought to bring the chilling 'breath of men', a fever, or wasting illness (M. Wilson 1951a: 100–8).

It was possible in traditional custom for an heir to waive his rights in favour of the next in line: 'the senior could refuse,' provided he did so before the death ritual was celebrated and he had been bundled into the house with the widows (M. Wilson 1957a:37, 42–6, 189). If he refused after that he feared lest he fall ill. If a man accepted the family estate as heir of his senior brother, all the property he held passed at his death to his junior brother, hence when he died his son did not receive what he (the father) had accumulated before inheriting from his senior brother. Even before wage-earning began, therefore, a rich cattle owner might refuse to accept the family inheritance from an elder half-brother on the ground that, should he do so, his own son would lose all, even what he (the father) had possessed in his own right. Refusal of inheritance increased with wage-earning, but old men insisted that it was a recognized traditional right, and the following case, dating from the time of the chief Mwaijonga (82) who died before the whites arrived, was cited.

CASE 6: REFUSAL OF A PATRIMONY

Mwamalobo [A] died. His son-in-law, Mwaijonga the chief [82], said Mwangoma [B] should inherit, but B refused saying: 'No, let Mwamakimbula [C] be my elder brother. I have borne a son, Mwaitege [D], who will inherit from me.' Because he thought: 'If I inherit then, when I die, my son will lose, the senior [C] will take all.' Yes indeed, if he [the heir] chooses he can refuse before the inheritance ritual, because he is the owner. So B refused. He and A were brothers with one father but different mothers: yes indeed, they milked each other's cows, but their sons, C and D, separated and did not milk each other's cows, because, when A died and C inherited, the mothers, Makimbula and her sister, went where they were refused and B built for them [implying that he provided them with accommodation but did not sleep with them]. Later, they returned to their own place [C's] because B refused to hoe for them: they moved on account of hunger. Then B was angry saying 'Why have they moved home?' They fell ill and people said, 'It's on account of B's tongue, because B was angry. Then

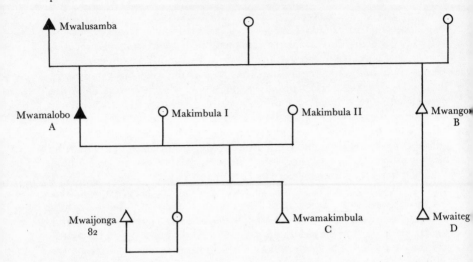

B and C separated because the illness was great. C milked the cows [marriage cattle] from his sister, daughter of A. B did not beget children with Makimbula and her sister.

By the period 1934–8 tension both between half-brothers and between the younger half-brother of a man, who had accumulated cattle and was his heir, and the senior son of the deceased was often acute; complaints that obligations were not being met were common.

CASE 7: COMPLAINT OF A SENIOR HALF-BROTHER

[Nsyani, an elderly man, complained in 1937:] My kinsman has gone back on me. He has refused. We were sons of one father by different mothers. I inherited from father and gave my half-brother three cows with which to marry. Recently I asked him for a cow for a funeral and he refused.

Young men commenting on this remarked that the custom of inheriting from a half-brother would disappear.

If a woman acquired cattle through practice as a doctor these were inherited by her youngest son: they did not belong to her husband's estate. And her household goods (consisting chiefly of sleeping mats and pots) went to a related co-wife, if she had one, otherwise they were divided between her husband and daughters. Normally a woman did not inherit cattle, nor were cattle inherited through her. One exceptional case of a pagan woman inheriting, and the modifications in law for christian widows are discussed later.

Those responsible for allocating an estate—cattle, wives and homestead, were the commoner neighbours of the deceased (*amafumu*), in consultation with the chief, and the senior sister of the deceased or the sister whose marriage cattle he had received. These were persons with no direct interest in the inheritance themselves. The neighbours of the dead, 'fathers in the age-village', had the particular responsibility of looking after the interests of a young son, and of pressing the heir, later on, to provide him with marriage cattle.

By 1934 the freedom of choice of a woman in marriage was supported by the courts, whether exercised at puberty after betrothal in childhood, on the death of a sister whom she was sent to replace, or when she was widowed. This was the first and most radical change we saw taking place in the Nyakyusa system of kinship and marriage. The second was the widespread shift from fraternal to filial succession.

If 'kinship is cattle', were the poor then without kin? In the 1934–8 period no Nyakyusa or Ngonde held this: rather the possession of cattle enabled a man to create *more* kinship links. And still a man's closest kin were born kin, his full-brothers and full-sisters, rather than his wives and in-laws. The fact that a sister was closer than a wife was repeatedly stressed. A wife might be divorced; a sister, above all the sister whose marriage cattle a brother received, could never be replaced. And such a sister had more influence with her brother and was more familiar in her behaviour than any wife. If a young man were in trouble with his father, he might beg his father's sister to intercede on his behalf, believing that her persuasion would be more effective than that of his own mother. And watching white husbands and wives together Nyakyusa remarked that the wives 'behaved like sisters'.

Divorce and the range of responsibility

A divorce was effected by the return of the wife to her father, and of the cattle he had received to her husband. Until May 1935, the father was required to return all the cattle and their progeny; after 1935 only the cattle, not the progeny were returned. Mwafula again explained the difference between a woman who had borne children and one without a child: 'If she did not leave children there was complete divorce, and no coming to mourn . . . If she left children I still claimed all my cattle and all the progeny, but kinship did not finish, the children visited their grandparents and, if I died the grandparents came to mourn, but without bringing a cow to bury me because the cattle had been returned. And if one of them died I went to mourn but without taking a cow for the burial. Also, if I died, the wife who had run away came to my funeral to weep with her children.' Some informants held that if children had been born at least one calf should be left to maintain kinship.

Betrothal gifts—a spear, a hoe, and a hen or a cow—were returned, like the marriage cattle, but not the bull given if the girl was a virgin when married. Should the husband have brought a funeral cow on the death of his father- or mother-in-law, and the cow been received, that was returnable also, even though it was over and above the number originally specified as required for marriage. However, should the funeral feast have been very large, as it was at the death of a chief, and the son-in-law have been given a whole carcass for meat (taking some home) then his funeral cow did not count as one to be returned.

Children of the union belonged to the father. If his wife was pregnant or suckling when divorced the child had to be returned to the father later on. He was entitled to any adulterine child conceived by his wife during their marriage since it was 'born with his cows', and if he accepted it he celebrated rituals on its behalf. The *ikipiki* powder given to a new-born infant represented 'the blood of the lineage', and when the husband's mother or senior co-wife administered it to the child this was an acknowledgement of its legitimacy. But the husband might refuse to accept the child and then his *ikipiki* could not be given. Furthermore, two doctors held that even were he to accept the child his *ikipiki* would be dangerous to it, though laymen argued that his legal claim included the right to provide *ikipiki* (M. Wilson 1957a: 144–9). A case was mentioned in which a minor chief was convicted and imprisoned by the German administration of drowning a child of one of his wives by his son. His wife's family had reported the case. Adultery with a father's wife was thought to endanger the life of the father, and so was akin to parricide (M. Wilson 1957a; 134–5).

The common cause of divorce was desertion by the wife, usually combined with adultery. She fled with a lover. Traditionally, the husband had the right to pursue them with his kinsmen, spear or impale the lover if he could, beat his wife, take her home, and claim a cow from her father or, if he did not choose to take her back, send her to her father and claim all the cattle and progeny. Sometimes he was so angry he speared her child, or cut off her nose or ears, or even killed her. One case was quoted in which a deserted husband killed his wife's mother. Or he might spear the village neighbour of the seducer:

In the old days if a man ran off with my wife I would go and kill a village neighbour of his. That meant: 'Go, you villagers, and look for my wife.' Yes, this might happen even in another village of my own chiefdom. Then the villagers would go and look for my wife, and when they found her with their neighbour they would bring her back to me with a spear or hoe as the fine. They would accuse the seducer saying: 'It is you who killed your fellow.' Then he would have to make peace with the family of the dead man, not I. He would give them a daughter of his own to wife, or else pay ten cows. Yes, ten cows were paid for a man's death, though only two for a woman in marriage. There was no case against me for killing a man; the chief would say to the seducer's village: 'It is your case, you ran off with a man's wife.' The chief himself killed those who seduced his wives.
Sometimes the husband followed the seducer himself to another chiefdom and killed him. But sometimes, even if the seducer was from another chiefdom, if the husband were gentle he would go to the chief and demand that his wife be returned with a spear or hoe.

Though the legal right of a husband to spear an adulterer was abrogated when the German administration established itself, spearing continued occasionally, as the following cases illustrate:

CASE 8: SPEARING AN ADULTERER'S FATHER

The wife of Mwakatwila ran off with a man A, and Mwakatwila followed him to his [A's] father's home and killed his father. Mwakatwila had built in the country of Kabeta, A in that of Mwangoka, his father in the hills. A fled with Mwakatwila's wife to yet another chiefdom, but Mwakatwila said: 'Do I not know where your father is?' He went with his brother and killed A's father, and returned. Then A feared and sent away the woman, and she returned to Mwakatwila. [The informant in this case was Nsyani, a man already married when whites arrived in 1891. The date of the case was not specified but was probably before 1891.]

CASE 9: THE ADULTERER WHO DANCED

Kagesya speared Mwakabela, because Mwakabela ran off with his wife. Mwakabela paid a fine of one cow, but then came and danced at the homestead of Kagesya. Mwakabela speared him, wounding him, but he recovered. He reported to the whites: 'I killed a man who ran off with my wife and he displayed himself at my house which is not the custom.' They agreed and said: 'He was just a wild boar, all right,' so Kagesya was saved. This was when Major Wells was at Tukuyu [early 1920s].

CASE 10: THE ADULTERER KILLED WITH A BILL-HOOK

And in the time of Mr Bell [early 1930s] Mwasokela the son of Mwasotile had found a man in his house with his wife. He hacked him and hacked him with a bill-hook and he died. He was imprisoned for three or four months and then set free because they said: 'He [the adulterer] was a wild boar indeed.'

CASE 11: ORDERING A SPEAR TO ATTACK AN ADULTERER

[In September 1937, in a village Godfrey Wilson was visiting,] a man was sick and complained that his wife was not looking after him well. His friends told him that one of his neighbours was making love to her, so, sick as he was, he went to a smith and had a large spear made. His wife asked him what the new spear was for and he replied: 'To lean on when I walk, am I not sick?' [At that date Nyakyusa men normally went about armed with spears.] Then one day his wife went off saying she was going to buy fish. He followed her taking two spears, the new one and an old one. His friends pointed the way his wife had gone. He found her with her lover lying in the grass, and he hurled his new spear at the man. It wounded him in the hip. The man tore it from the wound and made as if to hurl it back but the husband cried: 'If you try to spear me I shall wound you again, I have another spear in my hand.' So the lover threw the spear into the ground saying: 'I am badly wounded.' 'Yes, indeed, I wounded you, why do you make love to my wife? . . .' Then the adulterer was carried to hospital. The next day, before the 'judges' [village headman or chief in council], he admitted his wrong-doing immediately, saying: 'Indeed, I will send to my father to fetch a cow.' The judges said: 'Indeed you must pay a fine, and as for your wound the husband will not be fined because he wounded you only once. Had he wounded you twice he would have been fined. . . .' The adulterer agreed. Yes, the Government accepts this: if an adulterer caught in the act is wounded only once there is no case; if he is wounded twice then the husband must pay.

MacKenzie (1925:91–2) cited a case in which a husband, having pursued and 'killed' his wife's lover, came to give himself up but it turned out that the adulterer was only slightly wounded.

Taking the lover's cattle instead of spearing him appears to have been normally practised if someone other than the husband caught the adulterer with the woman and took them to the chief, and even if the husband caught them but knew that the man came from the same chiefdom. Some men felt this to be acceptable: 'If I have taken his cows I am satisfied; I say I have killed him:' But before 1893, if the seducer came from another Nyakyusa chiefdom, it was difficult to press a claim for cattle in court, and violence was likely. Furthermore, an adulterer whose cattle had been taken might be driven from his home since his village neighbours, and indeed the whole chiefdom, felt him to be a danger, likely to bring retaliation upon them.

Nyakyusa and Ngonde believe that there was a great increase in the frequency of divorce between 1893 and 1934, and argue that this was due to

the abrogation of the right to kill an adulterer (MacKenzie 1925: 90). Chief
Mwandosya (123) said in 1935: 'It is you [whites] who have brought running
off from a husband; you have brought gentleness and taken away the old
penalty for adultery which was death.' and a commoner said: 'Formerly love
making was small because men feared to die.' Mwafula, a village headman,
said: 'Running away from a husband used to be infrequent. People feared. If
a man ran off with my wife he went to Ngonde, perhaps to BuSangu, perhaps
to the hills, but not to Mwankenja's [the next chiefdom]. No, they feared.'
Kinsmen of the adulterer left behind might be attacked, or the marriage cattle
demanded from them so that, even if the adulterer escaped, his kinsmen were
likely to suffer.

It was also argued that formerly adultery was felt to be shameful. In 1937 a
case was cited in which a woman accused of adultery 'long ago but after the
coming of the Europeans' committed suicide, whereas in 1935 a woman who
had run off with a lover and then returned to her husband was greeted by her
co-wives with the phrase: '*Ndaga, umogile!*' meaning literally: 'Thanks, you
have displayed yourself,' but which may be interpreted as 'Congratulations!
Had a good time?' But still, in 1935, if a woman had run off from more than
one husband her father might refuse to receive marriage cattle and she was
deeply shamed; an *mbeti* (wanderer or flighty woman) was despised.

One case was recorded in which a man who had run off three times with a
woman, but who lacked the cattle to marry her, was caught by her husband
and forced to eat filth. Later he was accused of witchcraft which his father
interpreted as due to this 'filth'. A young man's comment on the case was: 'It
was an old custom, it is to cover a man with shame so that he will not do it
again. It is to make people say: "So and so's lineage is fierce. People fear to
make love to wives of that lineage."' Since the case reflects a number of points
in law, as well as the fear of mystical sanctions, it is quoted in full.

CASE 12: LOVERS WHO FLED THREE TIMES

A, the son of B, ran off with a girl q a sister's daughter of the chief X. He ran with her to
Karonga in Nyasaland where all fled before they had established the custom of the
reciprocal trial of cases. He left in his house a wife p, who had not yet reached puberty.
He had sought her [p] from her father and lived with her, perhaps one year and had
given five marriage cattle. The court, chief X and others, sent messengers to B to take
one cow as fine (this was in 1929), but B refused saying: 'No, my son is grown up, if he
were a child I would pay the fine for him, but I have given him adult status, he has a
wife.' Then he sent another son, the younger brother of A, to C, the father of A's wife p,
with a spear in his hand. C the father said: 'He has come . . . A!' And he returned them
one cow.

Then A came home secretly, by night, to hear the court decision, leaving the girl q in
Karonga. People told his father saying: 'Your son has come.' He called his neighbours
and they beat A saying: 'Why have you caused us to pay out our cattle in fines?' And
they took him to court. The court ordered: 'Go and fetch the girl and give her to her
owner (*umwene nagwe*). The younger brother A[2] went and fetched the woman q and
they gave her to her owner, her husband D. Then the court said: 'You have escaped A,
since your father paid the fine for you.' A second time A ran off with the same woman
q; he ran with her to Mbozi [in Mbeya district]. His father B asked another cow from
C, A's wife's father, who said: 'Since you do not love my child divorce her.' 'No, I do

not divorce her, I ask only for one cow.' Then her father C agreed and gave B another cow to pay the fine. Then the court ordered: 'You, B, fetch your son, let him marry this woman and let him divorce his wife.' But D the husband of the runaway wife objected: 'No, she is my wife. He will never take her, I will nourish her, so you can seek her.' B also objected and he sent his younger brothers B^2 and B^3 (the young 'fathers' of A) to fetch A. But at Mbozi A refused saying: 'I shall not go.' He gave them the woman and they were bringing her home, but on the road she ran away again to join A in Mbozi. They arrived without her saying: 'The woman ran away on the road.'

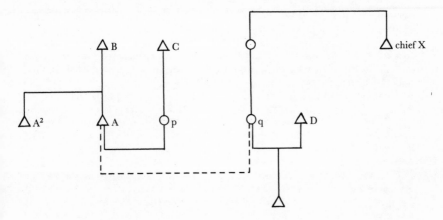

elopement

Then the court said: 'Let the owner of the woman hunt him out.' So the owner of the woman, the husband D, went with court messengers to Mbozi, and the messengers beat A and beat the woman q also. Both of them were bound, and they forced the man [A] to receive filth in his mouth . . . Then they brought them back and chief X said: 'All right you have punished him.' The woman q went with her husband D. A was very ill. His eyes and hands and legs swelled. His father sent for a doctor who gave him medicine so that he vomited and got rid of all the filth. Then he recovered and did not begin again with that woman.

Before he had run off with her, the woman had born one child to her husband, but since then she has not born again [it was 8 years ago]. Her breasts dried up. People think it is a curse (*ikigune*) [see M. Wilson 1951a: 101]. People were shocked that she had disgraced someone so, since A had eaten filth and was beaten . . . She came to S [a famous doctor] to drink medicines saying: 'Give me children,' but S refused saying: 'They have been shocked, in your husband's village,' because the woman q had told her friends that people had been shocked and said: 'She has disgraced a man's son.' And the people of the village are shocked, because the woman goes frequently to Z to see her grandmother, and the men of Z are neighbours of B who has built there. Their breath affects her because she visits there [M. Wilson 1951a:102:3]. They are shocked saying: 'That is the woman who disgraced our child.' It's a curse.

When A recovered from his illness he went to the Lupa gold-fields and finished one 'ticket' [a month's work], then his fellows accused him of witchcraft saying: 'You eat us.' He fled to his father B to tell him and ask for the poison ordeal (*umwafi*): 'Father,

my fellows have accused me of witchcraft, if there is a means, give me *umwafi* to drink.'
But B refused saying: 'I am a village headman of chief X, I am a real headman, I have
never throttled men, you are black (*ntitu*) to your fellows since you ate the filthy cloth.
Your blood has mingled with this filth, I begot you with pure blood, they have seen
your blackness and say: "You are a witch," but they are wrong. You will not drink
mwafi. We in our lineage have never drunk it' [M. Wilson 1951a: 115–9].

The relatives of A's mother sent to ask: 'Who has been accused of witchcraft?
Someone in your lineage? Never!' Then B told his fellows that people had just sworn at
his child A on account of the filth he was given which showed in his heart. He said: 'I
have long been a village headman of chief X, also my mother's brother is a village
headman, and I hear that the village headmen of chief Y [where he is] have never been
accused of witchcraft.' His neighbours agreed saying: 'Indeed, they swore at him [A]
on account of those filthy cloths.' But A said: 'In the young men's village where I live I
am ashamed since they have accused me on the Lupa of witchcraft.' Then his father
said: 'Go then and build in R village.' There they want him.

[Comment on B's explanation of why A had been accused of witchcraft was as
follows:] A man is said to have a black heart, or black blood, or a black face when he is
thought to be a witch, meaning he eats his fellows. Perhaps, when a man is a thief, or a
liar, or an adulterer, or dirty, men compare him with a witch. So B said: 'Since you ate
the dirty cloths your blood appears black, but your fellows are mistaken in supposing it
is witchcraft.'

[The woman in this case, q, was disapproved of by her husband's neighbours, and
the neighbours of her lover's father, *therefore*, it was argued, she became barren and a
doctor with a good reputation for curing barrenness refused to treat her. A runaway
wife fears also the anger of her father, lest it prevent conception or cause her to bear
sickly children.]

So fearful were the mystical sanctions surrounding adultery that a woman
who conceived by a lover sometimes revealed his existence and name to her
husband, lest she die in childbirth. A protracted delivery was attributed to an
unconfessed love affair. Formerly, 'Her husband would send her to get a cow,
so she went to the village headman of her lover. If the lover denied guilt he
and she took the poison ordeal. If he failed to vomit he paid two cows to her
husband and one to the chief for wronging the country. But if he had practised
coitus interruptus the ordeal would not get him because the child in the belly was
not his.' Still, in 1935, the fear of a delayed delivery if confession of adultery
was not made was very real, but adultery was admittedly common.

From the man's point of view adultery was very wasteful. Typical
comments were: 'There is no man who has cows who does not try to marry.
No one likes just seducing girls.' 'A married man with one or two cows who
runs off with a girl is a fool; he loses his cows.' And of a man who married and
stopped chasing girls: 'He is wise because he does not choose to dissipate his
wealth in fines.' But still in the period 1934–8 adultery continued. Clearly
attitudes about adultery and divorce were conflicting, and no doubt this
conflict was not wholly new.

During the period of German administration, if complaint were made, an
adulterer who had run off with someone else's wife might be imprisoned for
four to six months, but the chiefs granted divorce without fining the lover.
After British administration was established (from about 1920) until 1935 an
adulterer was fined one cow. If the wife returned to her husband only that was

paid: if she remained with her lover her father had to return all the marriage cattle and their progeny, and recover cattle from her new husband. In May 1935 the law changed: thereafter the fine was three cows, two paid by the adulterer and one by the woman's father and, as before, the marriage cattle were claimed if she did not return to her husband, but only the original number, not their progeny. In the case of adultery with a chief's wife the fine was increased from three to five cattle.

The impetus for change in the law came from the British administration. 'It came from you whites. The whites talked to the chiefs.' Under the new law fathers might refuse to receive home a daughter who wished to leave her husband lest they have to pay the fine, and lovers tried to persuade girls to seek divorce and only after it was granted to seek remarriage. Women in limbo remained at the homestead of the chief 'looking for their cows', and paying for their keep by working in the chief's fields, as did men under arrest. The divorcees living at the chief's were an attraction: some men were reputed to attend court in order to 'make love to the women there.'

Case 13 reflects some of the complications:

CASE 13: THE RISING COST OF DIVORCE
[One evening in September 1935 there was shouting and a scurry of cattle at chief Mwaipopo's. Mwansasu, a man of Mwaipopo's chiefdom, rushed into the chief's homestead complaining that they had seized all his cattle ... 'All, all ...' Angombwike commented: 'It is very bad to take all a man's cows for a case; they could take one or two but to take all is to make a man commit suicide. Will he not go and hang himself if they take all his cows, for it is in his cows that a man's hope rests.' Mwansasu lost his temper and said something indiscreet to the chief, who snapped back: 'Well, leave the country if you wish.']

Mwansasu's daughter had left her first husband A, who lives in the hills, and gone off with B, a young man of Mwaipopo's chiefdom. B handed over four marriage cows, and one cow as fine, to A in January 1935. Then the girl left B and went to her father, who returned her to her first husband A. B took out a warrant against her father saying: 'She went to you.' He claimed three cows as fine (under the new law—it changed in May) and the four marriage cattle. A had handed over one cow to her father saying: 'It is your case not mine.' The case was heard in Mwaipopo's court and judgement given for B. The court messenger seized all five of her father's cattle. He, Mwansasu, contended that four cows had already been returned to B, and that only three cows and one bull remained to be returned. [The adultery fine increased from one to three between the time B ran off with the girl and she left him to return to her first husband.] If the husband has driven away his wife, and she stays with her father until she is married again, the husband cannot claim from her father, but if she herself has left, and her father agreed, then the next day the husband sends a letter of claim to her father.

[Does the father always agree if his daughter wishes to leave her husband? Mwangwanda:] No, if the woman leaves just from pride then the father perhaps tells the husband to beat her, then they both go home, and perhaps they make it up. But perhaps the woman returns to the court. If the woman leaves her husband and runs off to the coast, or to some other distant place, then, when time has passed and she has not been seen, a summons is sent to the father. Perhaps it is sent after two years have passed, or one year, perhaps after only two or three months. Then, if the father is poor, they take his wife [pp. 53–5].

CASE 14: A RUNAWAY DAUGHTER AND A FAMOUS BULL

The daughter of Mwakwelebeja [an elderly village headman] was married to Mwakasapi before she reached puberty. Eight cows were given for her. She ran away from her husband with a lover, who came to Mwakelebeja and was taken by him to Mwaipopo's court. Mwaipopo gave judgement against the lover and told the husband, Mwakasapi, 'Go with your wife.' She agreed. But Mwakasapi demanded back his cattle, and without court authority sent three men to seize Mwakwelebeja's bull, which was famous. He was prevented by Mwaihojo [153], a chief who lived close to Mwakwelebeja, but court messengers finally took the bull early in May 1935, and the lover paid one cow and 10s as fine.

CASE 15: A WIFE RETURNS TO THE MILK POTS

Mwakwelebeja's wife, married before puberty, went off with a lover when she was pregnant with her first child. Seven cattle had been given for her. The lover gave seven cattle and 10s as fine. Then the woman returned to Mwakwelebeja with the child, which was walking, and he was ordered to return seven cattle, and pay a fine of 15s. Mwakwelebeja sold a calf to secure the money: he did not wish to give his wife's lover a heifer calf which would bear calves. A husband whose wife had been divorced and who later attracted her back paid a fine as did an adulterer. [The reason Mwakwelebeja gave for his wife returning to him was 'hunger'. Her second husband had few cattle for milk and little food. This occurred in June 1935.]

CASE 16: THE DIFFICULTY OF RECOVERING MARRIAGE CATTLE

A married a daughter of B, giving six cows. She ran off to Mwakaleli court asking for a divorce and was sent back to her father B, who refused to receive her and sent her back to court. There she ran off with C. A sued for his cattle and C was called to Mwakaleli court. He had no cattle and renounced her. The court again sent her to her father B who received her. C ran off with her again, from her father's house, to Masoko. A came to her father B for his cattle. The court gave judgement against her father B, instructing him to hand over six marriage cattle and three more as the adultery fine. The case went to appeal and A and B were both told to find C, but it was not specified which of them was to take out the summons and nothing happened, so A went to the District Commissioner in Tukuyu and got a letter instructing the chief to send a policeman to seize B's cows. But A had concealed the fact that the case had gone to appeal and he had been told to find C, and the chief refused to send the policeman. [The case was still continuing when we left the area in 1938.]

A court judgement might be difficult to enforce when men moved, but effective pressure was sometimes brought to bear on a son-in-law through arbitration in his village without resort to a constituted court, as case 17 shows.

CASE 17: PRESSURE ON A SON-IN-LAW

Publicly, before the village headman of B, a 'father' A, claimed more cattle from B, the husband of his daughter by inheritance. He had received three cattle for her but of these one had died, and according to custom he had carried the meat back to her husband so that it no longer counted as one of the marriage cattle. Then B was seized as a tax defaulter and A provided a calf, which was sold for 8s, to release B. All this was admitted. [What A sought in bringing the matter to arbitration was a public expression of opinion to exert pressure on his 'son-in-law'. This he achieved and payment of more cattle was anticipated.]

CASE 18: LIMITATIONS ON A BRIDE'S CHOICE

[In 1937 a girl, for whom four cows and 2s 'to ask for her' (*ukwasima*) had been given, reached puberty at the homestead of her husband A.] She returned home as was customary at puberty, and her father demanded one more cow and a bull from A. He pleaded poverty and was told just to bring a bull. She remained for some time at her father's, and nothing came. Eventually A sent saying: 'I am very poor, I'm leaving her. Please give me my cattle.' So her father said to her: 'Your husband is leaving you, where will you find your cattle?' She replied 'I don't know.' Then a headman B came to her father to ask for her and was told: 'We have received four cows from someone for her.' 'It's all right, I have cattle, I shall marry her.' According to her father, the girl agreed. 'Then her mothers took her to bathe, and placed her with her husband B. He brought six cattle, four we sent to her first husband A, and two we kept. Then the girl ran off to a kinswoman. We [her father's junior brothers] went and fetched her, caught hold of her and carried her to B. There she slept once only and ran off to C, the man who had married her elder sister. There she spent six days. When we followed her she said C had married her: "This is my bed here." But C denied it saying: "I've not married her, and know nothing about it. She has just slept with her elder sister." Then we seized the girl and beat her and beat her with a stick (for that is Nyakyusa custom) and we carried her again to B, and she is with him now.'

[Asked again whether she herself had agreed to accept B before the marriage, her father said she had, but all the other men present (ten of them) said: 'She denies this. She says she did not agree but her fathers compelled her because B had cattle, and they had received A's cattle and were in debt to him.' The question being discussed over a pot of beer was whether or not C would have to pay a fine. The general opinion was that he would have to pay, but the case had not yet been heard. Had he agreed to marry her he would have paid no fine for she had slept only once at B's, and then under compulsion from her fathers. It was admitted that both A and B were middle-aged men while C was younger.]

CASE 19: A HOMELESS WOMAN

Kalata had one wife who ran off with a lover and bore him a child. The lover was summoned to court and he agreed to pay the fine of two cows and went to work at a coffee farm in the district to earn them. The father of the girl paid one cow to Kalata as fine, but he refused to receive her since then he would be liable for all the marriage cattle. Kalata refused to have her back. Her lover had no cattle with which to marry. [In 1936 she had been living for five months at the chief's court in Ilolo, waiting for someone with cattle who was prepared to marry her.]

CASE 20: A VACILLATING WIFE

Kibopile [A], younger half-brother of the chief, Mwaihojo [147] married a little girl and gave five cattle. He lived with her for some time before she reached puberty, and then the girl said: 'I don't love you, Kibopile.' And she ran off with another man B. So the case went to court. They [Kibopile's kinsmen] followed B and caught him. He did not have many cattle and paid one cow only as fine (it was at the time when the fine was one cow). Then the girl returned to A and lived with him, but after a little she ran back to the young man B. Then A said to the girl's father: 'I'm tired, give me back my cattle, father!' So the girl's father returned the cattle to A. No, there was no fine, because at that time a man did not pay a fine twice: if he had run off with a girl five times he still paid only one cow. So B married her but the father had not finished returning the cattle to A, there remained one bull to be returned. Then the girl ran back to A. But by then the custom of fining an adulterer two cows, and the father of the woman one cow, had been established [in 1935]. So A received the girl and laughed saying: 'My wife has come!' But the judges said: 'You must pay four cattle', because under the present law a man does not marry with the first cow, the first is a fine, and he marries with the second. So A agreed: 'Yes, I'll marry her again and pay a fine of four cows.' And he handed over the five head of cattle, the marriage cattle returned to him earlier. But at first he objected saying: 'She's my wife, why should I be fined?' But the court said: 'Pay the fine! Look, her father had finished returning the cattle, and B who ran off with her had given cattle for her.' 'But a bull was left, still to be returned!' 'Do you speak of that? Now if a *cow* had remained you might have escaped the fine, but your father-in-law had only a bull to return and he received a letter saying that he had finished returning the marriage cattle. How can you claim that he had not finished?' So he agreed, but the father of the girl refused to pay his fine of two cattle, and spent 4s on an appeal which was rejected, then he paid two cattle as fine.

[In such cases, when the girl's father has paid two cattle as fine, does the new husband return them to her father?] No, he just brings one cow to establish friendship, the cattle paid according to the custom of the European administration are in order to make girls stay with their husbands. But perhaps the father himself will raise the number of marriage cattle asked for. If the first husband married with eight head, the second may be required to give ten. The father thinks of the cattle he has squandered. But the new husband does not return the fine to the father, he just gives marriage cattle, and if the woman leaves him they will be returned.

Under the 1935 law, a man who divorced his wife when she had not committed adultery, or beat her so that she fled, was fined two cows. Grounds for divorce asked for by a wife and admitted by the courts included: harshness of a husband towards his wife, shown in continually beating her; greed, shown by eating all the food and leaving her none; neglecting to hoe for her; refusal to sleep with her; and impotence. In such cases when a woman left her husband there was no fine; her father was required to return the marriage cattle only. But people always suspected that there was a lover in the background. 'No woman seeks divorce unless someone has made love to her. Some women do leave on account of a husband's harshness, or laziness in hoeing, but it is because a man has made love to her and criticized the husband.'

A case of divorce on account of the husband's ill treatment of his wife and their conflict over a child is quoted below:

CASE 21: CLAIM TO A CHILD

T [once a christian] betrothed the daughter of J [a christian] with two cows, but then he decided to go to the coast to work and said: 'I want to marry another wife at the coast, and I'm divorcing this one,' so the two cows were returned. The girl lived at her father's but ran off with a young man N, and had a daughter by him. Her father J claimed for cattle. N had given none, and he had none, except one cow which he gave as the fine (this was before 1935). The girl went back to her father, with her child.

Then T returned from the coast and said: 'I want back my wife who left me.' He married her, giving eight cattle, but he beat her, and beat her continually, so that after three years her father J said: 'My daughter will be divorced because you beat her continually.' T said: 'Very well, but the child is mine because I began long ago to marry the woman.' This was the girl fathered by N, and her mother hid her when she heard this. She hid her by night at the home of her father J. In the morning she dissembled and said: 'Where has my child gone? Perhaps T has hidden her with his relatives? Perhaps he has killed her?' We sought and sought for the child and eventually found her at J's home. Then at the court we said: 'They can be divorced, but you J, since you and your daughter lied saying T had killed the child, must pay two cows; there is no fine for the divorce because indeed he beat his wife.' T took out a warrant against J saying: 'Give me my child.' J said: 'She is mine, did T beget her? My daughter had left him and the cattle were returned, how can the child be his?' T claimed: 'She is mine, I started long ago to marry the woman and the child was nourished in my house for three years.' Then the court judged: 'You, J, since you agreed that T should go with your daughter and her child seem to have accepted that the child was his. Indeed she is yours, but since T nourished her for three years you pay two cows.' So J paid T four cows in all.

CASE 22: DIVORCE FROM A THIEF
[Divorce without fine was granted to a woman whose husband had been imprisoned for the second time.] At first her father refused to support her claim or receive her saying: 'She is his wife even though he is a thief. He ran off with her. She was previously married to someone else.' But when he heard that there would be no fine he received her, and she married someone else who gave five cattle which her father accepted.

It will be noted that women who were divorced lost all rights over their children conceived while the marriage existed. Arguing from evidence in South Africa, where Mpondo women were reluctant to agree to divorce because it involved separation from children, I kept pressing this point and was told: 'The mother always thinks she can bear another child,' and 'If she misses a child she can return and see it.' A Nyakyusa woman did not expect to live in the same homestead with a son after he moved to the boys' quarter at the age of ten or eleven, whereas in Pondoland (and among the Nguni generally) she lived with him until long after his marriage, often until her death, and her daughters-in-law served her, doing the heaviest work in the homestead. Her status as mother of the head of a homestead (if her son reached that position) was very high (Hunter 1936: 15–18, 23, 35–41, 59–60). A Nyakyusa daughter married and left her mother between one and ten years earlier than an Mpondo girl. Therefore a Nyakyusa mother never got as much practical help or emotional support from sons and their wives, or from daughters living at home, as an Mpondo woman; furthermore, though divorced, a Nyakyusa woman was likely to live within easy visiting distance of her children, and attend their rituals, whereas Mpondo homesteads were scattered. De Jonge and Sterkenburg noted (1971: 95) that in 1967 far the most frequent divorces were of young married women without children or at the most with one child and this was probably true earlier. In the 1934–8 period, in at least some of the cases in which a woman returned to a previous husband, the desire to be with her children was said by friends to have been a· factor, and the difficulties of children whose mothers were divorced were acknowledged (p. 100).

At least from 1934 onwards the extent of litigation over marriage in BuNyakyusa was enormous. Numerous cases went for arbitration to a respected neighbour, a village headman, or a small chief with no court recognized by the administration. The recognized chiefs' courts, and the

Appeal Court (see G. Wilson 1937:23) were choked with cases, and in District Reports there was repeated complaint over the very large number of cases coming on appeal. An analysis of appeal cases in Rungwe District for 1934 showed that four out of five were concerned with marriage, divorce, inheritance, and claims for children or for cattle arising from marriage. This distribution fitted with the comment a chief volunteered when discussing legal procedures. He said: 'All cases are about women.' In 1934–8 everyone was agreed that the number of cases coming to the chiefs' courts was growing. This was attributed to the practice of fining instead of spearing an adulterer; to inflation, more cattle being involved in each transaction and argument flaming over each beast; and to changes in the law which led to uncertainty in the minds of many as to what law really applied. One man volunteered: 'Since the whites came they speak with the chiefs, one comes and says: "Judge thus," and another comes and says, "No, thus."' The legal changes of 1935 abolishing the return of progeny and increasing the fine for seduction were an attempt to reduce litigation, as well as to stabilize marriage, but they did not have the effect intended.

Women as property and the payment of debts

Before the colonial period, it was customary to give a girl as compensation in a case of murder, or false accusation, when one had accused another of witchcraft and both had drunk the poison ordeal (*umwafi*) but the accuser had failed to establish his case by vomiting, whereas the accused had been proved innocent by doing so. It was expected that whoever received the girl should later—after the birth of at least one child—take a cow to her father to establish kinship, and then she became his accepted wife. It was absolutely forbidden thereafter to mention to her the original occasion of the union. The procedure was well understood:

In the old days, before Europeans came, if a man speared a fellow countryman in a different village, then either he himself would be speared by one of the dead man's family, or else the dead man's family would accuse him to the chief. The chief would make him pay five cows and a girl in marriage, to create kinship between the families. If no girl were available then ten cows might be given. The two families would drink the *ulukwego* (spearing) medicine [M. Wilson 1957a: 172–3, 193] together as kinsmen, and the case was finished. It was forbidden for the man who had married a girl thus given in compensation ever to speak of the matter to her. After a year or two the husband would go to the chief and say: 'I am going to place (*ukubeka*) my wife.' Then he would take her to her father (the killer) with two cows as marriage cattle. But this was at his discretion: his father-in-law could not claim for cattle.

The chief Porokoto confirmed this: 'Men brought a murderer to the chief who heard the case. Some village headman might say: "He ought to die," but others might say, "No, he ought to pay. See, it began with such and such a wrong" [i.e. extenuating circumstances]. Then, if the chief agreed, he ruled: "Pay a girl child and two cows." If the murderer was without children he paid a sister. The cows were for burying the dead.' A girl given in compensation in this way differed from a slave (and slavery existed in Ngonde only, not throughout BuNyakyusa) in that she had relatives concerned for her welfare, and it was expected that marriage cattle would eventually be given.

By 1934 payment of girls as compensation for murder had ceased, but compulsory divorce in order to pay a debt was common. A man in need sought help from his father-in-law, and sometimes cattle he had given for his wife were seized at his father-in-law's by a court messenger, and he was forced to divorce his wife to pay his debts.

CASE 23: SEIZING CATTLE FROM A FATHER-IN-LAW

The chief Mwangomo [124] married two daughters of the chief Mwaihojo [147], giving 15 cattle for them. Then a daughter of Mwangomo ran away from her husband, and court messengers came to Mwangomo for cattle. He told them: 'Go to Mwaihojo, my cows are there.' So the messengers, accompanied by Mwangomo, came to Mwaihojo demanding six cattle. Mwaihojo refused, and caught up a spear. He was charged with threatening a court messenger, fined 50s, and required to hand over the six cows. [This was in 1936.]

CASE 24: FINES COMPELLING SUCCESSIVE DIVORCES

[In 1926,] a man A, the first husband of p ran off with q, a wife of chief Porokoto. A had married p with four head of cattle. p was seized and taken to her father B, with the demand for three cows. B had no cattle so his wife was seized and taken to her father C. There three cows were taken. Porokoto had married q with eight cows and A paid a fine of two (the fine for adultery with the wife of a chief before 1935), ten in all. A divorced p and took back his four cows to enable him to marry q. Later cattle were demanded from A again because his sister s, betrothed as a child, refused her husband, so A fled to the coast and still had not returned in 1937, when p died.

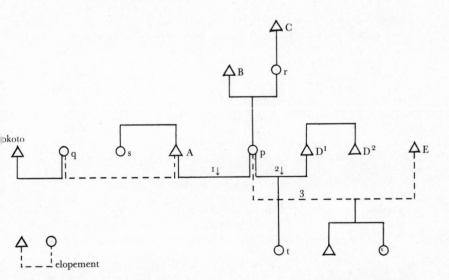

B's wife r did not leave him though there only remained one of the four marriage cattle originally given for her. She refused to remain with her father and ran to her husband for love. B was working and earned three cows to pay back again to C.

Then p was married to a second husband D^1, who gave five cows for her, but this man ran off with another woman and he took back one of his cows, so four remained.

Again he ran off with yet another woman and took back two cows from B, so two remained. He ran off with a third woman and one cow was taken from B, so one remained. Then D^1 went off to the coast and is still there: he has never returned. He left p with one child, a girl t.

Then E made love to p and took cattle to her father B, but he refused saying: 'There remains one to repay to her husband D^2, the younger brother of he who fled to the coast.' So E paid the younger brother D^2 and married p, and again brought two cows to B as marriage cattle, but B refused saying: 'I will not receive marriage cattle for that woman [p] because she always creates war. She ran away repeatedly from her first husband; she did not love him; but I, the father, lived in a state of war: they caught her [p] repeatedly and took her to her [second] husband D to seize cattle. She always ran back to her [second] husband D so then, when another case came, they seized her again and brought her to me to take more cattle.'

But in 1937, when p died, her father B said: 'I go with my children.' She bore a boy and a girl at E's. They are B's. B will take the girl's marriage cattle and give marriage cattle for the boy. He feared to receive cattle from the third husband E because, he thought: 'Perhaps they will come again. It is better to put one's hope in the children she has born.' t, the child of the second husband D^1 (who fled to the coast) is with his younger brother D^2. When t is married B will claim for some of the cattle for only one out of the five originally given by D^1 for p remained to B.

CASE 25: CONCERN OF FATHERS-IN-LAW AND FATHER
IN A YOUNG MAN'S ELOPEMENT

[In 1937] X ran off with a wife of M, a minor chief on the plain. He fled to the country of Mwambipili. There the case was judged and he was fined two cows. He was married with one wife, and the two cows were taken from his wife's father. He had paid four marriage cattle, so two remained. Then again, he ran off with the same woman and was fined two cows and the two were taken from his father-in-law. So no cows were left to the father-in-law. A third time X ran off with the same woman and he did not return her. The father of the first wife was also demanding his cattle. The case came to Mwaipopo's court. The court said: 'He must marry both women and pay the fine. We are tired of this case.' X agreed to the judgement but his father complained bitterly to the court: 'I am a poor man, where will he find cattle to marry the wife of a chief? He has taken two wives. Does he want one to be divorced?'

CASE 26: DAUGHTER'S DIVORCE MAY COMPEL DIVORCE OF WIVES

[October 1937:] A girl has left her husband, she is young, she has not yet borne a child, but she has reached puberty. Her husband has lived with her for three years without begetting a child, so she came to Mwaipopo's court saying, 'I am leaving my husband, I do not love him.' No, she did not say because he is impotent, but people think it is because she has not borne a child. So we called the husband. 'Your wife is leaving you.' 'No, she is my wife.' To the woman: 'How about it? Will you go with your husband?' 'No.' Then we called her father. 'Your child is leaving her husband.' The father agreed and said, 'I'll take her.' Now she has lived at her father's for two months. The husband summoned the father to Mwangoka's court. They called the father and his two wives. The wives are both sleeping at the court meantime. The father is poor. The day before yesterday the father came to Mwaipopo's court and told us: 'They want to take two cattle from the father of my one wife for my case, and two from the father of the other, together four, so I have come here [to Mwaipopo's court] to tell my child to seek a husband quickly so that I may resolve the case.' He said to his daughter: 'Have you found the cattle?' 'No, I have not found them.' 'Go to your husband.' 'I refuse.' At

Mwangoka's they gave him three weeks to find the cattle before they went to his in-laws. All he can do is to send his wives back to their fathers.

[What is the interval between a divorce and claiming for cows?] Some are quick and some slow. They take out a summons against the father when two months have passed, perhaps one, or perhaps only a week. Yes, we judges are surprised at such haste. If the plaintiff is good tempered he soothes his father-in-law; if he is harsh he takes out a summons immediately, demanding his property. If a woman had left her husband twice, and her father had caught her for him, returning her to her husband, then if she leaves her husband again he will say: 'My father-in-law returned my wife to me repeatedly; I cannot imprison him.'

[Do you think the custom of breaking up marriages like this is good?] No. We judges who watch over the country think it is bad. [Why don't you tell the Europeans so?] We speak but they over-rule us saying: 'But the accused cannot pay, where shall he find property?' [Why do you no longer ask for cattle from fathers-in-law without waiting till messengers are sent to seize them?]

Because now the cattle are many. We don't agree when they are asked for. A man may ask for one cow, perhaps two, but never three. If I did, my father-in-law would say: 'If you wish to divorce my daughter, come with the court messengers.'

CASE 27: HELP FROM A SON'S FATHER-IN-LAW

[A middle-aged man told of his own case (1935):] I had committed adultery with a chief's wife and was fined five cows. I handed over four but could not secure a fifth. My son, for whom I had provided marriage cattle, went to his father-in-law and asked for a calf, which was given to him and he gave it to me to pay my debt.

The father-in-law seldom acquiesced readily as he did in this instance, and the attempt to recover cattle from a father-in-law sometimes led to murder. In one case a court messenger who had come to collect the cattle was killed, in another (in 1934) the son-in-law who was claiming ten head of cattle was murdered by his father-in-law.

In 1934–8 informants agreed that the procedure of seizing cattle given for a wife, or the woman herself, was nothing new; it had long been customary to send away a thief's wives and seize the cattle given for them, he himself perhaps being speared. In 1897 a woman had sought medicine from missionaries in Manow (in Selya) to prevent herself being seized repeatedly by those with cases against her husband (*Nissions-Berichten* 1807: 217 quoted in Charsley 1969: 54). And to seek cattle from an adulterer's father-in-law was spoken of as 'customary' also. But informants believed that the frequency of forced divorces was increasing as more and more women left their husbands, and the Appeal Court at Mpuguso tried to speed up cases, so that a debtor was given little time to find cattle to pay. 'This custom did exist formerly but it was small: now it is very harsh.'

In 1965–9 Nyakyusa men in debt still sought help from their fathers-in-law, and a son-in-law might go to his father-in-law with a court messenger and ask for cattle. 'If the father-in-law does not agree he can be forced to help.' He could 'ask his daughter to return home until the bridewealth is refunded,' but this was 'not looked upon as a divorce.' (Konter 1974: 18–19). Attempts were being made to restrict successive divorces, though the assumption that 'a man's wealth was with his father-in-law' remained.

Range of relationship and degree of responsibility

Responsibility for a man's debts extended in some measure to his father-in-law, though no more cattle than had been given for his wife could be taken there; it extended to his father or his father's heir, and formerly to his brothers. One father in Selya in 1935 had to pay seven head of cattle because his son had fled with a wife of a chief, and disappeared in BuSangu. Another case was cited in which ten cattle were seized from the brother of an adulterer's father to meet the adulterer's debt. In pre-colonial times a cattle-thief risked torture and death but kinsmen might redeem him with cattle. Crimes were formerly avenged in a wide circle: the father, father's brother, brother, half-brother, or father's brother's son of a murderer or adulterer might be speared in his place if he were not caught, and so might some village-mate. The responsibility of a village-mate was less than that of a kinsman, for the relatives of the mate killed claimed compensation from the kinsmen of the original cause of strife, whether murderer or adulterer, not from the avenger. By 1934 the right of self-help had been restricted and we never witnessed a feud of this sort: at that date Nyakyusa informants counted the limitation of the obligations of agnatic kinsmen to pay cattle for the debt of a member of the lineage as one of the advantages brought by colonial government.

This raises the question of how far the lineage, the *ikikolo*, was a corporate group. If a Nyakyusa was asked for his *ikikolo* he recited the lineage of his father, usually going back five or six generations if a commoner, and much further—even up to 20 generations—if a chief. Then he might go on to recite the *ikikolo* of his mother, usually only for three generations; his knowledge there was much more limited and we had no evidence of cattle belonging to mother's kin being seized for debt.

The range of effective kinship was demarcated by avoidance, participation in common rituals, and exchange of cattle. A man's wife avoided his father: she must never meet him face to face, or look at him from a distance, or hand anything to him, or enter a house where he was or, even in his absence, the room in which he slept, or mention his name or words like it. She also avoided men identified with her father-in-law: his brothers and half-brothers, his father's brother's sons, even his father's half-brother's sons. A man asked whether X was a kinsman frequently replied: 'Yes, my wives avoid him,' or 'He is no kinsman, my wives don't avoid him.'

The second criterion of kinship was 'attending one another's funerals,' and the range of obligation to do so coincided more or less with the range of avoidance, but was more likely to be modified by personal friendship and proximity. Many friends and neighbours attended a funeral irrespective of kinship: the kinship connections were demonstrated in who celebrated the ritual, but this circle was narrower than that of those avoided. For rituals such as puberty, birth and abnormal birth, which carried the danger of monstrously swollen legs and belly, the range varied, being widest for abnormal birth (M. Wilson 1957a: 172–99, tables a and b). Kinship was also thought to determine the spread of certain other diseases. One medicine, *ikipiki*, symbolized 'the blood of the lineage' and a supply of it was kept and distributed by the senior wife of the senior member of a three generation lineage segment whose members ordinarily participated in common rituals (M. Wilson 1957a: 103–7, 145–9, 207, 210, 222).

But avoidance, attendance at rituals, and the mystical dangers of kinship were not limited to members of ego's lineage. They applied in a more restricted range to ego's mother's lineage. A wife avoided her husband's mother's brother (*umwipwa*) and his full-brothers, but not the *umwipwa's* half-brothers or father's brother's sons. An *umwipwa* attended funerals in his sister's son's family—not necessarily all funerals—and his children were treated if his sister's son begot twins. One or more *representatives* of the mother's lineage participated in rituals celebrated by her son, but not all the individual members of the lineage. And similarly with *abako*, a wife's father's lineage: her father or his son attended the funeral of her husband, bringing a cow and, if she bore twins, members of her father's lineage would be treated, but fewer of them than of her husband's lineage.

When a woman had been divorced, she and her father or brother might still attend the funeral of her former husband, or he their funerals, but neither celebrated the full ritual or brought a cow for the burial, and a divorced wife was not in danger from diseases attacking her ex-husband's lineage.

The third criterion of kinship was 'milking-one-another's-cows', and here the range of reciprocal exchange was much narrower than for participation in ritual. It is reflected in the range of exchanges already cited on pp. 30–34 which were confined to the grandsons of a common grandfather, and often extended only so far as half-brothers, sons of a common father.

Lineages were not named, eponymously or otherwise, but were referred to in kinship contexts as 'the fathers' (*batata*), 'the fathers- and sons-in-law' (*abako*), 'the mother's brothers and sister's sons' (*abipwa*), the terms *abako* and *abipwa* being reciprocal. And since men lived in villages with age-mates, and full-brothers were not expected to build in the same village, agnatic kinsmen were dispersed. If corporateness is taken as a matter of degree rather than of absolute distinction, then the Nyakyusa lineage-segment of four generations fell somewhere in the middle of a continuum between precisely defined corporations and descent categories without any corporate identity. Such corporate identity as existed was linked with the ownership of cattle, and it was no accident that a certain cow might be referred to as *jakikolo*—that of the lineage. Such a cow was not given in marriage, or sold, if members of the lineage could avoid it. A cow became *jakikolo* when it had belonged to the deceased father of the present holder and had 'looked into the owner's grave'. It is arguable that the degree of corporateness in Nyakyusa lineages varied, and that this variation was linked to the control of cattle. A royal lineage tracing back twenty generations and wealthy in cattle was corporate in a way in which a poor, commoner lineage was not.

Marriage cattle and the status of women

The status of a woman turned on the cattle given and received for her. She was of importance to her father and brothers as a source of cattle, and they, in turn, had an obligation to protect her. If, in the judgement of neighbours, her husband ill-treated her, her father and brothers might lie in wait for him and beat him.

CASE 28: BEATING A SON-IN-LAW WHO FAILED TO GIVE CATTLE

One day [in 1937] Lyata, who had married but not finished giving the cattle agreed upon, beat his wife. She ran home to her father who said: 'How can he beat you when he has not given marriage cattle?' Then her husband followed her to her father's and said, 'I want my wife.' Her father replied: 'Give me some cows. I am astonished that you have beaten my daughter when you have not given marriage cattle! Give marriage cattle! I hear that you have beaten my child when your cows are lacking!' Then the husband took hold of his wife who resisted him saying: 'No, I am my father's. No!' The husband told the father that he was going. Father: 'No! Give marriage cattle.' The husband caught hold of his father-in-law and began to fight with him, and hit him. The father said: 'How can you hit me, your father-in-law, I who begot the child, your wife?' The case went to court and the husband paid his father-in-law some shillings.

A young man confirmed that: 'the custom of fathers-in-law beating sons-in-law if they were cruel to their wives was regularly followed, but in these times it is disappearing. The whites say: 'The courts are there, and the stick has gone.' But he went on to tell of a case that occurred before 1916:

CASE 29: BEATING A SON-IN-LAW WHO TALKED PROUDLY

My father, Gwamungonde, beat a son-in-law in German times; my father had inherited from his elder brother, but was still a young man; his 'daughter' [elder brother's daughter] was married to a man who beat her and treated her badly. One day this son-in-law came driving a cow, saying: 'I want to exchange this for one cow of mine'—one already given for the marriage. He had only given three cows. Gwamungonde got very angry and said: 'You are proud, you continually beat my child, and you have not given marriage cattle; you have only given three of the seven I asked. And you come to take your cow because you know that it is in milk. This cow that you have brought I shall keep and then you will have brought four of the marriage cattle.'

The husband said: 'What? Do you just seize my cows?' and he grew angry. Gwamungonde said: 'I shall beat you for your pride. My friends tell me, "That young man is very harsh, he beats your child without cause, he just makes her a slave (*ntumwa*), he sends her to fetch water by night, he does not take account of wild animals." You have not given marriage cattle and you talk proudly. On account of that I have taken this cow. You have given four marriage cattle, and I shall beat you.' Then Gwamungonde hit him and hit him. Layandileko [Gwamungonde's wife inherited from his elder brother, and the senior in his household] rescued the man and said: 'Leave him, that is enough.' So the son-in-law complained to the Germans, but the judge laughed when he saw them both because Gwamungonde was the smaller. He said: 'How did you, youngster, beat him? We don't judge cases with children.' So the son-in-law lost his case. Later he brought a bull to Gwamungonde to enter relationships again and say: 'I am sorry, I did wrong.' Then, after some time, the girl reached puberty, and the husband gave her mothers a bull to eat, and he lived with his wife.

A husband was always in a sense a suitor in his wife's home. 'He says: "Give me your child, you are my superior (*uli mpala fijo*)." On this account he brings food, and hoes, and gives marriage cattle.'

A girl had obligations to her family which she best fulfilled by accepting the marriage arranged for her and remaining with her husband or his heir. If she ran off with a lover her family lost at least one cow and often many more, for she might not remarry quickly, or might be married for fewer cattle. That women were conscious of this was repeatedly made plain. One friend, married to a chief, had tried several times to leave him but each time her family had pressed her to return for they could not find the fifteen cattle given for her. Two women living as prostitutes on the Lupa gold-fields in 1937 had actually bought cattle from their earnings to return to their husbands that their fathers might be free of debt. Other women expressed the view that 'prostitutes don't want cattle to be given for them. A woman is bound if her father holds cattle given for her.' On the other hand a woman was proud of cattle given on her account; we watched the daughter of a chief peering through the doorway of a hut at the cattle brought for her marriage (*ukukwa*) and chattering excitedly with her companions and 'mothers' about their number and beauty. Another woman, daughter of a chief, was heard boasting about the large number of cattle given for her mother. Nevertheless handing over cattle gave a man power over his wife which he did not have in a case of 'cock marriage', described below. He commanded her obedience and labour specifically because he had given cattle: 'If a wife does not fetch firewood the husband says: "I have wasted my cattle."'

Contrary views on the effect of the passage of cattle and other goods at marriage come from Africans of different traditions. Of the Bemba it was reported in 1911: 'Parents . . . who accept a large dowry are considered to have sold their daughters and to have reduced them almost to the status of a slave. Hence we frequently find fathers refusing a substantial *mpango* and surrendering their daughters to poorer, but more complaisant suitors, as against whom they reserve the right of recalling their daughters and revoking the contract' (Gouldsbury and Sheane 1911: 166–7).

But of the Mpondo it was said in 1936:

'"A woman who is not *ukulobola* has no honour there (at her husband's *umzi*) for, no matter how many children she bears, her brother can come and take her daughters away." When there is a quarrel at the *umzi* other wives swear at her and say, "You have brought yourself: you are a cat for whom nothing is ever given, you are no *umfazi* (wife) but an *ishweshwe* (concubine)"' (Hunter 1936:190). 'If a man misuses his wife she may leave him . . . She has a refuge in every *umzi* to which a beast of her *ikhazi* has gone . . . One woman said: "Well, if you are not *ukulobola* what do you do when your husband misuses you, since you have no home to run to?"' (Hunter 1936: 213).

The Nyakyusa were possibly peculiar in the degree to which contradictory views about the effects of giving cattle at marriage were expressed at the same time and in the same villages, sometimes even by the same informants. We were told: 'The passage of cattle is what makes a wife a kinswoman.' 'A wife is my real kinswoman (*unkamu fijo*) and she gives me seniority and dignity before people. I appear a dignified person when I have a wife.' But we were also told, 'Many say: "My wife is my slave because I have given marriage cattle for her, given my property."' Within living memory two forms of marriage had existed side by side among the Nyakyusa. One can hardly escape the conclusion that two separate traditions, that of marriage by service with matrilineal descent, and that of marriage with cattle and patrilineal descent had not been full reconciled, and that some of those who married with cattle felt that they were due greater command over a wife than poor men who married by service.

A Nyakyusa son-in-law was required to hoe for his father-in-law, and perhaps help him build, as well as giving cattle. From the time the betrothal gift of a spear or cow was handed over he was expected to come from time to time with a party of age-mates to hoe the fields of his bride's mother, or the millet fields of her father. A plentiful meal was prepared for them them after their labour. This hoeing continued for a number of years if the girl betrothed was young. After all the marriage cattle had been handed over the son-in-law might come occasionally with one or two friends but this was not an absolute obligation. His diligence in hoeing was important at the earlier stage because it modified the attitude of his father-in-law to cattle payments. If he were negligent cattle were pressed for; if he were diligent time for payment was allowed. But whatever the number of cattle given and whatever the status of the groom, hoeing by him or someone in his place was required. In the period 1934–8 a man in full-time employment paid a friend 10s a year to fulfil a son-in-law's obligation in hoeing on his behalf. Ambilikile, a christian of about 35 at Rungwe, maintained that hoeing for in-laws had diminished considerably by 1937 among both pagans and christians. The same year, an elderly pagan, Kakune, from the same area, reported that of his four sons-in-law one had not hoed at all for him; the second had hoed for maize for two days with two friends, though in earlier years he had come with ten friends; a third had hoed for maize for one day with eight friends, and the fourth came alone for two days and hoed for sweet potatoes, though the previous year he had brought ten friends and hoed for maize.

Until wage-earning began, a poor man sought a wife by hoeing for her father without handing over any cattle. Children of the union then belonged to the bride's father and it was called a 'cock marriage' because, our informants said, 'children follow the hen.' But a man always hoped to be able to convert his cock marriage into a cattle marriage by acquiring a cow to give to his father-in-law, or persuading his father-in-law to take the marriage cattle of the eldest daughter of the union, and allow his son-in-law control over the remaining children.

If a man wanted a wife and was poor, in the old days, he would go to the village headman and ask him to go to the father of a certain girl. The headman told the father: 'So and so wants to marry your daughter.' 'Where are his cows?' 'He is a poor man, there are none, but let him hoe for you in your garden.' In the old days fathers agreed to this; they agreed that a man should hoe. But later on when he had married his wife and taken her to his house, if he acquired a cow, he took it to give his father-in-law. Then men said: 'He has done well, he has followed with a cow, he has given cattle for the bride.' But nowadays only cattle are accepted for marriage.

[Mwafula (see p. 35):] Indeed there was cock marriage because cattle were not yet many. They were owned by village headmen. So if a poor man hoed for me, the father, and built my house, I said: 'I am satisfied because you don't speak proudly, and you work for me. I will give you my child.' Then when a daughter was born and grew up, I, the father, took the eldest grand-daughter because my son-in-law was a cock, he had not given marriage cattle for my daughter. But all the other children were his, I took only one. Yes, my daughter was his wife, if others made love to her there was a case, because I, her father, had agreed saying: 'He is my child even though he has not given marriage cattle, he has worked for me.' She was really his wife.

Yes, there were always cattle here, God (Kyala) gave them to us that we should be men, long ago. But they were not numerous. The rich married with one hoe, one cow, and one bull; the poor with one hoe and no cow, sometimes nothing at all, not even a hoe. To marry with one hoe and not to give cattle were alike; both were cock marriage. But when a daughter had grown up then the father's friends said to him: 'Your cattle will appear.' We saw this with our own eyes.

According to chief Koroso (173) who lived on the lake plain: 'Cock marriage used to be common but not among men still alive.' Many other informants spoke of it as something familiar; it had existed *before* the rinderpest epidemic but disappeared when opportunity of employment by whites developed. It was said by Nyakyusa informants still to exist among the Safwa in 1935 and two types of marriage, 'one with bridewealth and the other without,' existed in UNyamwezi in 1957–60 (Abrahams 1967: 22). Chief Mwakisisile (170) also living on the lake plain, explained that if there were several children 'they divided them, some belong to the father of the bride because the man was just a cock, some were the husband's because his blood had mingled with that of the bride.'

The chief, Porokoto, near Rungwe, discussed the legal provisions in greater detail:

If a man who was poor hoed for a village headman and the headman gave him a daughter who bore a girl-child, then the headman claimed cattle saying to his son-in-law: 'I claim because you were never *tata* (father).' The eldest granddaughter belongs to her mother's father. All the children belong to him because the husband was just a cock, but sometimes the mother's father divided the children with his son-in-law: if the daughter had borne two girls he took all the cattle from the first, and the second belonged to his son-in-law, but when the second daughter married her cattle were shared by her father (the son-in-law) with her mother's father. If only one cow were given for her, her father gave his father-in-law a calf later on, because his sons went to their grandfather to seek cattle to marry. They sought some from their father and some from their mother's father.

[The chief compared cock marriage with cases in which a father refused to receive cattle for a daughter who had been divorced:] Long ago if a woman left one husband and came to her father's home, and someone came to marry her, then the father said: 'just take her, she is not my child, she brought war.' He refused to receive cattle because the woman was a wanderer. [And he cited case 24 then going on, in which the father had refused to accept marriage cattle from the third husband of his daughter. But though the chief compared cock marriage with that in which a man refused to receive cattle for his daughter, he went on to distinguish the relationships in these two cases:] A poor man who takes the daughter of a headman in this way cannot beat his wife much. He will wrong his father-in-law who gave him the girl. She will run to her father and her father will say: 'Why do you beat my child? Did you give marriage cattle?' Then he takes his daughter away. But a wanderer, of whom the father has said:

'She is not my child,' and for whom he has refused to receive cattle, is beaten. The husband just beats her because she has no father. Where should she run to?

Whether marriage was with cattle or by service it was always virilocal. The husband brought his wife to live in his own age-village even if he were hoeing for his father-in-law; the density of the Nyakyusa population even in precolonial times made this possible. And of course in any marriage relationship the place of domicile is crucial: no Nyakyusa man lived under the eye of his father-in-law as a Bemba suitor or son-in-law did.

During the 1965–9 period elopement became 'frequent', partly to reduce the expense of marriage, but marriage with cattle continued, most grooms being required to earn their own cattle (Konter 1974a:11–12, 24). Exactly similar changes had been recorded twenty years earlier among the Xhosa and Mfengu in Keiskammahoek district where elopements reached 30·3% (M. Wilson, Kaplan et al. 1952:80–9) and it is possible that this represents a widespread adaptation to the difficulties of men earning marriage cattle and the determination of girls to marry according to their own choice rather than that of their fathers. For example, Perlman (1966:578) noted increased elopement among the Toro by 1950.

Cattle created kinship among the Nyakyusa–Ngonde people and, during the 1934–8 period, a substantial part of a man's holdings in cattle were continually travelling the roads of kinship creating new relationships and fulfilling old obligations. In an early account of Nyakyusa society Godfrey Wilson (1936: 256) spoke of cattle being in 'constant circulation'. Continuing circulation of cattle was noted by N. K. Mwangoka in 1966–8 when a fifth of the cattle in five villages investigated in detail had either been given or received during one year. During the same period over 6% of the cattle owned in these villages were killed for funerals (Luning, Mwangoka and Tempelman 1969: 26, 45).

NOTES

[1] Most cases are accounts by one or more informants, and small type implies quotation, but explanations, and in cases 13 and 18 the eye-witness reports of Godfrey Wilson, are put in square brackets. Where a letter is used in place of a name it is not bracketed.

Chapter 4

RICH AND POOR LINEAGES

The changing basis and control of wealth

THE basis of wealth among the Nyakyusa–Ngonde people has changed through remembered history, and during the past century of written record. Traditions of the coming of iron and of cattle to the Rungwe valley reflect a change in tools which must have increased productivity, a new source of food in milk and meat, and a means of storing wealth. In Ngonde, according to precise tradition, ivory was exported from the time of the first Kyungu and cloth trickled in; this trade expanded somewhat when the direction changed; it increased in volume in the late nineteenth century and then included a trade in slaves, wire waist-rings, and guns. The ritual power of the divine kings, Kyungu and Lwembe, turned on the concept that they controlled rain and fertility, and this power was associated with drums and zebra tails set in horns, however these drums and tails were not trade goods any more than the sceptre and crown of England: they were possessed only by the living representatives of the heroes and some of their sons who were chiefs.

Food in the form of grains, pulses, bananas and fish; salt; medicines; cosmetics; clay pots; baskets and sleeping mats have been continuing forms of wealth. We do not know when particular grains, such as maize and rice, were first cultivated in the area, but there are references to chiefs or priests who brought 'new crops' (M. Wilson 1959: 8–9, 13, 47). Coffee, tea, and cotton, important as export crops, were all introduced in colonial times, and there was an enormous expansion of the trade in cloth and other manufactured imports. Bicycles, brick houses, and motor cars became symbols of wealth and since the 1950s control of land has become all important. A hundred years ago access to education and opportunity for paid employment began to be significant and these have steadily increased in relative importance, though opportunities for employment have fluctuated.

Relationships between generations and between men and women are bound up with the control of wealth and therefore some analysis of changing control is necessary to our theme. We know nothing about the control of wealth in the dim past before chiefs came except that the *abilema*, the original occupants, lived in small, independent groups, hunting and cultivating, and it is likely that wealth was dispersed. Once cattle came, the control of breeding stock was the main wealth, and this control was vested in patrilineages, beginning with the lineages of the founding heroes, Lwembe and Kyungu. Chiefs first owned cattle. They also controlled iron and salt: the iron spear was a symbol of chieftainship, and iron hoes and salt were distributed through the Rungwe valley as part of the ritual for the founding heroes. In Ngonde, iron, cloth, and later wire waist-rings and slaves were distributed by the Kyungu.

During the late nineteenth century, as trade with the coast developed, wealth was seized by outsider slave traders, notably the Sangu chief Merere, and the Arab, Mlozi. Then came whites: missionaries, traders, administrators, and planters, all controlling wealth far in excess of that held by Nyakyusa–Ngonde people, and offering goods coveted by them. Employment for wages began and wage-earning, together with an expanding market for produce, altered the balance between generations and between men and women. These changes must now be examined, and since development differed somewhat north and south of the Songwe we deal first with the Rungwe valley and then with the plain of Ngonde.

The spread of the 'sons of Lwembe'

It has not yet been demonstrated whether chiefs indeed introduced cattle to the Rungwe valley, or whether this claim is symbolic like the myth of their introducing fire. Archaeologists have not yet dated cattle within the valley, but remains of 'domestic ox' have been found less than a hundred miles away at Ivuna near Lake Rukwa, dating from 1235 ± 110 A.D. (Fagan and Yellen 1968: 11–12), and the tradition that cattle were brought to an already established agricultural population finds confirmation in domestic rituals, for in 1934 the puberty, birth, and death rituals were celebrated primarily with bananas, plantains, millet, and fowls, though a cattle-owner also killed cows at funerals, and virginity was honoured by the slaughter of a bull. For the rituals of chieftainship cattle were essential.

There is no reason to doubt the tradition that asserts that stock holdings expanded with 'the sons of Lwembe', the founding hero, who settled at Lubaga[1] in Selya (map 5), and whose sons spread through the surrounding country. Chiefs did not establish a separate caste (as in Rwanda and elsewhere) for though the daughters of other chiefs may at one time have been chosen as mothers of their heirs,[2] chiefs married daughters of commoners as junior wives and children of junior sons became commoners.

Lineages differed in wealth, and chiefs' lineages were rich. Cattle bred and wealth begot wealth. A rich man married many wives and begot many sons and daughters. He received cattle for his daughters' marriages and gave cattle for the marriages of his sons, but girls married much younger than men—ten to fifteen years younger—and during those years the cows given for them increased before it was necessary to pay out for sons. A ruling chief gave more cattle for his wives than a commoner, but he claimed more cattle for each of his daughters, and if each wife had more than one daughter, he gained, even after fulfilling fraternal obligations. The younger full-brother of a chief asked more cattle than a commoner did for his two eldest daughters, but not for other daughters. The marriage cattle for the two eldest went to the chief himself, as the senior brother. But half-brothers of a ruling chief neither claimed extra cattle nor owed them to the chief: their daughters were commoners. The distinction and identity of chiefs' wives and daughters, and sons-in-law was reinforced by the use of special terms: *mwehe* for a chief's wife in KiNyakyusa, *masano* for the Kyungu's wives in KyaNgonde, *undenga* for a chief's daughter or son-in-law. The terms carried prestige and 'in the old days not everyone thought of marrying a chief's daughter, only one who knew he had cattle.' It was said that chiefs sometimes took commoner women *without* giving cattle, and also that a chief might reclaim marriage cattle in fine if a wife committed any wrong, nevertheless the expected pattern was that a chief married with cattle and the fathers of his brides grew wealthy.

A chief was buried with a live cow, traditionally black, and it was the duty of the royal lineage to provide cattle for offerings at the groves of founding heroes, and past chiefs who were thought to control fertility. So fearful were men of the power of the groves that, when the chief Mwaijonga (82) fought the priest of Lubaga, Mwakisisya (56), and killed some of his men 'because he had spoiled the year', Mwaijonga nevertheless returned all the priest's cattle (see M. Wilson 1959:17, 40). No one dared offend the priest lest he send too much rain, or an epidemic of running sores, and cattle die throughout the country. Mwakisisya, as representative of the founding hero, Lwembe, who brought cattle to Selya, controlled cattle there. This was before 1890. In 1935 and 1936 and again in 1954 'hunger'—a shortage of certain crops—was attributed to the failure to kill at the groves and the chiefs were blamed. The obligation lay particularly on junior lines; a ruling chief argued with his kinsmen: 'Why do you refuse to send the cow back? Our grandfathers gave you a cow. Why do you not return it? They gave you cows saying: "Bring them back one by one and kill them in the sacred grove here . . ." It is always the custom for the younger brothers to look for the cow. The elders gave them wealth saying: "You be the priest, take cattle to the grove."' The cow bought should be a 'cow of the old lineage', 'descended from a cow formerly taken to Mbyanga' [grove].

Besides providing for the dead a ruling chief was required to feast the living.[3] Feasting and fighting were equated. 'It was always the custom to eat meat at the place of the senior lady before going to fight. Before Europeans came the chief would summon men and kill two cows for them. Then the people would eat. The reason was this: if the leading commoners were starved they would go out in dreams and call Mwangomo (124) to attack Mwaipopo (116). Since Europeans came this has never happened.' 'If a chief angered his men and they refused to fight he paid them a cow. Or if all threatened to move he killed a cow for them.' The link between provision of beef by the chief and his men going to war lapsed with the pacification of the country, but the chief was still expected to feast men at a funeral or wedding. In 1913, 50 head of cattle were killed at the funeral of Mwatongo, chief of Ngana in Ngonde (MacKenzie 1925:78); 300 head at the funeral of Mwakyembe (99); 30 head at the funeral of the mother of Mwaipopo (116); and in 1933, 43 head at the funeral of a chief on the Nyakyusa plain.

A young chief was expected to 'lead his men in war and take cattle. He would go to a funeral dance in another country and take cattle. The old chief left his sons to do this. The lusty bachelors were the fighters.' A man of 25–30 who discussed this had never himself seen it happen but had heard many stories about it. The chief certainly got a share of the spoils and some spoke of his dividing the booty among his men, of each fighter seizing cattle for himself, and handing over a portion to the chief. A man who died in 1935 had been given a cow by the chief Mwaihojo (147), 'because there was war and he [who died] had been very fierce in war'. He had returned two of the calves it bore to Mwaihojo.

Since cattle marriage was combined with polygyny, wealthy lineages increased fast, for sons married younger than in poor lineages, and they married many wives. This was one reason why the descendants of the incoming heroes increased and absorbed small groups already in occupation. The pattern is one that has been widespread in Africa (M. Wilson 1969: 78–80). Among matrilineal peoples, where a lineage cannot be increased through polygyny, legal adoption, and affiliation of slaves occurs, and serves the same purpose of increasing manpower in a dominant lineage group (Fortes 1970: 256, 258–9). In Ngonde, at one time when most of the sons of the Kyungu had been killed, his retinue was enlarged by slaves.

Though 'the sons of Lwembe' were the first cattle-holders, breeding stock passed to commoners, and commoner lineages also expanded through polygyny. Cattle-owners in Africa have practised contrary methods of conserving stock: some distribute cattle by contracting marriage alliances as widely as possible, and thus establishing a wide network of obligation—of men indebted to them; others have sought to conserve herds and keep them in the family by marrying cousins, especially parallel cousins (M. Wilson 1971a: 71). The Nyakyusa used the first device.

Rich men, including chiefs, did not keep large herds in their own homesteads but preferred to spread risks by dispersing them, placing one cow here and another there with a client, who had to return the cow when called upon to do so, but who could hope for a calf after some years if the cow had calved regularly. Placing out cattle (ukufufya) was explicitly designed to avoid crippling loss in a raid, or through sickness in one byre, but behind the explanation: 'We ukufufya on account of cattle dying' was the idea that cattle sickness was caused through witchcraft by those envious of the rich, or angry with the chief who owned them. One close friend admitted this. He was a chief and rich, and in answer to the challenge: 'So you send the cattle to another village or chiefdom where people don't hate you?' he replied (laughing): 'Yes, because formerly men said: "The cows will escape in another village or chiefdom." If cattle die they dissect them and sometimes find wounds in the stomach [evidence of witchcraft]. So they place out (ukufufya) the others, one here and one there. The cows will calve, and when a calf has grown I shall take it and leave the mother.'

Commoners who grew wealthy also had an obligation to feed men, especially at funerals. A commoner from a wealthy family remarked: 'We do not like to appear too rich, we commoners, because if we do men poison us. Yes, even if we feed men, they don't like us to exceed others. Even if we kill cattle for our friends they may work sorcery against us.' The fear of envious poor exercising witchcraft or sorcery was thus an effective sanction encouraging both generous hospitality and the distribution of breeding stock.

Possession of cattle not only implied meat feasts: milk, eaten as curds, was a choice food, and herding for a rich man usually implied the right to use the milk. Only if the herdsman lived very close to his patron was he required to return the milk, and for fear of raids and cattle sickness he was more likely to be at some distance. Should an animal die the meat was not the herdsman's: he must carry it back to his patron.

Although ownership of cattle was so clearly linked with chieftainship, his wealth did not absolve a chief from work in the fields: like all Nyakyusa men he was expected to hoe. Mwaipopo, over 70 in 1934, hoed vigorously though, with his many wives, he had to engage others to help him, and the most damning criticism of his heir, Mwankuga, came from the wife of one of Mwaipopo's village headmen. She burst out one day (in 1955) when I was talking with her and her husband: 'And he is never seen with a hoe in his hands.' To her this was the final condemnation. Only the divine kings, the Kyungu of Ngonde and the Lwembe in Selya, and the ladies of the Kyungu never worked before colonial times; the weeding and planting of their fields was done for them. The wives of the Lwembe were not mentioned in this connection: they had not lived in such close seclusion as the *masano* of the Kyungu. But by 1934–8 both the living Kyungu and the Lwembe were active, and most of the ladies of the Kyungu, even, hoed their fields.

As already noted, before European control was established the political units of the Nyakyusa were tiny chiefdoms, each independent of the next, but recognizing a common culture which distinguished them from neighbouring peoples who spoke different languages. Chiefs were connected by kinship ties and related chiefs participated in common rituals both for founding heroes and immediate ancestors. Every chief married two senior wives and when power was handed over to the next generation the eldest son of each senior wife took over the half of the country in which his mother had been established, and commonly expanded into adjoining unoccupied country. But if there were no unoccupied land close by one of the young chiefs might move with his contemporaries to a new area. Colonization was thus traditionally carried out by age groups, and the spread of successive generations has been demonstrated on a map. (M. Wilson 1959: 87–9, map II and genealogy).

By the period 1934–8 colonization by individuals was also going on. It was conspicuous in the coffee growing area around Rungwe when men moved out of their villages and established what were referred to as 'farms' on what had been pastureland. They built far apart from neighbours, planted bananas and coffee, and cultivated fields around their homesteads. It occurred too in Selya when men, anxious to increase their cattle-holdings, built scattered homesteads in unoccupied savannah, where, it was recognized, cattle would increase faster because better pasture was available. The settlement of a number of his men in an area gave a chief some claim to that area, the more so if the settlement included wives of his own. In 1934 Mwaipopo had just placed a homestead of his junior wives in the savannah then being colonized by individuals, and thereby staked a claim to the area, which was also claimed, though no precise boundaries had been drawn, by another chief. Mwaipopo slept at this homestead for extended periods, coming back to his 'capital' to hear court cases. In 1953 at the 'coming out' of Mwaipopo's grandson, Mwanyilu (177), the second heir, Mwanyilu's junior half-brother,

Mwabungulu (178) established himself with the members of his age-village in this colony. He was not acknowledged by the colonial government but was recognized within the chiefdom as the junior heir (M. Wilson 1959: 89–90). Colonization outside Rungwe district, which was conspicuous from 1925, was undertaken both by individuals, and by junior sons of chiefs moving with small groups of contemporaries. They moved into areas sparsely occupied by other peoples, Safwa, Nyiha, Lambya (Hall 1945; M. Wilson 1951a: 3–4).

By the period 1934–8 the main disadvantage of individual colonization was lack of company; a man who moved to a 'farm' near Rungwe or into the savannah in Selya expected to profit, but he missed the close company of friends (M. Wilson 1951a: 66–7, 82); only when groups of contemporaries moved together was this overcome. Before 1893 the limiting factor on colonization was danger from raiders; then no one man building away from village neighbours could hope to defend his wives and cattle, alone, against man and beast. A rich man was not surrounded by brothers, sons, and grandsons as among the Nguni or Nuer. It was security—effective law operating between chiefdoms, and the shooting of lion, leopard, elephant, and buffalo—that made individual colonization possible.

The rivalry between chiefs was primarily for men, cattle, and women. Boundaries of chiefdoms and villages were recognized but since land was plentiful it was over *occupied* land that disputes occurred. Until 1938 every chief and every village sought to attract men and increase its fighting strength (G. Wilson 1938:33–5, 51), and in some areas the dominating desire to increase in size, to attract a following, was still conspicuous in 1955 (Gulliver 1958: 25–6).

Disputes within a chiefdom were settled by arbitration, or in the chief's court, but settlement of dispute with a man of another chiefdom was hazardous: a litigant could not be certain of securing justice from a chief other than his own. Partly because of this uncertainty, marriage within a chiefdom was greatly preferred to marriage in another chiefdom, and marriage in a distant chiefdom was strongly disapproved. A man enjoyed greater security of life and property in the chiefdom in which he had been born, in which he had village-mates with whom he had grown up, and in which he had claims for care and protection on his father's village-mates. The property or wife of a stranger might be arbitrarily seized by the chief, even though the exercise of such power was bridled by the desire to attract men. Two such cases which had occurred in Selya before 1914 were cited:

CASE 30: A FOREIGNER'S CATTLE SEIZED

A certain man had come from Masoko with eight cows and one wife to settle in X's chiefdom. The chief killed him and took all his cows.

CASE 31: A FOREIGNER'S WIFE SEIZED

Chief Y killed a stranger who came into his country in order to take the stranger's beautiful wife, Sasunda. This happened even though the stranger had been invited to come by a friend living in the chiefdom. Therefore, people feared to move.

But, just because 'international law' was not effective, those accused of adultery, murder, theft, or witchcraft fled to other chiefdoms and hoped to be secure, particularly if they succeeded in fleeing to a distant and not merely a neighbouring chiefdom. A chief's person and the hut of his senior wife provided sanctuary for a fugitive, whether from the same or another chiefdom, and his pursuers were compelled to bring the matter to court. Those who fled a chiefdom included those related to a wrongdoer, who feared lest they might be fined.

CASE 32: A FATHER WHO FLED

Mwakwelebeja [a commoner, over 70 in 1934] fled [many years earlier] from Mwaipopo's chiefdom to that of Mwaihojo [adjoining] when his daughter, Seba, the second wife of Mwaipopo, ran off with a lover. Mwaipopo had 'come to take his cows'. [Mwaipopo had married three kinswomen of Mwakwelebeja, two Sebas and one Kijabelwa, and the relationship was not in fact broken off. Mwakwelebeja visited Mwaipopo's homestead and celebrated a ritual mourning the death of the senior Seba (M. Wilson 1957a: 44–5).]

Within a chiefdom there was reciprocity in function and balance in power between chiefs and commoners led by the village headmen who were necessarily commoners themselves. Chiefs were thought to have in their own bodies the power of fertility: commoners had power which, used legally and morally, was spoken of as 'the breath of men', and used illegally and immorally as witchcraft. Commoners feared the anger or illness of their chief lest it bring blight on their fields, a murrain on their herds, and sickness to their children; and the chief for his part feared the anger of his men, thinking it would fall on himself or his children as a chilling breath, bringing fever. A chief was rich in cattle but if he angered his men they refused to fight and his cattle were taken. Occasionally a commoner came and told the chief, 'We don't sleep (tutigona)—we fought and were beaten,' thus prophesying evil, and demanding reform. 'The younger brothers of the chief were strong in reproving him.' On the other hand, a chief might take a commoner's wife if he liked her, sending cows to the husband. 'The husband feared and received the cows.' 'Now the chief persuades a woman he likes to seek a divorce.' The chief's authority was important in safeguarding property and maintaining order. 'Formerly if a man was taking cattle somewhere to a distance he sought a relative of Mwaipopo [the chief] to accompany the party lest cattle be stolen on the road: the relative represented Mwaipopo.' And no one dared begin the mourning ritual or the ritual for abnormal birth, both of which involved large gatherings, without permission from the chief.

The chief Porokoto elaborated on the traditional rights of a chief over cattle held by his men. 'If a chief needed a bull for hospitality he sent a village headman to ask one of that headman's villagers for one. If the owner first asked had a good excuse the headman asked someone else, but, if a man constantly refused, the headman, with the help of neighbours, would seize it saying: "He is proud (namatingo)." After a time the chief would send the headman with a heifer to the man who had given the bull, saying "Let him herd it." The man kept the heifer for his own, but after it had calved once or twice the chief would send to ask for a calf. If a chief's cows died of disease he would send village headmen through the country to take cattle and collect a herd for him. Cattle given to commoners by the chief were of three categories: a gift from the chief, a gift in return for a bull (as described above), and an allocation by the chief from cattle taken in war or a portion of those each man had captured. No one now [1935] agrees to give a chief a bull in return for a cow later, unless his own village headman still follows the old custom. When courts were established in 1926 chiefs claimed all the calves of the cows their fathers had given people, even calves that had died. This was a change in custom for of old a chief would not ask for all the calves of such and such a cow, but only for one or two. So now men are afraid to receive a heifer in exchange for a bull, and will only give a bull in return for shillings.' But a chief still paid in cattle for services rendered, rewarding the grave-diggers for his father with a cow.

In the 1934–8 period ideas about how the balance of power between chiefs and people were changing were by no means wholly consistent. On the one hand many commoners argued that between 1916 and 1934 chiefs had gained greatly in power vis-à-vis commoners, and village headmen in particular, for the British government supported chiefs and ignored headmen. Chiefs who were 'recognized' were paid, village headmen were not, and the chief, backed by an external authority was partly freed from ancient democratic controls. Such an increase in the power of chiefs has been widespread. In the Citimukulu's immortal phrase 'I am not afraid of my *bakabilo* now because I know the bwanas listen to me and not to them (Richards 1935:12). The power of a chief became greatest where land became scarce and he controlled its allocation, as in Lesotho, but in BuNyakyusa in 1934–8 the chiefs had little control over land, and it was agreed that a chief could not seize a man's cattle or wife in the way he used to do. His power depended upon wealth and the exercise of authority in court.

Cattle in his own long byre (*ikibaga*) or distributed among his subjects on loan, or in return for wives, were the main form of chief's wealth in the period 1934–8; but iron goods and salt had been scarce and important in the pre-colonial period. An iron spear, symbol of chieftainship, was grasped by each of the two young chiefs at the 'coming out' ritual, and by extension a spear symbolized a warrior, a male. Still in 1934–8, a man grasped a spear when he danced, and carried one as he went about his daily business. Many spears were heirlooms: others were ordered from local smiths who, though they did not smelt iron ore, would readily forge a spear out of an old hoe.[4] The distribution of iron hoes was linked to the rituals celebrated at sacred groves, but there was also a secular trade: some hoes were bartered by Kinga to individual Nyakyusa in the Lufilio valley or, if hoes were not available in Selya, 'a man would go to BuKinga carrying food for sale to buy hoes, but he might have to wait for them to be made and have nothing to eat meantime.'

Hoes were continually referred to by Nyakyusa informants as an essential commodity; axes were not mentioned; and it was hoes which figured in rituals, not axes. This reflects the difference between a people with fixed cultivation, normally working land without trees, and a people who depended upon swidden cultivation, pollarding trees to provide wood-ash. Dr Richards (1939: 290) reported that, in 1931–4, 'A Bemba never parts with his

axe. He carries it everywhere with him swung over his shoulder as he walks.'
Whereas a Nyakyusa man of the same period went about with a spear, except
when on his way to his fields, when he carried a hoe. The long-handled hoe
was a man's tool: Nyakyusa women used only a short wooden hoe for weeding
(M. Wilson 1951a: Pl VII), until a radical change in the division of labour
began. By 1934 western-pattern trade hoes were in general use because they
were cheaper than Kinga hoes, but they were not as long-lasting. The bill-
hook used for pruning bananas was also a man's tool, still in general use in
1955 and made by local smiths, but it was not referred to as something
brought to the sacred groves. What Kinga priests had brought along with
hoes was salt and this, with hoes, had been distributed to chiefs who brought
cattle to Lubaga (M. Wilson 1959:10, 15, 25, 27, 29–30).

In small societies certain goods long remained scarce and circulated slowly.
Iron was worked at Kalambo near the southern shore of Lake Tanganyika
from the fourth century A.D., salt was produced at Ivuna from the 13th
century (St. John 1970:209; Fagan and Yellen 1968) and cattle were kept
there then, but in 1938 in Rungwe district women still used wooden hoes, a
small packet of salt was a valued present, and some men lacked a cow from
which to start a breeding herd.

In the early colonial period cloth and brass or copper wire circulated in
exchange for cattle, food, and labour. Dr Kerr-Cross wrote in 1893 of the
Nyakyusa–Ngonde people: 'They are in . . . the "Brass-wire Age". This is
their gold, or medium of exchange. You can buy anything for brass wire'
(1895:118) and Fotheringham (1891:27–8) describes how the wire which
came from Britain was drawn fine by local smiths, and wound round a core to
make the treasured waist-rings. Early in colonial times a market was
established at Tukuyu and there was a flourishing trade there in food in the
1934–8 period. Local exchange in produce from different areas continued
throughout the Rungwe valley and Ngonde plain. Maize from BuKukwe was
exchanged for *trichelia* berries and ointment made from them in Selya; rice
from the Nyakyusa plain for ground-nuts in Ngonde. Grain baskets were
bought from the Kinga, winnowing baskets from the Sangu, beer baskets from
Ndali, pots from Kinga hawkers who brought them from the Kisi market,
and dried salt-fish from hawkers coming from Rukwa. Since altitudes and
rainfall varied greatly between Lake Rukwa and Karonga (see map 1)
produce varied, and trade flourished. Some of this exchange dated from pre-
colonial times but there is no evidence on its changing volume.

The growth of the wealth of Mbande

How wealth and power were progressively concentrated in the hands of the
successors of the founding hero, Kyungu, in Ngonde has been described
elsewhere (G. Wilson 1939:39–48). It is argued that the Kyungu came to
control wealth through trade at Mbande, as the Lwembe at Lubaga did not,
and that trade developed at Mbande, not at Lubaga, because of the difference
in their geographical situation. Mbande was accessible, through a ravine to
the plateau between Lakes Tanganyika and Malawi which formed a corridor
between east and central Africa, and was accessible also to a relatively safe

lake crossing; whereas Lubaga was cut off by mountains, a great marsh, and the stormy tip to the lake. According to tradition, traders from Mwela on the east shore of the lake did not reach the northern shore until some time after they reached Ngonde. It is incontestable that, at least until 1955, the Kyungu disposed of wealth such as the Lwembe did not, and the Kyungu exercised political power in a way the Lwembe did not.

Iron weapons and tools 'of an unusual pattern' were preserved in the sacred groves of Ngonde, and the first Kyungu was said to have brought them (G. Wilson 1939:10, 15, 36–7; M. Wilson 1959:10, 14–5), but it was not claimed of the Kyungu, as it was of the Lwembe, that he *introduced* iron (and indeed iron goods dating from the third century A.D. have been found in the Ngonde plain). Acquisition of iron hoes in Ngonde seems to have been less closely linked with the celebration of ritual than among the Nyakyusa. A possible implication is that they were more readily obtainable through secular trade. From the time of the first Kyungu, cloth, iron goods and 'white crockery' were brought back by the men who went north with ivory. Later, Ngonde traded hoes from the Kisi at the north east corner of the lake, the Kisi having procured them from BuKinga, and after a lake crossing had been established hoes 'of a different pattern' came from Mwela, further south on the eastern shore of the lake, in exchange for Ngonde canoes (G. Wilson 1939:19; M. Wilson 1959:97 n. 2). Surprisingly, there was no explicit mention of hoes traded from the Nyiha on the northern plateau, though the Nyiha had ancient and extensive smelting furnaces (Kerr-Cross 1890; B. Brock 1966; P. and B. Brock 1965: 97–100) and were nearer Ngonde than the Kinga were.

The wealth of the Kyungu came from the export of ivory. At least from the beginning of the nineteenth century, and probably much earlier, tribute was paid to the Kyungu in the form of ivory—the right tusk of every elephant killed on the plain, and a lesser proportion of the ivory accruing to chiefs and nobles in the hills over which he exercised some suzerainty. He could call upon the chiefs and territorial nobles of the plain to provide him with food and beer when required, and they came with their followers to work the great millet fields from which store-houses at Mbande were filled. Prisoners taken in war and the kin of those executed for treason became the Kyungu's slaves. He distributed women slaves, whom recipients married, cattle, cloth, and waist-rings, and this distribution bound chiefs and nobles to him. The gift of a cloth from the Kyungu when a chief or noble sent him a hen, to notify him of a death, was particularly prized, and great chiefs similarly sent funeral cloths to the families of important commoners.

The 'sons of Kyungu' did not initially spread as did the 'sons of Lwembe' for only two sons of a Kyungu were permitted to live: the others were killed. Only at the end of the 'early period' in Ngonde history was the killing of infant sons of the Kyungu checked. In this 'early period' there were some chiefs (*abanyafyale*) related to the Kyungu, ruling territories, but more nobles (*amakambara*), i.e. followers of Kyungu who were not related to him, leaders of earlier occupants of Ngonde, and immigrants who came with a following. The heirs of all three categories of commoner leaders long retained power over territories—'fiefs' as distinct from 'chiefdoms'—but in the 'middle period' of

Ngonde history, as more sons of the Kyungu grew up, they began to replace nobles as territorial authorities. The manner in which this was achieved was that familiar in southern Africa, whereby the son of a chief was settled in an outlying area, and later replaced the local ruler (G. Wilson 1939:19–22; Hunter 1936: 380).

The 'early period' in Ngonde includes part of the century of Bisa dominance of the ivory trade (Roberts 1973:189–91) from the great plateau west of Ngonde. Bisa ivory caravans at one time travelled to Kilwa by a northern route skirting UFipa (Burton 1859: 256; St John 1970: 217–8) from the great plateau to the west of Ngonde. If the Kisi-type pottery found on Mbande hill was indeed associated with a Kyungu, then the 'early period' began during the fifteenth century, but there can be no certainty about dates until more archaeological work has been done. The 'middle period' of Ngonde history began a generation before the first Ngoni raids. These raids occurred after the Ngoni crossed the Zambezi in 1835 (dated by an eclipse of the sun), and before they moved to UFipa about 1842 (Read 1936:464, 468–9; Barnes 1954:16). Therefore, the 'middle period' of Ngonde history must have begun somewhere about 1800.

The Kyungu was a divine king with ritual power and control of trade; in the early period of Ngonde history it appears that his judicial authority was slight; he commanded tribute and could summon men to war and to hoe, but his power to keep the peace was limited. In the years following the first Ngoni attacks after 1835, judicial power developed, and in the 'third period', between 1875 and 1936, the transformation 'from god to magistrate' became complete (G. Wilson 1939: 25, 56–60, 68–70, 76–8). During this period cotton growing developed and in 1936 £1000 worth of cotton was exported, the Kyungu himself having taken an active part in its production.

After independence the institution of chieftainship was abolished in Tanzania, but it continued in Malawi, so that differentiation between Nyakyusa and Ngonde in this regard increased. No evidence on the effects of this differentiation is yet available.

Proportion of men to cattle

In 1934 everyone was agreed that among both Ngonde and Nyakyusa the number of marriage cattle given was increasing. Cock marriage was familiar to men still alive, and men in their sixties, married in the 1890s, themselves had given a spear for betrothal, and a hoe and one cow for marriage (*ukukwa*). Village headmen married at the same period were said to have given two cows, and chiefs ten to twelve. Mwafula in Ilolo village remembered that it was not unusual for his contemporaries to give a single cow to a father-in-law and recover it when it had calved, leaving the calf as a marriage cow. In Ngonde in the 'middle period' before the Ngoni came, one cow was given for a woman (G. Wilson 1939:46). Whether the rate remained constant throughout the middle period (c. 1800–1875) we do not know. The devastating rinderpest epidemic of 1892–3 was remembered everywhere but it was argued that its effect was temporary: a scarcity of cattle, and marriage with one cow, existed before the rinderpest, and herds recovered quickly after it. Mwangwanda, son of a village headman in the Rungwe valley, married as his first wife a young girl ('she had no breasts') about 1890. He gave a spear for betrothal and two cows, a bull, and a hoe at the marriage. In the period 1907–16 three to four cows were given for a commoner's daughter and ten to twelve for a chief's daughter or wife (Bishop O. Gemeseus, personal communication 1937; Fülleborn 1906: 344, quoted in Charsley 1969: 59). In 1934–8 five to eight cows and one bull were usually given for a commoner's daughter (24 cases recorded: average 6·5 cattle) and ten to twenty cows and a bull for a chief's daughter or wife (9 cases recorded: average 14 cattle). More cattle were asked for eldest and youngest sisters than for those between.

The reason given for the increase in the number of marriage cattle was that cattle had increased in the country. Mwafula said: 'Formerly cattle were not many: raiders finished them all.' And the chief Porokoto: 'Cattle have increased because the country is at peace; no one seizes cattle now. Formerly there was war; our cattle were finished.' Mwafula and Porokoto came from BuKukwe, part of the country that had been subject to Sangu raids in the last decades of the nineteenth century (Wright 1971: 47: 50), but the increase in the number of cattle given occurred throughout the Nyakyusa valley. Cock marriage, and marriage with one cow, had occurred on the lake plain and in Selya as well as in Bukukwe, and there is a strong presumption that cattle increased throughout the valley, though they may well have been more numerous on the lake plain and in Selya in the 1890s than in BuKukwe. Cotterill (1878), who travelled through the valley in 1876, and Kerr-Cross (1890:282), who travelled through in 1888, both reported that 'cattle abound', and Lugard (1893: I, 131) spoke of 'enormous herds' in 1888.

The cattle population in BuNyakyusa in 1934–8 was probably about half the human population,[5] and stock-holdings were widely distributed. Few men over 25 owned no cattle and many older men had four or five cows in their stalls. But if the Nyakyusa are compared with pastoral peoples like the Gogo, Nuer, Turkana, Dinka, or early nineteenth century Xhosa, it is plain that in 1934 they had proportionately far fewer cattle.[6] Professor Rigby has shown that the number of marriage cattle given is not directly proportional to a people's cattle-holdings,[7] but it can hardly be doubted that increase in the number given in BuNyakyusa between 1890 and 1938 was connected with an increase in the number of cattle in the district. A second factor was the rate of circulation. It seems that until 1914 men were reluctant to part with a cow before it had calved several times and they delayed marriage for this reason; by 1934 there was an urgent need for cash; cattle-owners sold calves to pay debts; and young men were impatient to marry as soon as they secured cattle, so circulation became more rapid.

By 1934 the Nyakyusa population had begun to increase fast and cash crops had been established. Up to 1938 grazing land was plentiful and cattle were normally in excellent condition as photographs taken at that date show. By 1955 population had increased, and the demand for land for cash crops had grown even faster. There was still unoccupied bush land in the middle region, but pastures in Selya and BuKukwe were visibly shrinking, and what in 1938 had been tall pasture grass was reduced to stubble. Cattle were in noticeably poor condition. In 1966–8 the proportion of cattle to humans in five villages investigated in detail was 0·33:1,[8] or 2·1 per householder. This figure is surprisingly close to the estimates of 1931 and the census of 1941, but less than a quarter of the 1933 count among mature men. Moreover the pasture per head of cattle, the milk available, and probably the rate of increase had considerably diminished.

From the point of view of Dutch economists, the return on capital invested in livestock was 'negligible' (Luning, Mwangoka and Tempelman 1969:16) in the Nyakyusa-speaking part of Rungwe district, but no consideration was given to the traditional importance of milk in the food supply, and means of replacing and distributing it if domestic herds were no longer maintained.

Population increase and sex disproportion

The annual natural rate of increase in Rungwe district was estimated at 2·3–2·4% per annum in 1967[9] and expansion of population in Ngonde had been still faster, probably owing to immigration, but changes in district boundaries made precise comparison difficult.[10] A sophisticated analysis of the 1967 population figures for Rungwe district is available; no comparable analysis of population in Ngonde.

An analysis of genealogies collected in 1934–38 suggests that, before 1934, a woman on the Nyakyusa plain who brought up two children who survived to marry was fortunate, and the conspicuously large families with many children surviving were those of monogamous christians living in the hills within reach of medical services.[11] Figures provided by the Medical Officer in Karonga in 1937 suggest that fatal diseases for children under one year on the Ngonde plain were malaria (54%), enteritis (22%) and, in the hills, pulmonary diseases. One cause of the increase in population has been closer spacing of children, already evident in 1934–38 and associated with pacification of the country, for the fact that a woman could not flee carrying two children was given as the compelling reason for spacing children four years apart (M. Wilson 1957a:131; 1959:204–5). In 1967 the average interval between births was 2·6 years, and the fertility rate for Rungwe district as a whole was estimated at 6·4–7·2. In 1968 it was 7·5 in a hill village (Hautvast and de Jonge 1972:92). The number of children per mother was higher in monogamous than in polygynous marriages (de Jonge and Sterkenburg 1971: 91–5).

A characteristic of the Nyakyusa population, at least since 1931, has been the preponderance of women, as the fragmentary figures in table 1 indicate. Professor Gulliver, who made a very careful study of the number of Nyakyusa men away from Rungwe district in 1954, concluded that the disproportion in

Table 1 : *Proportion of Males to Females in Rungwe District, 1931–67*

	Males	Females	
1931	73·6	100	Tanganyika Territory, *Census of the Native Population*, 1931
1948	80	100	Tanganyika Territory, *East African Population Census*, 1948
1954	87·9[1]	100	Gulliver 1957
1967	88	100	De Jonge and Sterkenburg 1971:67

[1] Allowing for bachelors and married men away without wives.

men and women was due partly to a disproportion in the survival rate, or else to a disproportion between males and females at birth. Comparative evidence suggests that a marked excess of females at birth is improbable, and a small sample taken in 1937 by the Medical Officer, Karonga (see table 2) confirms

Table 2: Demography of Thirty Villages, Ngonde, 1937[1]

Twenty-four villages within five miles of Karonga (lake plain)

	Adults		Children		Total
	Male	Female	Male	Female	
Population	989	1394[2]	1087	1116	4586
Deaths	17	16	34	40	107
Births			118	120	238
Still births			7	9	16
Deaths under one year (not including still births)			18	29	47
Causes of death under one year	Malaria		13	18	31
	Diarrhoea		2	9	11
	Influenza		3	2	5
Masculinity rate (adult)	70·9:100				

Four villages in hills, 4000 feet (near Nyondo and Misuku dispensaries)

Population	348	347	136	142	955
Deaths	5	1	15	13	34
Births			31	27	58
Deaths under one year			9	8	17
Causes of death under one year	Malaria			3	3
	Diarrhoea		1	3	4
	Respiratory diseases		7	2	9
	Other		1		1
Masculinity rate (adult)	100:100				

Two villages on the Songwe river

Population	134	137	72	73	416
Deaths	2	0	2	7	11
Births			9	11	20
Deaths under one year			1	4	5
Causes of death under one year	Malaria		1	2	3
	Diarrhoea				
	Respiratory diseases			2	2
Masculinity rate (adult)	98:100				

[1] These statistics were kindly supplied by the Medical Officer, Karonga, 1937. There was a complete census of each village.

[2] 1226 were women of childbearing age. No record of this statistic was available for the other villages.

that view, for although in 24 villages within five miles of Karonga on the lake plain, an area from which many men worked as labour migrants, the proportion of men to women was 70·9:100, in six remote hill villages (within the old Ngonde kingdom), the proportion of men and women was almost equal.

Dr de Jonge, whose standing as a demographer commands respect, working with Dr Sterkenburg, a geographer, and also a specialist in population, concluded that the discrepancy in Rungwe district in 1967 was due to the number of men who had left the district during the period 1940–1966 and not returned. He thought a differential survival rate unlikely (de Jonge and Stekenburg 1971: 68). However, comparative material from elsewhere in Africa suggests that where migrant labour exists on a large scale, the survival rate of men and women does differ.[12] Possibly the difference is most marked when mines are the destination of migrants, but this has not been demonstrated. The disproportion in BuNyakyusa may be expected to diminish, whether a differential survival rate is indeed associated with migrant labour or whether the present disproportion is due to emigration of men during the years 1940–66.

The figures, inadequate as they are, reflect two facts of great importance to our theme of the relations of generations and sexes: first, the rapidly increasing population leading to pressure on land and, second, the existence of a large number of women who have somehow to support themselves.

Changing costs and earnings

In the 1934–8 period there were recognized rates of exchange between cattle, grain of various types, pulses, spears, hoes, cow bells, wire waist-rings, bark-cloth belts, and household goods such as baskets, sleeping mats, and clay pots (see table 3a). How long these rates had been accepted we do not know but they were said to have been in use in a market that existed at Ilyolelo on the Lufilio river where Kinga had exchanged hoes and salt with Nyakyusa for food since before 1893. Mission records refer to 'inflation' in 1900 (Wright 1971: 94), and prices rose sharply again between 1938 and 1955.

Opportunity for employment within the Rungwe and North Nyasa districts between 1934 and 1938 was very limited. Government service as clerks, teachers, police, and messengers; mission service; domestic employment; work on a few plantations and work on the roads only absorbed a small number of men; but employment was available on the Lupa gold-fields 50 miles from Tukuyu. Some unskilled men from Rungwe went to the sisal plantations on the coast, and from North Nyasa men went south to Southern Rhodesia. A handful found skilled employment outside their home districts. Some married men, with the cooperation of their wives, earned money for tax and clothes by growing millet, rice or beans, coffee or cotton: it was difficult for an unmarried man to grow a crop on his own, and if he hoed for someone else he earned less than an unskilled labourer on the gold-fields. Unskilled earnings were 8s to 12s a month without food for a labourer on the Lupa in 1934–8. A full grown cow cost 40s, a bull 30s. Therefore six cows and a bull for marriage required two to three years' earnings for an unskilled man. This made no allowance for food, clothes, and tax while earning, or the additional marriage gifts, nor did it allow for cattle increasing. The man who said: 'Not everyone thought of marrying a chief's daughter, only one who knew he had cattle,' concluded: 'but now whoever wishes to do so goes and works for Europeans and gains cows. Yes, it is true that some people spend all they earn on clothes, and it takes time anyway to earn a cow, but it can be done. When I was a boy earning 11s a month I bought clothes at first, a shirt

Table 3: Costs and Earnings, 1934–8[1]

(a) *Exchange rates*

Cattle and chickens	Grain or pulses	Metal	Clay pot, basket, bark cloth	Cash
Cow	20 baskets (*ikibo*) = 400 kilo millet (if food was scarce smaller baskets were used to measure)	5 spears or 5 wire waist rings or 10 sets small bells		40s
Heifer	15 baskets = 300 kilo millet			30s
Bull (full grown)		8 Kinga hoes		30s
Bull (small)		6 Kinga hoes (after 1920?)[2] or 5 cow-bells (tuned set)[3]		8s
Bull calf	1 basket (*ikibo*) millet or beans = 20 kilo	1 Kinga hoe		2s
Chicken	1 basket millet or beans = 2 baskets rice or maize			25c to 50c
	Double handful millet		Large basket (*ikibo*)	
	Fill in maize (Kisi market)		Pot	
	Fill in beans (Selya)		Pot	
			Bark-cloth belt	50c
			Sleeping mat	2s

(b) *Cost of trade goods in local shops*

Trade hoe (less lasting than a Kinga hoe)	1.50s
Cloth (for a woman)	2s to 12s
Blanket	2s to 12s
Shirt (man's), cheapest	2s
Shorts (man's)	2s
Sweater	1s to 2·50s
Canvas shoes, cheapest	2s
Leather shoes	6s
Toga (for dance)	8s
Salt (per pound)	13c

Hawkers sold chiefly cloth and salt, and bought produce of all sorts which was sold in Tukuyu, Mbeya, and on the Lupa.

[1] In Selya unless otherwise noted.
[2] The relative value set on Kinga hoes varied. The value fell after 1920 as imported hoes spread.
[3] See M. Wilson 1964: 64.

Table 3: Costs and Earnings—cont.

(c) *Earnings*

Cultivation. Millet, beans, and rice were cultivated by some men for sale, to buy cattle. A man thought he had done well if he produced enough to buy a bull or a young heifer in a single season. It might require two seasons work.

A reaped 10 baskets of millet one season and 5 the next. He sold all 15 for a young heifer worth 30s. The buyer wanted the millet for beer.

B, with the aid of five wives and other relatives, cultivated a field in which he reaped 18 baskets of millet one season and 16 next. He was noted for 'strength in hoeing'.

C cultivated rice and sold 40s worth in one season.

None of these men used ploughs.

A man hoeing for a chief hoped for a heifer after two years.

Prospecting. The largest profit was made by a Nyakyusa holding a prospector's licence on the Lupa gold-fields. In two years he made a profit of 3,000s, from which he bought 40 cows.

and trousers, but then wisdom came to me and I wore only one cloth tied round my neck. I saved all my wages and in two years at 11s a month I had bought two cows. I said to myself: "I have no sister, and father has no cattle, I am a poor man, I must work."' It was possible for a Nyakyusa man to earn his own marriage cattle during the period 1934–8, but it took several years, and rigid self-discipline in saving (see table 4). The man who worked usually bought cattle and handed them over to his father-in-law, but by 1938 a few fathers were beginning to accept cash (at the standard rate of 40s for a cow, 30s for a bull) in place of some of the cows and the 'bull of puberty'.

The most prosperous period in the Rungwe valley was between 1944 and 1962, when the price of coffee rose and there was a demand for labour. Many Nyakyusa then worked underground on the Copperbelt in Northern Rhodesia, or travelled south to the coal mines of Southern Rhodesia and the gold mines of South Africa. Since 1963 only Ngonde have been free to go south, and opportunity for migrant workers on the Copperbelt has diminished. Moreover the proportion of men from Tanzania (many of them Nyakyusa) fell from 43·6% of foreigners on the Copperbelt in 1950–54 to 26·31% in 1966. The proportion from Malawi (including Ngonde) rose from 25·83% to 38·70% during the same period (Ohadike 1969:5, table 1). Restriction on employment coincided with a fall in the price of coffee and the spread of disease in coffee plantations in the Rungwe valley. The rise in price of cattle, followed by unemployment, affected bachelors most severely, for it made it very difficult for those who did not secure employment to marry. Table 4 reflects what evidence is available on the number of marriage cattle given, prices, and wages at different periods. The gaps are evident. The only substantial material on productivity is that for 1965–8.

One major difference between the economy of the Nyakyusa–Ngonde people, and the Nguni and Sotho peoples of southern Africa, whether living in the Republic of South Africa or in Lesotho and Botswana, must be stressed. It is that Nyakyusa–Ngonde villagers continue to feed themselves from the land they cultivate, whereas in the south self-sufficiency in food began to disappear in 1900 and has decreased to the point that most families in South Africa and Lesotho are dependent upon wages to buy staple foods such as maize, grown

Table 4: The Changing Cost of Marriage Co

Year	Cattle given				Hoes given	Spears given	Value of marriage gifts				Daily local[1] unskilled	Mo lo uns
	Commoners Average	Ideal	Chiefs Average	Ideal			Cow	Bull	Hoe	Spear		
1891	½?	1		3	1	1						
1897	3½	4	11	12	1	1						2s 7 cal rob (kh
1905	3½	4	11	12	1	1						
1925												
1935	6½	8	14	20	1	1	40s	30s	2s	8s	5c	6s t 4s. en)
1947							70s			8s		
1955	7?	10					200s				2s	
1960							300s					
1968	7	10		20			200s to 300s	150s to 200s	2s to 3s			12c (P.

[1] 'Local' includes the Lupa gold-fields.

[2] Money is expressed in Tanganyika currency though currencies in Nyasaland and Sout Africa differed. Cash represents current values.

[3] On the Lupa gold-fields and for domestic workers a food allowance of 2s a month was add not for plantation workers.

[4] Cost of schooling (a condition of most skilled work): Karonga, 1937, Primary 3s to 5s per a
Rungwe, 1972, Primary I–IV 19s p.a.
V 38s; VI + VII 58s.
Secondary School—no fees.
Uniform provided by parents.
80s p.a.

Earnings and Cost of Food, 1891–1968

ings ...ant	Local[1] skilled	Value of cash crops sold p.a.	Period to earn marriage gifts	Tax	Cost of food (local and neighbouring areas)	Monthly wage in neighbouring areas[2] (unskilled)
		1 calf after 3–4 yrs hoeing for chief	3–4 years		2 inch calico strip = 1 day's food for 2 men, Rungwe (1879). 4c or 1 yd calico a month per man, Kondowe (1895)	3s 3c or 8 yds calico, no food, Kondowe
			6 mths in job	4s		2s 7c and food, Kondowe (1897)
				6s	4½ yds calico a month per man, Plateau (1911). Sheep = 3s; goat = 2s 5c	3s and food, Plateau (1911)
	50s (cook) 180s max. (chief) 87s max. (clerk)[4]		2½ to 3 yrs in job 4 to 5 yrs hoeing	8s	2s monthly (P.W.D. rate) Rungwe (1935)	
				9s		
		Average in District Coffee 245s per taxpayer 450s to 3000s p.a. Average 460s	1 to 2 years			
ant ...r ...ed, ...ania,	100s minimum[4]	150s; women brewing 42s p.a.	2 yrs unskilled job; 15 months skilled; 10 years hoeing			

es

...ntyne and Shepherd 1968: 72, 250, 252
...nson 1881: I, 274
...dsbury and Sheane 1911: 6
...emeseus, personal communication (1930s)
... born and mission reports quoted Charsley 1969:59
...ver 1957: 55–9
...ilson 1939: 75
...ilson 1972: 4, 54, 66
...Konter 1971: 32–3, 35
. Mwansasu, personal communication, 1972

upon white-owned farms (M. Wilson and Thompson 1969–71: II, 55–62, 68–72). Inflation affects Nyakyusa–Ngonde villagers primarily in the cost of cloth, tools, household utensils, and transport, not in the cost of food.

Although it was said in 1934–38 that 'kinship is cattle' and in Nyakyusa–Ngonde thought and practice at that time the phrase held reality, nevertheless it had been possible in the late nineteenth century for men to marry legally without cattle and, if the oral tradition is accurate, there must have been centuries before the coming of cattle to the Rungwe valley and lake plain in which marriage by service was the general practice, as it was among peoples to the west and south (Richards 1940; Crosse-Upcott 1956; Mitchell 1956; Colson 1958; Marwick 1965). Marriage by service among Nyakyusa and Ngonde continued in poor lineages until the twentieth century. Marriage with cattle became relatively easy for two generations, sometimes involving as little as six months' to a year's labour, if a man saved all he earned, but by 1968 the *minimum* time for a man in unskilled employment and saving all he earned was two years. Most unskilled men must have taken considerably longer. Only a skilled man might expect to earn marriage cattle in under two years. Between 1935 and 1968 the cost of marriage cattle rose from approximately 260s to 1400s. Local unskilled wages increased about 5 times. The difficulties of young men turned on the fact that even unskilled jobs were scarce, and the ability of a family to assist a son with marriage cattle had diminished.

The form of marriage was closely linked to a changing economy but it was also linked to values such as patriliny, monogamy, and freedom of choice which cannot be explained solely in terms of economic pressures. These are discussed in succeeding chapters.

Access to land

Until 1938 competition for wealth was expressed primarily in terms of cattle, wives, cloth, wire waist-rings, food and beer, and a dignified (*nsisya*) homestead (see M. Wilson 1951a: 77–8). Coffee trees and substantial houses added to the dignity of a homestead but were not as important in inheritance as cattle and wives. Cloth, waist-rings, food and beer were of lesser importance. By 1955 land had become a scarce resource in some areas. Access to it came to depend on inheritance in a lineage, rather than on membership of a village (Gulliver 1958: 20–8), and there was competition for it between fathers and sons, comparable to the competition for cattle. By the period 1966–9, 26·1% of the land in a village established in 1900 on the lake plain, and 3·7% in a village established in 1930 near Rungwe mission had been inherited (Konter 1971: 24–7). The inheritance normally went from father to son, but the respective rights of men and women were questioned as land became scarce and women began to hoe for themselves. In 1934–8 it was said that 'all cases are about women,' and indeed most litigation turned on women and cattle. In 1954, 68% of civil cases in the lowest courts were marital disputes (Gulliver 1958:28 fn.). By 1968 there had been a marked shift to litigation about land and damage to crops. In Ngamanga village on the lake plain, 25% of the cases concerned land and 10% damage done to crops (van

Hekken and van Velzen 1970: II, 46). Consideration of inheritance of land leads directly to the question of how relationships between generations are changing.

NOTES

[1] In KiNyakyusa *ikibaga* means a byre and Lubaga suggests a long byre.

[2] Bishop Gemeseus of the Moravian Church stated that this was the case when he arrived in 1907 (personal communication, 1937). According to elderly men in Selya, daughters of commoners were also eligible.

[3] The root for milk (*ulu-kama*) in Nyakyusa is the same as that for ruler (*ba-kama*) in Nyoro.

[4] Fotheringham 1891: 29–30, 80. Nyakyusa–Ngonde artifacts are illustrated in Fülleborn 1906:Pls 64–7, 71, and M. Wilson 1964:figs 1–7, Pls II–IX.

[5] 'The number of cattle in the district (Rungwe) in the 1941 census was about 2·3 head per taxpayer, or 55 head per square mile' (Thwaites 1944). The 1931 census gave the population of Rungwe district as 195,062 and cattle were estimated at 58,000, i.e. 0·3 cattle per person. The population census figure was thought in the district to be an overestimate. In Ngonde, the population at the same period was thought to be about 40,000 and the cattle population 37,000, or 0·9 cattle per person. Seven Nyakyusa households investigated in 1933 averaged seven members and nine cattle (ranging from 4 to 23) but this was a middle-aged village, with more cattle than a young men's village.

[6] The Gogo had on the average between 1·55 and 2·52 stock units per person in 1962, the average depending upon the local area (Rigby 1969:50–1). Among the Nguni, in the early nineteenth century the stock population was estimated as far exceeding the human population. It fell dramatically in the later nineteenth century in part of the Nguni area, rose to 1·4 stock units per person in 1930, and then fell steadily (M. Wilson and Thompson 1969–71: I, 107; II, 57–8). A 'stock unit' = one bovine or equine or four or five sheep or goats. The Nyakyusa resembled the Arusha in cattle holdings (Gulliver 1963: 14, 242), and differed from the Masai among whom the cattle to humans ratio was about 14:1 (in 1969?) (Rigby 1969: 226).

[7] The Gogo average was 15 cattle and 10 small stock as marriage cattle, the Masai 5, and the Nuer *ideal* was 40 cattle (Rigby 1969: 225–6).

[8] Luning, Mwangoka and Tempelman 1969: 10, 13. Only five of the eight villages investigated in the district were in the traditionally Nyakyusa-speaking area and figures for these five only have been used. As cattle were expressed as 'stock units' in which calves counted as 0·25 unit, the figure of cattle to humans should be rather higher than 0·33:1 when comparison with figures of 1931 and 1941 is made, but the villages appear to have been occupied by mature men.

[9] De Jonge and Sterkenburg 1971: 101–2.

Table 5: The Observed Annual Growth in Rungwe in %, 1948–67

	1948–1957	1948–1967	1957–1967
Males	1·50	2·50	3·40
Females	1·55	2·05	2·45

1931	Rungwe District	195,062	Tanganyika Territory, *Census of the Native Population*, 1931
1948	Rungwe District	236,386	Tanganyika Territory, *East African Population Census*, 1948
1957	Rungwe District	271,287	*Tanganyika African Census Report*, 1957 (undercount?)
1967	Rungwe District	359,971	*Tanzania Census Report*, 1967

[10] *Table 6: Population of Ngonde, 1931–66*

1931	Ngonde, north of chief Mwafulira's country, i.e. not whole of Ngonde District	40,000	*Nyasaland Population Census*, 1931
1945	Karonga District	82,508	*Nyasaland Population Census*, 1948
1966	Karonga and Chitipia, formerly included in Karonga	137,082	*Malawi Population Census*, 1966

[11] Genealogies were collected on the Nyakyusa plain of 35 men, 25 of them with children married and ten with grandchildren married in 1934. They had 154 wives who had 274 children living, i.e. 1·78 per wife. Only 163 children who died were reported but the genealogies (designed to show inheritance) were collected from men, and only mothers were likely to recall all young children who had died. The families were wealthy; each man had on the average 4·4 wives and 7·8 surviving children. One fortunate and long-lived man, Mwamakula III (107), had 27 children from his five wives (not counting those inherited) and of the 27, 16 survived to marry. This indicates how wealthy lineages did in fact increase, even in the period when chiefs married 3 to 8 wives rather than 15 to 40 as they did in the 1930s. But, if this small number of families was representative, the Nyakyusa on the plain cannot have been increasing before 1934. It is possible that the population explosion took place in the hills.

[12] Houghton and Walton 1972: 51–9, and M. Wilson, Kaplan 1952: 91–3. Hastings (1973: 130–3) provides useful figures on sex ratios for Tanzania, Malawi, and certain other countries but, since figures for some of the labour-supplying countries are not given, the sex ratio for south east Africa as a whole cannot be deduced.

Chapter 5

GENERATIONS

Fathers, brothers, sons, and sisters' sons

GENERATION conflict is not something that emerged with an industrialized society. It was taken for granted in many pre-literate societies which devised a variety of institutions to control it. The Nyakyusa device was to separate fathers and sons. It was thought right and proper for men to enjoy the company of their male contemporaries; wrong for them to eat and drink, or talk in a familiar way with those of another generation—their fathers or their sons—or with women, whatever their age. Kinsmen did not live together: fathers and sons were required to separate, and full brothers, who were expected to be three or four years apart, very often lived in separate villages also. Of the men of one lineage only half-brothers, or the sons of brothers, were likely to live in the same village, and then their contiguity was accidental, not sought because of kinship. In the 1934–8 period, in a young men's village it was expected that groups of friends should eat together; older men more frequently ate alone, but they drank beer with their friends. It was accepted that chiefs would normally eat alone but when young clerks, fearing sorcery or wanting to eat butcher's meat regularly, began to do so, there was much criticism. However, men eating alone was more common by 1955 and had become the normal pattern by 1965–9 (P. M. van Hekken, personal communication 1969; Konter 1974a:14).

Ideally, the men of a village lived together from the time they were herd-boys of ten or eleven until death. They had legal responsibility for one another, less than for a kinsman but important when raiding was common. Defence was necessarily by a group of neighbours and great emphasis was laid on the fact that in a tight corner a man wished to be supported by village mates whom he knew and could trust. In practice, between 1934 and 1938 movement between villages was common, partly for fear of supposed witches who were no longer compelled to drink the poison ordeal, and partly to obtain land for coffee or rice; the extent of movement was probably greater than at an earlier period when accusations of witchcraft were tested, and the danger of moving considerable, or later on, when land became scarce.

The sons of the men of one village were likely (though not obliged) to build together, and usually elder and younger brothers separated themselves. Villages within a chiefdom were classified as those of fathers, sons, elder brothers, younger brothers, grandparents, grandsons; and the authority and mystical power of a father was thought to be shared in some measure by his village neighbours. The anger of 'fathers of the village' was feared as was that of a father. When in August 1935 a younger brother who had insulted his elder brother brought a calf to beg pardon it was held to be most important that his brother's neighbours share in the feast, eating the meat and wishing him well (p. 33).

The first wife brought as a bride to a young men's village was likely to be ordered about by her husband's friends. 'They say to their friend "Did not your father marry this woman for you to be the wife of us all?" And to her they say: "It is your work to cook, ours to eat."' This did not imply any sexual rights over her, but she was expected to be diligent and good tempered in drawing water for them. Women in a village did not form an age group, for a man growing old continued to marry young wives, and a young man might inherit women much older than himself from his father, his father's brother, or his own elder brother. The first wife brought to the village was entitled to some respect from women married after her, and the senior wife of the village headman shared ritual functions with her husband, but beyond that there was no hierarchy or bond other than personal friendship between the wives of village mates. With death, inheritance, and divorce, the movement of women from village to village in the 1934–8 period was considerably more frequent than that of men.

Before long-term crops were planted and land became scarce, the young men were allocated good land in the central part of the chiefdom on which to build their villages, their fathers moving to the boundaries of the chiefdom. And the young men seized 'cattle, food, and women' from the old men; this was their right. The mates of the first heir of a senior chief boasted in 1935: 'We came out with grandeur, we ate many men's cattle.' Young chiefs also went raiding neighbouring chiefdoms for cattle, and divided the spoil with their men. To them cattle were the object of war, as F. D. Lugard observed (personal communication 1933).

Chiefdoms and villages thus went through a cycle of development. At the 'coming out' each chiefdom split and both might survive to split again a generation later or one might be conquered and extinguished. Boys' age-quarters were reorganized on new sites as villages of the ruling generation, and their fathers withdrew; the old men's villages diminished in size and finally were extinguished (M. Wilson 1959: 49–57). At any point in time the relative status of villages was clear.

The ruling generations exercised political power and controlled much wealth; the retired generation exercised ritual authority and controlled a share of wealth. An heir took the social position of the man from whom he inherited. He commonly (M. Wilson 1951a: 35–6) moved to the deceased's homestead, took his name, and was accepted as a member of the deceased's generation. The dead man's sons became his sons, and this was reflected in the celebration of rituals and rules of avoidance, as well as in mutual economic obligations. The heir became *tata* (father) which was an office, not only a biological tie, and conflicts inherent in the father–son relationship were liable to grow greater in the relationship with his heir.

Competition between generations for marriage cattle was acute between 1934 and 1938. Senior men—those over 50—continued to marry young wives though their sons were lusty bachelors of 25, eager to marry, but unable to find the cattle. Commoners were limited by public opinion and the right of a son, in an extreme case, to summon his father to court, and claim marriage cattle coming in from a sister. But a chief was less subject to the opinion of neighbours and could not be summoned to court by a son—it was his court. This happened in the case of Mwaipopo, who had already been a chief when the missionaries arrived in 1891 and who must have been over 70 in 1934. He married his forty-first wife in 1935 but his younger sons in their late twenties were still unmarried, and repeatedly charged with seduction. His village headman had remonstrated with him, without effect. He argued that his sons were 'still boys', and that they did not hoe for him. 'They hoe for inlaws (*abako*), not for their own mothers. Delay in giving cattle is to teach them that they should hoe first.'

In Mwaipopo's chiefdom his 'son' Mwankuga (151) had 'come out' in the 1920s, and according to pre-colonial law Mwaipopo should have retired and the bulk of the cattle passed to Mwankuga, but Mwaipopo, like other elderly chiefs, was maintained in office by the administration of Tanganyika. Public opinion in the chiefdom was critical but Mwaipopo continued to draw his allowance as a chief, exercise power, dance at festivals, and marry young wives. He could do this only because peace was kept and chiefs supported by a police force, backed by an army, commanded by a Government based outside any Nyakyusa chiefdom. Before 1891 the power of young men had turned on two things: fighting strength and moral right. They were the lusty warriors, mostly between fifteen and thirty-five with a few rather older, and they were likely to be physically stronger and more numerous than their surviving fathers. From the time of their coming out they had the *right* to take land and cattle previously belonging to the older generation and, according to accounts of those who had participated, they seized them at some point after their leaders had burst out of the seclusion hut shouting 'war is come'. It is true that mystical authority rested with the fathers but it was not unbridled power: the shades were thought to support a father only when he murmured against a son with just cause. The approved constitutional order was that power should be handed on, and if a chief delayed unduly in celebrating a 'coming out' he was thought to fall ill from the 'breath of men', including men of his own generation. A case in which this was thought to have happened was cited.

In the 1934–8 period a son expected that his father would provide him with marriage cattle if he owned a herd, and the son's claim was particularly strong if he had full sisters. If the father were dead his heir inherited his responsibilities along with his property, so a son's claim might be pressed on a father's younger brother, or ego's elder brother, as it would be on his own father. For his part, the son was expected to serve his father as herd-boy and milker, milking twice a day, and to hoe diligently for him, working in his own mother's fields, but also helping his father in other fields for which he was responsible, and in building. If the father was not wealthy, it was thought proper by 1934 that, in his late teens or early twenties, the son should go as a migrant labourer to earn cash, and hand over the greater part of it to his father, but the father should then set aside a cow for his son, or at least buy a calf for him. The son might buy cattle for himself with whatever earnings he kept. In many families these reciprocal obligations were willingly fulfilled; in others there was acute friction turning on *when* a son might marry, and which of various claimants were to receive cattle which came in for a daughter, whether a son had fulfilled his obligations in hoeing, or whether a father had spent an undue share of his son's earnings without providing cattle in return. The day on which marriage cattle were brought for a daughter might be the occasion for discussion between father and 'sons' (own and classificatory) on the allocation of those coming in, and neighbours might join in expressing their views on a fair division. Mwaipopo remarked in 1935: 'In the hills younger brothers sometimes seize the cows when they are brought for the *ukukwa* but not if the chief has real authority. This is not customary here in Selya, only in the hills.' But a son might justly press his father 'to look for cows to give him, to look among is *abako* (sons-in-law)'; and a son or younger brother who felt he was being misused might appeal to his father's friends and neighbours to arbitrate between them. It was not ill mannered for him to raise the matter with his father or with his fathers friends, but to take his father to court was only done as a last resort.

The principles applied in balancing cattle and services were discussed by a number of informants in Ilolo in 1936:

If there are two sons by the same mother, the elder will always be given cows for marriage first though the younger may be more diligent in hoeing. No distinction is made between the second and third brothers in seniority. The eldest son is given a cow-for-the-house (*ja nyumba*) after he has married so that he has milk, and a son who hoes well may be given an extra cow after all the sons are married. A father marries for all his sons, but he only gives the cow-for-the-house to his senior son and those most diligent in hoeing.

[Kasitile at Selya in 1937:] Formerly a father gave his son one cow which calved until there were four: one of these the son kept in the house and three he gave in marriage. Later, perhaps his wife left him. The cows had calved at his in-laws—perhaps there were three calves. He claimed all six. Then he married again with three and three remained in his house and calved. Later he married a second wife with two cows. He now had two wives and cows for milking at home.

[Angombwike at Selya in 1936:] A father takes all the cattle from the marriage of his eldest daughter, perhaps three from the marriage of the second, and one from the third. A brother of one of the girls may ask for two cows and be given them. A son who goes out to work is like a girl, he gains cows for his father. He may gain 20 cows; they will all be his father's. But his father gives him cows to marry.

[Tulinagwe at Selya in 1937:] If a young man earns 30s he buys a cow for *ukukwa*. Yes, people are willing to sell cows when they need money for tax or to pay an adultery fine. We don't *ukukwa* with money but with cows. Money is not seen. Cattle are seen by the whole country and men say: 'So and so has given marriage cattle.'

A younger son of a wealthy man in Selya in 1937 was engaged to a girl for whom eight marriage cattle were asked. His father gave him three cows. He worked for a year on the Lupa gold-fields and sent 30s home with which his father bought him a fourth cow. The girl was still living with her father, but her father-in-law hoed one strip of garden for her and allocated to her a second strip planted with rice. Her husband, still away at work, sent her 2s to buy a cloth.

The following court case sums up reciprocal obligations:

CASE 33: MUTUAL OBLIGATIONS OF SENIOR AND JUNIOR BROTHERS
There were two half-brothers, sons of the same father by different mothers. The senior brother had several sisters, the junior none. In 1934, the junior claimed six cows with which to marry from his senior brother. The senior brother refused. The junior brother had not hoed for him, and though he had worked on the Lupa gold-fields he had sent him nothing. The court awarded six cows to the junior brother but required him to pay 20s to his senior brother in lieu of obligations. On appeal, the assessors were unanimous that six cows were due to the junior brother but that he must pay his senior brother since he had not hoed for him or sent him money or cows. The judgement was confirmed.

Accepted rights and obligations were confused by inflation: no one quite knew how to interpret customary law in terms of the changing value of cattle. And though the opportunity of earning might be expected to make a man more independent of his father for cattle to marry, the rapid rise in the number of cattle given in marriage, and limitation in opportunity for employment, partly offset this. When in 1963 the opportunity of employment diminished, but the cost of marriage remained as in a boom year, suitors found themselves unable to marry. Thus inflation of marriage costs exacerbated conflict between generations to the point that in 1965–8 one son threatened parricide (Konter 1974a:11), because his marriage had been so long delayed.

As in other patrilineal societies, the pivot in Nykyusa inheritance was a woman. A polygynist established a 'house' (indlu) for each wife, except for an unsakulwa—a younger sister or brother's daughter of an existing wife—who joined her kinswoman, and whose children were treated as junior full siblings of the elder sister's children. Property was not allocated to houses as it was among the Nguni to the south, or the neighbouring Gogo (Rigby 1969: 187–201): it remained under the control of the father, so long as he lived, but the eldest of each group of full-brothers had a particular claim to cattle from his full-sisters' marriages, and a particular responsibility for his younger full-siblings. On the death of his father and all his father's full-brothers a senior son gained the right of disposal over the cattle of his own full-sisters, of his daughters, of his full-brother's daughters, subject to claims created by 'milking-one-another's-cows' (ukukamanila) by his father or grandfather. A man with more than one wife might give a cow that had come in for the daughter of one house for the marriage of the son of another house; and by so doing he established a claim for the return of a cow from the receiving to the giving house when the daughter of the receiving house married. A similar link was established between half-brothers if a father used the cattle from a daughter to marry another wife himself. The new house thus begun was linked to the house from which the cattle originally came, and at least one cow had to be returned when the eldest daughter of the new house married. The exchange once begun went on; as their sisters and daughters married linked half-brothers continually gave each other cows; between their respective sons the exchange usually continued but between their grandsons it lapsed.

Before 1934 it was usual for a father to create an *ukukamanila* relationship between his senior son and the eldest son of each of his other houses, so that by this exchange of cattle the family was held together, but from then onward the practice became less common. Furthermore, it became increasingly common for a man to refuse to accept the estate of a brother because he wished his own estate to go direct to his son. These changes in the law of inheritance implied the break up of the wider lineage, something still regretted in 1955 (Gulliver 1958: 21). Since the heir, whether brother, half-brother, or son, took on the social identity and responsibilities of the deceased, often it was not apparent to an outsider that a particular *tata* (father) had not begotten his 'child'. Angombwike's own father had died when he was small: Gwamungonde, the deceased's younger full-brother who replaced him played the part of a father. As Angombwike put it: 'Gwamungonde gives my wife milk regularly. He married for me. I have given him four cows bought from earnings.'

The obligations of kinsmen to express mutual sympathy extended even further than economic obligations. Kinsmen were expected to notify one another of funerals, attend each others' funerals, request help in preparing for marriage feasts, and warn those concerned of such dangers as abnormal births, spearing, and the disease *ilyepa*, which were believed to spread among kin, if not controlled by treatment. A man was heard to complain at a beer drink that his half-brother had neglected to call him to attend a death ritual. The men present discussed the case and reprimanded the negligent brother.

In another case (recorded in 1936 by John Mwaikambo) a younger brother attempted suicide after quarrelling with his elder brother over a cow, and accusing him of not showing sympathy when his three children died.

CASE 34: ATTEMPTED SUICIDE AFTER BROTHERS' QUARREL

One day Mwakyusa the elder brewed beer and called people, including his younger brother, Mwakyusa, to drink. The name of the younger Mwakyusa was Litelile; the lineage name of both was Mwakyusa. When they were drinking beer Litelile said to his elder brother: 'Why do you not ask how many shillings were left from the cow I bought, and express sympathy for my mourning?' The elder brother replied saying: 'No, I have not expressed sympathy for your mourning'. Litelile said: 'And why did you refuse to give help for your children when I sought help for them, and they herded cattle for you?' [The implication is that Litelile had asked his elder brother for a cow and been refused, and he bought one.] Perhaps it was you who ate your children?' For three children had died. [Mwaikambo commented: 'We never say that a man eats his children through witchcraft: kinsmen do not do this, only people (non-relatives). Litelile said this in anger, without thinking of what he said. Sometimes, if two men are angry and the children of one have died while those of the other live, the father of the living may say: "Perhaps you ate your children and I should move mine away." This comes from anger: it is swearing at someone' (cf. M. Wilson 1951a:91–108).] The elder brother replied: 'See, I did not refuse to give you help.' Then the quarrel flared up. Mwakyusa the elder went out and the younger followed, quarrelling with him, and when the elder went elsewhere he followed him. Then the elder was angry and hit his younger brother twice with his fist, in the face. The younger brother said: 'This is the day of my death. I am astonised that you hit me, your brother.' He said this while he stood by the grave. We say that people who do this are inciting 'the breath of men'. People said this because, though others have killed themselves when their children died, Litelile had not done so at once; some time had passed since the death of his children. Litelile ran and took a spear and people seized him. Then he went home. When his wife asked him what he was angry about he replied: 'Who has told you that I was angry?' Then his elder brother came to see him, and Litelile, noticing a shadow, asked his wife who was there. She replied: 'It's Mwakyusa.' Litelile took a spear and stabbed himself. His elder brother entered the house and took him outside and bound up his belly with a cloth. In the morning he went to the chief and sought men to carry Litelile to hospital. The doctor asked why Litelile had stabbed himself. The elder brother replied: 'We were quarrelling. We began over a cow. He said: "I will kill myself. Since my three children have died it is better that I die also."'

A brother who received a sister's marriage cattle (or the greater number of them) had a special responsibility for that sister and her children, and she, for her part, was entitled to respect from her brother's wives and children to whom she was 'like a father'. A sister talked more freely with her brother in public than any wife might do; they were familiar together and a man's wives were observed to move away when his sister sat down to talk with him. It was to his father's sister, never to his mother, that a young man turned if he sought an intermediary in begging a favour from his father, and she exercised authority in the allocation of his father's inheritance including the division of cattle between half-brothers. As Mwaisumo's brother put it: 'My father's sister is a man like my father.' When Gwamungonde was disturbed at the decision of his heir to become a christian, he sent for his elder sister to come and 'talk the case' with the young man. The brother–sister tie is reflected in the claim a man has on his mother's brother (*umwipwa*) who received cattle from her marriage. If he asks for a cow for his marriage from this *umwipa*, formally visiting with a pot of beer to make his request, and hoeing for some time for him, his claim can be sustained in court. Even if he does not hoe he may still get his cow. As one man put it: 'He is my child, I bore him myself.' The cow from the mother's brother (*ijabwipwa*) was kept if the nephew could possibly do so; men laughed at him if he used it in marriage, saying: 'You are very poor, giving away your *umwipwa*'s cow': he should rather let it calve and give the calf as a marriage cow. A son who quarrelled with his father typically took refuge with his mother's brother, eating at his house, hoeing for him, and sleeping in a neighbouring boys' village. He might play him off against his father. A teen-age boy remarked: 'I have just been with my *umwipwa* for three months, hoeing for him and sleeping there. If I choose I can just hoe for my father who begat me, not for my *umwipwa*. My father would be angry if I ran away altogether, but not if I tell him what I'm doing.'

CASE 35: TAKING REFUGE WITH MOTHER'S BROTHER

Mwanyekule, son of Mwakwelebeja, was a tempestuous young man who had quarrelled with his father and others. He hoed first for his father, then for his mother's full-brother who had not received any of her marriage cattle, then for this man's senior half-brother who had received the cattle. His father, Mwakwelebeja, had allocated Mwanyekule two cows from the marriage of a sister, and later given him a bull, and replaced a poor cow with a better one. A senior half-brother also gave him a cow. But, of the cattle he received, one cow was returned at the death of his sister, one was returned because the woman for whom it had been given left her husband, and one

Mwanyekule paid in an adultery fine. The bull his father gave him was paid as a fine to his father whom he had actually struck, in a passion of anger. His father's comment was: 'He is very quarrelsome, he struck me, his superior, dangerously. He is very proud, he is not my child. He does not give me cows or hoe for me.'

In Nyakyusa idiom a young man had the right 'to take food', that is, to *order* that milk in the form of curds be supplied to him and his friends, if he visited his mother's brother's house and found him absent, *because* his mother's brother had married with cattle which came in for his sister, the young man's mother. The nephew had no rights in the home of a mother's brother who received no cattle. A sister's son was also a residual heir, inheriting if his mother's brother had no son, or brother's son, or half-brother's son to inherit in the ordinary way.

Something of the emotional quality of the relationship was conveyed by the way in which our friends drew attention to it. Kasitile pointed to a homestead we passed one day: 'Mwaipopo [the chief] came from there; that's his mother's brother's'; and Mwaipopo himself elaborated: 'My mother's brother is my *umwipa*. From him I get a cow. His sons are my *abatani* and if he dies they take his place and become my *abipwa*. My *abatani* are my friends and they bring a cow to bury me. I likewise go to their funerals with a cow.' And of Lubabelo, Mwaipopo's sister's son, it was said: 'He will not ask Mwaipopo for food. He will go and take it. He is *umwipwa* and that is the custom.' And Lubabelo added: 'In the old days I would have taken food from his people too. If I am in want of a cow and go and ask Mwaipopo he must give me one. If we are friends he may give me two. He will say: "When that daughter of mine marries, one cow (or two) are yours."'

The continuing importance of the mother's brother in the 1965–9 period was reflected in the fact that a landless man might beg land from his mother's brother if he failed to get any from his father (Konter 1974b:135).

Though inheritance remained so important in BuNyakyusa, relationships between fathers and sons were considerably different in 1934–8 from what they had been a generation earlier. This, at least, was the view of old men like Mwakwelebeja in Selya. 'Since European custom [*ikisungu*) has been established we have joined our children, we eat with them. Boys, both christian and pagan, greet their fathers without stooping down; in the old days a boy would not dare to go near the place where his fathers were eating.' In 1937, in Ilolo, we watched a young man and his friends helping his father in building. When the work was done they ate and drank with their fathers. An elderly man commented that in the old days, the sons would have been called to help, but given no beer; they would have been given a calabash of milk [curds] to eat separately. 'You Europeans brought the change in custom. You sit down with your children at table. The Swahili do the same.' In time of war, he said, elders objected to young men drinking beer at all. 'Now a young man who has returned from work *buys* a pot of beer, and comes to drink with his friends in his mother's house, his mother providing water [hot water is added repeatedly to a Nyakyusa pot of beer]; and he invites his father to join them.' And on another occasion chief Porokoto (K49) said:

Young men returning from work have less respect for seniors than formerly. What brings disrespect is beer; formerly the young did not drink beer, but now they come with their own money and buy and drink. Beer brings pride. A junior quarrels with a senior and seizes a spear. Beer used to belong to the older men. Yes, it belonged to men, there was none for sale, and juniors did not get any. A man did not sit drinking in his house with youngsters; only when they had been through the 'coming out' were they given beer. Now they drink their own beer [which they have bought]. Formerly bachelors had no beer, and a married man should take his millet to his senior, his father or senior brother, if he had one. Formerly all the millet from the fields of two brothers was taken to the house of the senior and he divided it, allocating only a little to the wife of the junior 'for porridge'. A younger brother took it all to his father if the father were alive. An elder brother thought: 'I am grown up, I'm a man,' and he divided his crop, taking some to his father. Even a junior divides for himself now. Other food belongs to the grower, but beer was most important. Beer taken to in-laws (abako) implies a request for a cow.

Traditionally, a father or his heir had mystical power over his children and an obligation to pray and celebrate rituals on their behalf. Belief in mystical power exercised by a father was still lively in the 1934–8 period and rituals were regularly celebrated by pagans (M. Wilson 1957a: *passim*), but there were hints of a lessening of belief (M. Wilson 1959: 166–215). Gwamungonde told how, after inheriting from his elder full-brother he went to live with a senior half-brother (he was still in his teens), leaving the homestead of the deceased. For two years he hoed millet and the crop was small so he went to a diviner to discover the cause. The reply was that his elder brother was angry because he had not swept his grave (implying remaining in his homestead), so he brewed beer and killed a cock, leaving them overnight in the banana grove. Next day the children tasted the beer and ate the cock. The following year the millet harvest was plentiful. Gwamungonde spoke of having prayed regularly in the banana grove in the evening, blowing out water, when children of his household were sick, but he had 'left off since Angombwike became a christian.' Mwakyonde (148) and Mwakewelebeja (p. 69) continued to pray as a matter of course. Mwakyonde: 'If my child is sick with *mindu* [illness caused by the shades] I go to the banana grove with water in a calabash cup and I blow out water and pray: "You, father Mwakomo (112), why are you angry?"' And Mwakwelebeja said: 'I pray to my father with a calabash of water saying: "Stand by me, why does disease kill my children?" It is forbidden to pray in the house for the women are there and we have to speak the names of their fathers-in-law. I always go to pray in the evening when the cows are coming home. The women shut the door of the house when I pray. Sometimes when we pray we leave a little beer in the banana grove for my father. We pray with water and leave the beer there overnight, then my children drink it.' 'When a man is blessed by his father the cows do increase. My father stands with me. Also food is plentiful, crops flourish.'

Mwankuga II (151), heir of Mwaipopo (116) and of the sons' generation to Mwakwelebeja and Mwakyonde, took the traditional view of a father's mystical power, and a friend accompanying him shared it: 'If a married man, married with his father's cows, goes away to work and gains much wealth, and does not send any home to his father, he will fall sick, the shades will be angry and say: "He is not wise, his father gave him cows for his marriage and he has given his father nothing." He will fall sick there at work. But if he is an unmarried man it is different, his father has given him nothing, so he may keep the cows and get himself a wife, and nothing will happen. But the first cow he gains he should send home to his father. If he does not he will fall sick. Young men know very well that this is the custom.' Mwankuga II himself had not begotten a son by the wives inherited from his deceased elder brother, Mwankuga I (150), and his village headmen had taken him to a diviner who diagnosed *mindu*, illness from the shades, so prayer was made and he was treated by a doctor, but no son had been born. Mwankuga II was therefore very conscious of mystical power intervening in a man's life. The shades were thought of as being roused to action by the just anger of the living who spoke of their misdoings in places frequented by the shades (M. Wilson 1957a: 187–8; 210–21). Kasitile explained: 'I crouch over the fire in the evening and mutter to myself (*ukwibunesya*): "Did I not marry for him and he does this to me?"'

Mystical power was thought to operate in several ways: sores around the mouth (*mindu*) and sterility were the typical but not the sole diseases attributed to a father having muttered in anger; paralysis and sterility were spoken of as due to a curse (*ikigune*) of neighbours, who had supported a father in his anger at the wrongdoing of a son, or were incensed because the heir had not killed a cow on moving into the homestead of the deceased 'that people may bless him, may rejoice, because he is now the owner of the homestead'.

An internal complaint in children, *ilyepa*, was attributed to a medicine taken by an angry grandfather. 'If I hit my father and he is angry, he alone, he drinks a medicine for *ilyepa*, and my child falls ill of *ilyepa*.' This medicine was thought to work only between kin, and to be ineffective if drunk by any unrelated person (M. Wilson 1957a: 176–8). The mortality among Nyakyusa children was high and their constant illness with malaria or enteritis was commonly attributed to the wrongdoing of parents. This linking of the health of a child with the right behaviour of the parent continued into adult life. 'If my daughter is married and I do not give my elder brother a cow, and he is angry, she will fall sick. She recovers when I beg pardon of my brother with a cow . . .' 'When relatives argue, perhaps a father with his son or younger brother, then the son or younger brother, or a child of the son or brother, falls sick and people say: "See, he argued with his father." The sickness will never fall on the father.'

The characteristic sin of Nyakyusa society, in which men under 25 were usually unmarried and elderly men were polygynists, was for a son to seduce one of his father's young wives. Occasionally a man gave permission to his heir, even though a son, to cohabit with a particular wife in secret; much more often, it was said, it occurred without his permission. Either way, when the father died, the son feared to approach his grave, and a wife who had laid with her husband's son also kept away. A case occurred in 1936 in which the son became very ill until treated with cleansing medicine as he stood under a waterfall (M. Wilson 1957a: 134–5). This danger was not thought to affect an heir who was the younger brother to the deceased, only his son.

If the son were discovered while his father was yet alive he fled, perhaps seeking employment at the coast, or he might seek refuge with his mother's brother.

Formerly, when we were children, if a man lay with a wife of his father and was discovered, he fled to his mother's brother (*umwipwa*). When he had lived there for a long time his mother's brother sought a little bull and a calabash of beer to take the young man to his father. This taking him to his father was called 'the astonishment' (*ubuswigana*); if a young man had made love to his father's wife it was called 'an astonishment'. His father had begotten him and if he did not enter into his father's house while he was alive, he could never enter. But if he entered before his father's death then the astonishment was finished. So his mother's brother thought: 'Should my child just be a stranger in the home where he was born?' And he brought the young man and the calabash of beer and the little bull to say: 'Let them bless one another.' He said: 'I have come with your child who committed a crime (*apitile*) at your place.' They always used the word *ukupita*. They did not speak of committing adultery in such a case though now in court, when the chiefs judge such a case they speak of adultery. They compared his crime to witchcraft. They said he had bewitched (*ambitile*) his father, which meant he went in secret to kill him, because it was said to sleep with your father's wife was to kill him.

Then the father called his relatives, his brothers and children, brothers of the wrongdoer, and his neighbours, to bless one another. He told them all of the wrong, saying: 'He worked witchcraft at my home, he worked witchcraft against me, his father.' The mother's brother sat separately on the side. They of one blood took council together. So they would take the little bull and eat it. The mother's brother they praised, saying: 'He is a great man, he thought about the case of his sister's son.' And they sought for something for him to take home.

Some men formerly divorced a wife in such a case.

If a young man committed adultery with his father's wife the father divorced the young man's mother; then they both went to her brother. The woman was divorced on account of her son's wrongdoing, though she herself had committed no wrong. They said her son's wrong was hers. If the young man were poor and had no mother's brother he and his mother went to the chief to hoe, and became people of the chief's household (*abankitangalala*).

Adultery is common now; they have left off speaking of 'the astonishment'. But occasionally, if the mother's brother loves the young man, he seeks a bull, a *big* bull (because formerly cattle were scarce), and beer, to bring him to his father . . . Now they enter according to the custom of the administration. But formerly they did not enter. Formerly, if your father saw you he said: 'He's a stranger to me.' If you entered his homestead to be brought to him, and you saw each other you would not approach him or shake hands, or enter his house. When he saw you he would be very angry. If he saw you and was angry and died without being satisfied you would pay the junior fathers and the chief and village headmen to enter.

This account reveals a certain flexibility in custom: a procedure for reconciling father and son existed. In theory an erring son could never enter his father's house if he did not do so during his lifetime, but in the last paragraph it is suggested that if he did come and was rebuffed, and his father died, he might yet pay his father's younger brothers, and neighbours, and chief, and be accepted. Moreover, by the 1934–8 period men were less shocked than they used to be (*ubuswigana* implies *shocked* astonishment), and a son might enter 'according to the custom of the administration'.

Sometimes the respect due to a senior brother from his junior was in question if the junior appeared to be richer.

CASE 36: A SENIOR BROTHER SURPASSED BY HIS JUNIOR

A certain junior brother built himself a fine *ikibaga* [the long house divided into rooms for wives and cattle, which is a mark of dignity, a symbol of wealth and prosperity, cf. M. Wilson 1951a: 77]. The senior brother was very angry, reproving his junior brother and saying: 'Why have you built a house better than mine? Is it the custom?' And he burnt down the junior brother's house. 'It is an old custom to do this kind of thing if a man's junior brother surpasses him in any way.' Later the senior brother and his children fell sick, and he admitted arson, for it was believed that if a man ignited another's house, 'the flames are found in his children's bellies,' and their healing depended upon his confession. 'If he does not admit the wrong the children die because of his sin.'

If the quarrel were in a chief's family the whole country might suffer. Mwaihojo (147) and his younger brother Mwakyonde (148) had long been on bad terms. Mwakyonde attributed the fact that his medicine to clear the country of the wild pig devastating cultivation had failed, to his quarrel with Mwaihojo. He said: '*Sili nemindu ingulube*', implying that the wild pig were an affliction from the shades.

Quarrels between half-brothers also led to mutual accusation of sorcery (M. Wilson 1951a: 126–7). By 1965–9 sickness was attributed to natural causes in many cases, but where disease did not yield to treatment and illness lingered, then mystical causes were still invoked, and the anger of senior relatives feared. In particular, neglect of the death ritual was believed to bring misfortune on a family. In terms of the changing economy the celebration of traditional funeral rites had become a heavy cost in time, as well as in stock, and filial obligation had become incompatible with economic self-interest (Konter 1974b:174; 1972:30).

In the 1934–8 period conflict between fathers and sons turned on cattle with which to marry. By 1955 a second source of conflict existed: land. In some chiefdoms arable land, especially land suitable for rice on the lake plain had become scarce, and fathers and sons were in competition for it. Professor Gulliver reported:

The younger Nyakyusa men find increasing difficulty in obtaining arable land now that there are no longer vacant areas to be taken up, and the older men are no longer prepared to cede their land rights in favour of the younger generation, as they traditionally did. When occasional fields are left vacant, the young men must take their turn with their elders, who themselves are so chronically short of land—and the headmen commonly favour the older villagers with families as against the younger men. This means that in the high-density regions the majority of men under the age of about 30 years have little or no arable land, nor can they hope for it until the deaths of their fathers. In the congested village sites even their banana plots may be smaller than is desirable for the provision of the staple food.

The young man, then, is compelled to remain dependent on his father's and elder brother's holding . . . Thus the valued independence of the young Nyakyusa is severely restricted and it seems that tensions and difficulties are beginning to arise between fathers and sons, and between brothers, because of this . . .

Only in the low-density region can the young men obtain the fields they require. There, as they did traditionally, the young adult sons continue to assist their fathers in the heavier labour in the fields, but gradually before marriage they accumulate and extend their own holdings and so achieve economic independence . . . Elsewhere . . . this process . . . very frequently awaits inheritance at the death of the father . . . (Gulliver 1958:36-8).

Access to land in the more densely populated chiefdoms thus became dependent upon inheritance, and most arable land passed from father to son. This meant also an additional and bitter ground of conflict between brothers, who were often in competition for shares in a holding too small to support all of them (Gulliver 1958: 20-2). Ten years later elders possessed most land, and received the largest share of payment from the agricultural cooperatives for their crops. Those over sixty lacked the labour to work the land they had, while many young married men had no land at all, or insufficient to keep their families (Konter 1971: 14-16; 21-7, 33-5). Men commanded the labour of their wives and children, and sons sought to evade their obligations, for they had little expectation of the traditional reward for diligence in hoeing: cattle with which to marry. Boys sought instead education, which might lead to a paid job with an income eight times that from farming in the 1965-9 period.

Shifts in power between fathers and sons were complex. On the one hand the pacification of the country from 1900 (when Nyakyusa armed resistance to the German administration ceased) meant that young men lost their importance as warriors. Raiding neighbouring chiefdoms for cattle was stopped: the violent seizure of the old mens' cattle at the 'coming out', said once to have occurred, no longer happened. Young men no longer had the opportunity of acquiring marriage cattle by fighting (unless they served with the King's African Rifles as many Nyakyusa and Ngonde did in the 1939-45 war), but they did have the opportunity to earn marriage cattle by working in paid employment. Everything turned on wages in relation to the price of cattle and the number of cattle required for marriage. As shown in table 4 (pp. 80-1) the cost of marriage cattle (excluding other gifts) rose from about 260s in 1935 to a minimum of 1400s in 1968 and local unskilled wages increased more slowly; moreover, in the 1934-8 period most young men were able to combine earning with assistance from their father or an elder brother. Furthermore in 1934-8 every cow might be expected to calve annually, and though some cattle died, once a man owned a cow he could begin to accumulate a herd. By 1968 Konter reported that 'few fathers could assist their sons with marriage cattle.' Some fathers did so, for a fifth of the cattle held in five villages were given or received as marriage gifts within one year (Luning, Mwangoka and Tempelman 1969:26, 45), and since the polygyny rate was falling a substantial proportion of these are likely to have been for the marriages of sons. But in 1966-8 cattle disease caused serious losses and stock-holdings fell, so expectations of sons could not be satisfied. No evidence is given on the age standing of the villages in this survey.

The number of cattle in Rungwe district increased with the population but pasture diminished in area and quality. Until 1938 it was the increase in stock coming in for daughters before it was necessary to pay them out for the marriages of sons, who married ten to fifteen years older than their sisters, that enabled many men both to keep cattle in their byres and assist their sons. In 1966 the average difference in marriage age was still eleven years, but if the rate of increase in cattle had indeed fallen drastically (as it did elsewhere in Africa on overstocked grazing land, cf. M. Wilson and Thompson 1969–71: II, 58) then difficulties in providing marriage cattle at rates set during the prosperous years, 1952–62 became obvious. Furthermore, potential consumption was changing, most conspicuously in clothing, housing, furnishing, transport, alcohol, and education; and fathers of marriageable daughters found it was all they could do to meet the needs of their households.

An elderly man was traditionally looked after by his young wives. Provided he owned cattle, he continued to marry wives. The sons and sons-in-law of his younger wives were expected to hoe for him, and he got millet for beer from married sons; only a man lacking wives and children was destitute, though a monogamist, with one wife no more than ten years younger than himself and sons already married, commanded little labour. As some cash became essential for everyday life, and pension schemes had not begun, old men became relatively poorer. The wages earned by their sons were required by them to marry, to pay school fees for children and to clothe them; there could be little to spare for elderly relatives: needs were far greater than income (Konter 1971:31). The increase in consumption without corresponding increase in total income exacerbated tension between generations.

In the 1934–8 period it was openly said that old men were hanging on to political power, notably elderly chiefs continued to draw government salaries when their sons had already 'come out'. On the other hand, it was mostly young men who had acquired some education and who got appointments as clerks. Changes in inheritance also tended to favour the young as sons, rather than younger brothers of the deceased, inherited. But changes in inheritance also tended to increase the relative wealth of senior sons at the expense of other members of the lineage. By 1969 those in power in the ruling party, TANU, were mostly young men (Konter 1971:18) but land-holding had passed mainly to older men; young men had difficulty in getting land and paid employment was scarce. Shifts in power between generations were therefore not clear cut but depended upon opportunity for education and employment, access to land, the form of legal marriage, the ground of selection for political office, and war or peace.

Traditionally, old men had retired and handed over political power and a portion of their wealth in cattle to their sons at the 'coming out', but they retained ritual power both within lineages and chiefdoms. The lively belief that they controlled fertility in man, in cattle, and in fields made their authority secure so long as it was legitimately exercised. Once elders exceeded recognized rights the authority of the older generation was diminished, but christians were slow to question it. Many christians interpreted the commandment: 'Honour thy father and thy mother, as the Lord thy God hath commanded thee, that thy days may be prolonged, and that it may go well with thee, in the land which the Lord thy God giveth thee' (Deuteronomy 5, 16) in the light of ancient ideas of the control of fertility, but christians not only thought of mystical power as exercised by elders in the church, as well as by their own parents, they questioned what was legitimate in the exercise of power (M. Hunter 1937).

Mother and child

In traditional law, a mother might be divorced for a son's wrongdoing, as the text quoted on p. 95 shows. In the 1934–8 period a child was also thought to suffer, pining and growing thin, if its mother quarrelled with her husband or was rude to her in-laws, or it might be made ill by her father's shades if marriage cattle were outstanding (M. Wilson 1957a:129, 188–9, 215–9). But the mother herself had no mystical power to discipline her child. Kasitile explained: 'At my place there are no shades of a wife. She prays at her father's place or in the grass on the road. My mother is no relative of the shades here. Our wives don't eat a cock killed in the homestead . . . A young woman's sickness comes from her parents, never her husband, but her child is another matter. If I have not given marriage cattle I take the mother and child to her father's place and leave them there. They go and pray in the evening. She remains during the following day and then returns to me. Then the illness finishes. The shades are angry if the marriage cattle are not given.' 'Women never mutter about their children, only the father does that . . . But my father's sister can, she is a man like my father.'

A boy's primary responsibility was to assist his father in hoeing, and hoe in his own mother's field. As he grew up he was also expected to provide his mother with salt, but in pagan tradition he was not responsible for her in old age: that was the obligation of the heir and a man did not inherit his own mother. By 1955, when pagan as well as christian women were expected to wear cloth, an heir's obligation was felt to be onerous particularly when, as the heir of a wealthy chief, he inherited many elderly women. Mwanyilu (177) complained bitterly of the cost of maintaining the women he inherited. His 'mothers' could not be expected to earn their own clothes like commoner women, and fields had to be hoed for them.

Law and practice were changing from 1934 on and many widows— christians and already by 1938 a few pagans—elected to live in the homestead of their own adult son, being 'built for by a son'. This implied that the son not only provided a round house and kept it in repair, but also that he hoed a field for his mother to plant and reap, and, if she were a christian, he was expected to provide her with clothes. The unity of the 'house', the group formed by a woman and her own children as distinct from other like groups, persisted. It was concerned with property, either inherited or coming in for daughters, and from the earnings of sons, and with the responsibility for sons' marriages.

The 'house property system' was widespread in Africa but varied widely in degree (Gulliver 1964). There was a continuum between those societies in which almost all property was allocated to houses during a man's lifetime, and those in which little was allocated. Each 'house' was considerably more independent where most cattle were allocated to it early in a woman's marriage, as among Nguni and Sotho peoples of the south (although among the Mpondo some cattle remained úndistributed and were inherited by a man's senior son, cf. Hunter 1936: 120); they differed from the Nyakyusa, among whom property was held undivided by the head of a polygynous family until his death, and fraternal inheritance was the rule. Where house property was fully developed a mother who was built for by her son was the mistress of the homestead, occupying (among the Nguni) the great hut facing the cattle-byre; often she was built for by a son after her eldest daughter had married (Cape of Good Hope Government 1883: II, 72), before her husband's death, for to live with a son, waited on by a daughter-in-law, was a position much desired. Where house property remained unallocated during a man's lifetime and inheritance was fraternal, his wives remained with him, and only a widow who was old was permitted in Nyakyusa law to join her son. He then built for her 'at the side' of his homestead, and the difference between the position of her hut, and that of a mother's hut among the Nguni, reflected a difference in status. In BuNyakyusa a mother was not mistress but a dependent.

The emotional bond between mother and child was commonly thought to be closer than that between father and child: mothers mourned dead children more than fathers did because 'we women have much work with children, men very little . . . My mother had ten children. Five died. If she and I mourn at a funeral I get tired quickly, but mother remembers all the children who died and never leaves off weeping.'

The tie between mother and daughter remained strong as a girl grew up. A pagan mother liked her daughter to be betrothed young that 'she might eat from her sons-in-law before she died.' A son-in-law, like her own son, had an obligation to hoe for her and provide her with salt. For her part, she cherished her daughter when she was sick, and after childbirth, and helped her in cultivation during the early years of her marriage. As one young woman explained: 'If your own mother is alive you are looked after when you go home to visit after the birth of a child. If she is not alive you have to fetch firewood and cook for yourself.' When a young married woman returned to her husband she should be taken back with gifts and one of the points of tension in a homestead was where these gifts should come from if the own mother of the girl concerned was dead or divorced. Some fathers specifically reserved a section of the banana grove for their own use, that they might be able to provide a daughter who lacked a mother with gifts to take back to her husband. Above all, the mother was sympathetic when a daughter came home. We heard Mwaihojo's newly-married daughter complain to her mother and father's sister of her in-laws 'swearing at' her, 'and I the daughter of a village headman'. 'Headman?' said her father's sister, 'We are *chiefs*. . . .'

A father had expectations from his daughter and in the 1934–8 period there was clearly great pressure on a girl approaching puberty to marry a man with cattle, and to remain with him. It was her responsibility to nourish (*ukuswela*) her father by staying married, but conflict over choice of a husband occurred and recurred. A father might command his daughter, or implore her to stay with her husband; he might refuse to accept marriage cattle for her from another man and so shame her greatly; and most people believed that his anger might prevent her conceiving a child or cause it to be sickly. All this did not prevent repeated divorce (pp. 43–52; 190–2). But there was a continuing sense of obligation of child to parent and the worst thing that could be said to a son or daughter by either parent—more usually the father—was *akaja mwanangu* (he/she is not my child). Such denial of kinship was fearful to pagan and christian alike. 'You are not my child' was the phrase a christian mother used in reproving an erring daughter; but in practice it seemed that a mother never cast off her daughter as a father might do. Nyakyusa prostitutes, talking together on the Lupa gold-fields in 1937, spoke of how they all longed to visit home and of how nearly all did so. Some fathers refused to receive a daughter who had run off from her husband—one was cited who had refused until his death—but a mother would welcome her daughter whatever had happened, and hide her from her father if necessary.

A girl also had an obligation to a sister. She was the preferred mother for motherless children if an elder sister died, and in 1934–8 the implication was that if she loved her sister she would agree to go as a replacement for the dead. A case was cited of a pagan man promising a dying wife to replace her with a sister, and in 1937, in two christian families, younger sisters of the dead women were sought to replace them and care for their children. A pagan girl might also be sought as an *unsakulwa* to be a junior wife in the house of her elder sister or father's sister. If she were married in this way she lived very closely with her senior kinswoman, and the solidarity of sisters in opposition to other wives in a polygynous family was never in question, but a father's sister must be shown respect in a degree in which an own sister was not. As Jane and her co-wife (wives of Kasitile) put it: 'You respect your father's sister very much and carry things for her. If you are rubbing each other with ointment it's forbidden to smear her back; she is father, even though she is a child, younger than yourself.' (In Nyakyusa thought the back is associated with sexual activity.)

Parents and children helped one another in cultivation and in the provision of feasts both before and after sons and daughters married. Above all, they celebrated rituals together at death and birth, marriage and misfortune.

The absence of children or the death of parents meant less help in agricultural work and in the provision of feasts. Both for a woman and for a man the absence of children implied destitution. This is a widespread pattern in peasant communities, where labour is continually needed, and therefore large families are looked upon as an insurance in old age. But change comes with pressure of population on land and the recognition, as in Ireland (Brody 1973:48–73, 120), that sub-division of a small holding is disastrous, for not more than one family can make a living off it. By 1965–9 in BuNyakyusa assistance in cultivation from children, whether married or unmarried, was diminishing. Men engaged in producing cash crops were beginning to depend upon paid labour rather than on the help of kin and neighbours (Konter 1971:35–6).

Detailed evidence on change in the pattern of feasting is lacking, but there is reason to suppose that by the 1960s feasts had become less numerous and much less lavish than they were in the 1935–8 period, when enormous quantities of food were exchanged between lineages at marriages, and distributed to kinsmen and neighbours at funerals (M. Wilson 1957a: 31–5, 44–6, 90–4, 98–100, 120, 122, 153).

In-laws

Mutual aid and sympathy was due first within a man's own lineage but it extended to his in-laws (*abako*), i.e. parents-in-law and sons-in-law, and also to his mother's people (*abipwa*). This was evident when lists of those cooperating in cultivation and attending rituals were collected. Girls of perhaps 8 to 12 years old worked with their mothers in the fields, weeding, planting, washing millet and carrying it home, collecting firewood; and as each girl married her 'mothers' (her own mother together with co-wives and friends) came to help their daughter in her fields. They came perhaps for two years, after which she might be told to manage by herself. Her husband's mother with her co-wives might also come to help. In 1935, of five women washing Gwamungonde's millet crop three were wives, one a daughter, and one an in-law; Mwandalema's crop was washed by three wives and a daughter; Mwaipugo's by two wives and five daughters; Mwandamba's by one wife, one sister, and one neighbour. 'Daughters' included married and unmarried girls. Three women found planting sweet potatoes with a girl explained: 'We're in-laws (*abako*).' The girl was betrothed and her 'husband' had hoed a field which her 'mothers' had come to plant. They would weed and harvest the crop for themselves, giving him a share if the crop were good. After the girl reached puberty she would plant and harvest for herself but her 'mothers' would come to help her, and her husband might give them some of the crop. He, for his part, should continue to give his wife's mother salt, even after his wife has joined him. Attendance at rituals extended much further than mutual aid in cultivation (M. Wilson 1957a: 190–202, tables a–e) and the rhythm of work was modified by the obligation to attend funerals and other rituals. All Gwamungonde's wives had stopped work on the millet one day because a grandson of his classificatory brother, Mwakasoule, had died and they had gone to the funeral, and another day one of the daughters-in-law had gone off to the funeral of her mother's sister's husband.

Although members of one's own lineage, in-laws, and mother's people cooperated in work and ritual, attitudes towards them differed greatly. A lineage was an in-group, in opposition to other lineages, particularly in case of attack by raiders, claims for property, and accusations of witchcraft which was thought to be hereditary (M. Wilson 1951a: 103, 252–3). How a younger brother was identified with the husband himself has been described, and in his shame this husband came to his father. When he was accused of witchcraft his father took the accusation as an insult to his lineage. Mwaihojo's sister asserted the prestige of their lineage when her brother's daughter was 'sworn at by in-laws'. From in-laws help with cattle was sought, and the cases collected suggest that cattle were requested or seized from a father-in-law more often than from a father or brother when a man had committed some wrong. But the in-law relationship remained one hedged about by conventional forms of deference and respect. These were most marked between those of successive generations and opposite sex.

Deference and respect were expressed by kneeling to greet, replying to an order with the humble expression *taa*, looking away rather than looking someone directly in the face, receiving anything in both hands, and avoiding any lewd reference. Between father-in-law and daughter-in-law total avoidance was required. A daughter-in-law stepped off the path and hid in the bush or bananas if warned that her father-in-law was approaching; she never entered the house in which he lived, or one in which he was visiting, or mentioned his name or words like it; or ate food associated with him such as meat or milk from a cow which had looked into his grave, or a cock which crowed in his homestead 'praising him', or bananas from his sacred grove which had grown over his grave.

There were two strands in this avoidance (*ukutila*): the first was respect. Lyandileko, a woman doctor, explained: 'Your husband is great (*mpala*) to you and his father is much greater. I think that my father-in-law is very great because he begat the man to whom I am married.' The second strand was fear of any sex association. On another occasion Lyandileko said, 'We think that to see your husband's father is very rude because it is as if you saw him sleeping with your mother. You compare: you see your husband's body and you see your husband's father's body, it is very bad.'

Deference and avoidance were extended to men identified with a father-in-law: his brothers, parallel cousins, wife's brother, and wife's brother's son, since the last might assist in his burial; and to his senior sister for 'she is a man', and also assisted in the burial (M. Wilson 1957a: 237). Because a woman was closely identified with her sisters she also avoided 'fathers-in-law' of her full sisters. A polygynist with many married sons and brothers' sons was thus avoided by a large number of women and this was felt to add to his dignity; he was *mpala*, *nisisya*, partly because of the respect these women must show him. Walking with Kasitile, the priest, one day we passed a group of girls one of whom bent down and hid her face in her cloth. Kasitile remarked, 'I am a great man (*ndinyambala fijo*), I have many daughters-in-law, all over the country.' On the return journey one in a group of women met on the road suddenly shouted: 'Mother, that's Kasitile, friends!' and two women rushed aside from the path, hiding their faces in their hands.

A woman also showed great respect to her husband's mother, and when she was first married never used her name, but after the birth of a child of each sex the taboos were gradually lifted, and they visited one another unless the father-in-law lived in the house of the mother-in-law, in which case a daughter-in-law in Selya (the area of strictest avoidance) could not enter.

When a girl reached puberty she, and her maids who accompanied her during the ritual, avoided her father and his neighbours in the village, calling them 'fathers-in-law'. The avoidance was most stringent in relation to areas associated with the sexual activity of the girl's parents: she avoided her mother's inner room with the bed (*kosofu*) and her loft (*pijulu*) where personal things were stored; and her parents observed a taboo on full sex relations lest they 'overstep' her and cause her to be barren (M. Wilson 1957a:115–6,

123–6). Avoidance was thus explicitly linked with separation of the sex activities of successive generations.

The onus to avoid was always on the woman, but a father-in-law was also watchful and if he met a daughter-in-law suddenly, carrying a load of wood, when she could not readily move from the path, he moved aside, or if it was necessary that she cook in a house in which he was visiting he left. The sanction for a breach of avoidance was believed to be sterility, a hard labour, a thin and sickly child, blindness, baldness, or worst of all, 'not be able to die' (*akamanya ukufwa*) but to linger on. This all fell on the woman. It was explained that intention was what mattered; an inadvertent breach would not bring misfortune, but pride (*amatingo*) leading to an intentional breaking of the taboo would; a case was cited in which an angry wife swore at her mother-in-law. And it was the shocked astonishment of the living who noticed the breach that mattered, for the living roused the shades, and their murmuring brought a curse; nothing happened if the lapse passed unnoticed. Misfortune falling on the man was rarely mentioned but there was a hint that if he failed to observe the rules of good manners his kinsmen would not come to meet him · when he died (M. Wilson 1957a: 216).

A son-in-law did not avoid his father-in-law, but he had to be respectful in manner, and helpful in assisting him even after all the marriage cattle due had been handed over. We watched a son-in-law, recently returned from work outside the district, formally present his father-in-law with a cloth worth 3s, 'to show kinship'.

The less stringent avoidance relationships were terminated by a gift as when a father and his village-mates gave small gifts to a daughter who had 'come out' of initiation, or a woman gave a gift to her husband's father's sister to end the avoidance between them. Among christians this was sometimes extended with the intention of ending avoidance between father-in-law and daughter-in-law (pp. 166–7).

Between those of the same generation, or those of alternate generations there were no restraints comparable to those between members of successive generations. The lewd talk which was taboo in the presence of father and son, or father-in-law and son-in-law, or even mother's brother and sister's son was perfectly acceptable before grandfather and grandson. A grandfather was a man's 'comrade' like his village-mates, and visiting a grandmother was a solace to a woman who found difficulties both with her husband and her father (p. 45). Grandparents on the mother's side tended to be identified with the mother's brother who was typically 'more sympathetic than a father', but they had this added advantage favouring familiarity that they were not of a proximate generation.

In the 1934–8 period the practice of avoidance was general, most conspicuously between a father-in-law and daughter-in-law, but also in the other relationships detailed. The degree varied somewhat with the local area, and also between pagan and christian families, but as a fundamental principle of good manners and good morals it was accepted. By 1955 radical changes had occurred. Many young men were migrant workers travelling as far as the Orange Free State gold mines, and they remained away for twelve to eighteen months at a stretch. They were reluctant to leave young wives alone, unsupervised, in their own age-villages, and a number of men, pagan as well as christian, chose to build huts for their wives near those of their own mothers (M. Wilson 1959: 221). This meant a breach of the fundamental Nyakyusa rule that father-in-law and daughter-in-law could not live in the same homestead. It was defended on the ground of necessity, and the fact that the young wife's hut was 'hidden in the bananas', away from the courtyard frequented by her father-in-law. Later on, as land became scarcer and scarcer, particularly in rice and coffee-growing areas, sons built their houses where they could, and it often had to be on land provided by their own fathers, so the separation of father-in-law and daughter-in-law in different villages was further eroded.

The norm of dominance

George Steiner speaks of 'a norm of dominance, albeit tempered by conventional insurgence, between generations, between fathers and sons,' as having been part of the accepted order in Europe until 1914 (Steiner 1971: 14). It was part of the accepted order among Nyakyusa–Ngonde people for another sixty years and Africans (Mphahlele 1962:212; 1971; 344; the late Professor Z. K. Matthews, personal conversation) are questioning whether the idea that deference is due to age will ever be rejected in Africa, where such deference is intimately connected with ideas about the moral and mystical power of seniors over their descendants and belief in such power is still widespread (M. Wilson 1971b: 41–2).

Chapter 6

MEN AND WOMEN

Choice, marriage age, and polygyny

DURING the 1934–8 period there was a confrontation in BuNyakyusa on three issues: (1) choice in marriage, whether a girl should or should not be compelled to accept her father's decision; (2) marriage age of girls, whether before or after puberty; and (3) polygyny. The courts supported the right of a girl to refuse a husband[1] and would not take cognisance of contracts made on her behalf before she reached puberty; they also supported the right of a widow to refuse her husband's heir; nevertheless the pressure of traditional ideas remained strong. Polygyny was legal but most christians thought it incompatible with christianity. In any study of the relations of men and women these three issues: choice, marriage age, and polygyny repeatedly emerge.

Until 1938 a Nyakyusa father was expected to provide the marriage cattle for a son's first wife. If possible he 'married for' each son in order of seniority, but at least he should be able to provide cattle for the senior son. And where he provided the cattle he had great influence in choosing the bride, sometimes betrothing the small daughter of a friend when his son was in his late teens, but more often when the son was in his mid-twenties. In selecting the girl he looked for friendship with her father; diligence, cleanliness, and hospitality in the mother; and the absence of any suspicion of witchcraft. According to a group of mothers: 'If a man is looking about for a bride, and a girl sitting down to greet him does not pick a piece of banana leaf to rest on, but sits down [on the earth] and gets herself dusty he will not have her; or if he visits a home and water is handed to him in a dirty calabash cup, or the water is dirty, he will not have a girl from that home.' 'Yes, a man likes beauty, but if the mother is a slattern and does not wash or draw water, even though the girl is pretty, a man says "I'll leave her."' An educated Nyakyusa remarked: 'Some other peoples look for strength in hoeing when selecting a bride, but we look for strength in mudding [a house], and cooking regularly without getting tired.' The father of a girl looked for a family with cattle, with a reputation for enjoying the company of neighbours, and again, free from suspicion of witchcraft. He rejected a man who was harsh, or had a reputation as an adulterer or a rolling stone, or for meanness or sorcery, and also one who was lazy in hoeing or did not build a house. The reputation of the lineage was as important as that of the suitor himself and the girl's parents might object on the ground that the lineage was harsh, or was reputed to have some hereditary disease like *ubusya*, characteristic of the Ndali, or the blindness found among the Lugulu. In arranging a match a father was expected to consult the girl's mother, as well as his own father (if alive) and elder brother, and their views carried weight. The girl's brothers who had a claim to receive cattle might also express opinions. Marriage with a chief was an honour but a doubtful blessing because, if his wife committed some wrong, he was likely to take back his cows as fine, and in a large harem a wife might be neglected. In the words of one informant 'she will have trouble over bearing children and over food.'

The suitor for a chief's senior daughter had to be approved by his village headmen. In 1937, one offer of marriage made to the senior daughter of a leading chief in Rungwe district by a wealthy trader was refused because the trader was not an African; another offer from a member of the chiefdom, also rich and liked by the chief himself, was rejected by the headmen on the ground that 'his grandfather was not a man of wisdom, he was foolish, he did not enjoy the company of others (*ukwangala*), and his father, though better than the grandfather, does not enjoy the company of others very much.' Christians were said to look particularly for wealth, for a son-in-law who would give their daughter suitable clothes and food, 'not a man who counts every bit of food'. He should either be in paid employment or very diligent in cultivation and rich in cattle.

Marriage was prohibited between the descendants of a common grandparent, or a great-grandfather in the paternal line, but it was just possible between descendants of a great-grandparent in the maternal line. The objection to marriage between near kin, such as between children of brothers, was firstly that cattle would not pass from one lineage to another: the same people could not both provide and receive marriage cattle. Secondly, if kin married 'people were astonished' and therefore barrenness or madness was feared. A secret affair did not matter: 'Who knows? Nothing happens!' But a liaison was comparable to marriage if it became known. Two cases were cited in which illness was thought to have resulted from 'marrying relatives', one of descendants of a common grandfather though with different grandmothers.

In a third case there was no illness but strong disapproval of a man who had seduced a girl who was the great-great-granddaughter of his great-grandfather in the male line. The crucial point was that the girl's father had given a cow to the seducer's father: 'They milked-one-another's-cows, they were real kinsmen.'

In a fourth case, acute gonorrhoea was attributed to the curse of men shocked by a chief's son seducing his father's half-sister, even though it was known that he already had the disease at the time of his wrongdoing. Our informant was a classificatory brother of the wrongdoer.

CASE 37: INCEST WITH FATHER'S HALF-SISTER

A, the son of chief Z, seduced a woman X, who was his father's half-sister. Furthermore, X's husband B, had married as an *unsakulwa* of X, the full-sister of A. Now A had gonorrhoea, and X caught it, and her husband B also fell ill with it. B cross-questioned his wife as to how she had caught gonorrhoea, and she admitted that it came from A. B went to his father-in-law, the chief, and complained about the incest and the disease. The chief was very angry and all men were astonished, saying: 'It is absolutely forbidden to lie with your mother, the sister of your father.' Then the chief took four of A's cows and gave them to B. This was before the courts and after the war

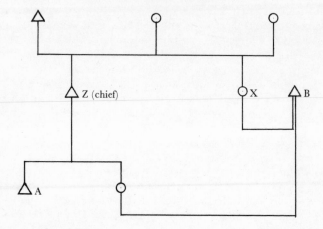

[i.e. 1918–1926]. I was still a boy. Because people were shocked they cursed A and he fell ill. He was ill for two years. In 1929 his eye came out of its socket and he went to Kabembe [mission hospital] very sick indeed. The village headmen gathered at the chief's place and said: 'This sickness of A is because of that case of his when he lay with X, it is on that account that he is sick.' So the chief sent for A and told him to bring four cows. He did so and the chief called his people and his brothers and said: 'Bless your child.' They swore at him and swore at him very much, and they seized the woman and swore at her saying 'How could you agree to your child sleeping with you? . . . You both have disgraced yourselves.' Then they killed the cows and ate them, I was there but we did not come close: it was our case! [The informant was a junior half-brother of A.] But we heard the insults. Very quickly A recovered and his eye is now all right, though the doctor had wished to cut it out.

According to Mwakyonde, the doctor: 'In the old days a man did not marry the daughter of a neighbour in the age village. He said: "She is my child, her father and I eat bananas together,"' but by 1934 this taboo was not enforced. What was considered impossible was for a man to confuse generations by marrying a half-sister of his son's wife. Her full sisters he never saw—they avoided him; her half-sisters he might greet but not marry.'

One case was recorded in which a father attempted to prevent a marriage because of a classificatory relationship confusing generations, but failed.

CASE 38: OBJECTIONS TO MARRIAGE WITH
CLASSIFICATORY DAUGHTER

Yotam Mwamukamba, a pagan of the chiefdom of Mwangake, married a daughter of Nsusa Mwakin'ali, the village headman of Mwaipopo. In 1934 when the girl reached puberty she ran off with Angyelile Mwambije of Kabembe, a christian, in the chiefdom of Mwangomo. Yotam brought a suit against Mwambije in the court of Mwaipopo (in Selya) without first taking the case to Mangomo. Mwambije paid a fine of *two* cows because there was a kinship connection between him and the woman. (One cow was the normal fine at that time.) Mwakalobo [another neighbouring chief] called Yotam saying: 'Your wife has come to me, she has found the cows from Mwambije, do you agree to receive your cows?' Yotam agreed saying: 'My cows are

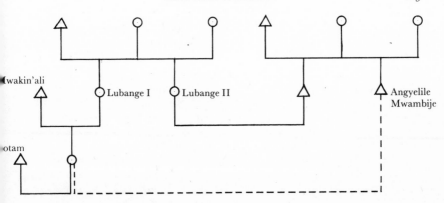

eight.' So Mwambije brought eight cows to return to Yotam. When Mwakin'ali the girl's father, heard he went to Mwakalobo saying 'I refuse to allow my daughter to be married by Mwambije, let her go with her husband.' Mwakalobo said: 'If you refuse, you, the father, must take her and return the cattle yourself, I, Mwakalobo, refuse to compel the girl to go where she refused to go.' So then Mwakin'ali agreed that she should be married to Angyelile Mwambije. He had refused on account of the kinship. An elder half-brother of Angyelile Mwambije had married Lubange II, a half-sister of Lubange I the wife of Mwakin'ali, which meant that she (the wife of Mwakin'ali) had married the elder brother of Angyelile Mwambije; a 'mother' of the girl who married Angyelile Mwambije had married his elder brother. In 1938 these two were still married.

A sister's son should treat his mother's brother's wife as a 'mother' and incest with her was a great offence.

CASE 39: SEDUCTION OF MOTHER'S BROTHER'S WIFE
A had moved to a distance and left his full-sister's son B to hoe for his wife and watch over her. B seduced the woman and in 1937 was brought to chief Porokoto's court. There he was fined three cows, one of them 'on account of kinship', and 12s for seducing a woman he was supposed to watch over. The woman's father was fined one cow.

Although sisters could not marry father and son, and 'mother' and 'daughter' should not marry brothers, one sort of generation crossing was approved: a man could and often did marry his wife's brother's daughter, as he did her younger sister. A continuing in-law relationship (*ubuko*) between two lineages was thought ideal, and for this reason a man often married 'where his father had married', in a different generation. He could not himself marry his cross-cousins whom he called sisters (*abilumbo*) but he called himself their 'owner' (*ndimwene abakikulu aba*) and often took a half-brother by a different mother to introduce him and commend him as a suitor.

A son did not choose his first wife whom his father betrothed for him and it was insulting to his father ever to divorce her. He was free to choose and marry other wives if he were wealthy, but he could scarcely refuse to inherit at least some of the widows of a man whose heir he was (his own mother excepted) however old and unattractive they might be. A girl had still less choice. She was normally betrothed before puberty and though there was a symbol of acceptance during the betrothal ritual when she took the spear stuck into the earth by her suitor and handed it to her father, it was almost impossible for a small girl of eight or nine to do otherwise than follow the directions of her father. An older girl might 'turn her head aside' and refuse to grasp the spear. When cross-questioned she could then express a preference for some other man, but this depended on her having an alternative suitor, or at least a firm determination not to marry the man approved by her father. In 1936 Kasitile's wives said to me: 'We are sent to men. Our fathers may accept a man's cattle and then we are sent to him even although we do not wish it, though we object very much. The only thing we can do is to run away.' Three women who had later left their husbands and become prostitutes on the Lupa gold-fields spoke bitterly of having been sent by their fathers to husbands when they were still very young. One remarked: 'You know Nyakyusa fathers are always in a hurry to get cattle for their daughters', and a father, pressed for cattle, might indeed go to a friend and ask for a cow on the understanding that it was the betrothal cow for his young daughter. The father of one young man we knew had betrothed a wife for him in this way when he was three or four years old.

A daughter might be sent to fulfil obligations as the *ulupagasa* replacing a sister or father's sister, who had died, or as supporter of one who was barren, or as indemnity in case of murder or witchcraft. More often she was sent as *unsakulwa*, the supporting wife to a happily married sister or father's sister; in this case her marriage was a compliment both to her kinswoman and to her husband, since the man had sought another wife from the same family, and the elder sister had advised her father to accept the offer. A characteristic mother's comment made in 1938, was: 'A woman rejoices very much when she goes to fetch a younger relative as a wife (*ukusakula*). Then she knows that if she dies there will be someone to care for her children.' But if a wife is not happy she may make difficulties over a kinswoman joining her. One instance was recorded in which a married man with four wives sought love-magic to persuade one wife and her father to agree to his marrying her younger sister. After his treatment they did, in fact, agree. Our information came from the doctor concerned. Another case came to court in which the husband had seduced his wife's sister 'before she had breasts' when she came to visit, and his wife had left him and refused to return on this account. To live as a co-wife with a kinswoman was generally accounted an advantage, but the junior of the pair was not always happy. One of Kasitile's three wives mentioned above was in fact an *unsakulwa* of the favourite, Jane; whe was very discontented and suspected of using witchcraft against Kasitile. The girl designated as a replacement or support for another wife was often a child of eight or nine, sometimes even younger, and it is likely that she was always well below puberty. In the genealogies analysed in table 7 below there was only one record of a replacement for a dead wife but 24 women out of 363 (6.3%) came as junior wives to an older sister or father's sister, or father's brother's daughter. We traced, in all, seven cases of replacement of a dead wife and two cases in which a replacement had been promised but never sent.

A group of elder men in Selya, experienced in court, discussed the rights of a wife with us. All agreed that, traditionally, a girl betrothed as a child had no right to refuse her husband when she reached puberty: 'Formerly, if a woman was betrothed as a child then she was the man's wife. That's all. She had no power to refuse him. She could only run off with another man. Some did run off even long ago. . . .' But if she were wooed at her father's when she was in her 'teens', then she had real power; if she refused to take hold of the spear her father had no power to compel her, 'the suitor just left'. Case 40 reflects the difficulty a young girl had in escaping an arranged marriage.

CASE 40: SUICIDE AFTER A FORCED MARRIAGE

X was married when approaching puberty. She ran off with a lover and her half-brother (who had inherited from his father and was 'father' to her) pursued her along with her husband and brought her back. She bore a child to her husband and then sought again to leave him. Her half-brother refused to allow this and she hanged herself. [Her half-brother was 50–60, in 1936, and the case probably occurred between 1916 and 1918.]

During the 1934–8 period various women remarked that the custom of sending a girl as *ulupagasa* or *unsakulwa* had 'disappeared'; girls refused to go 'because each wants her own husband nowadays'. The custom had not in fact disappeared but perhaps was less frequently observed than formerly since, when the girl reached puberty, she might refuse to live with the husband designated. Some women expressed a sense of obligation to go to look after the children of a deceased sister, but it was plain that others felt that a girl had a right to choose, and by 1965–9 marrying a kinswoman of a wife was not even approved.

The courts played a great part in establishing the right of a woman to marry whom she chose.

CASE 41: SUPPORT OF COURTS FOR BETROTHED GIRL
REFUSING MARRIAGE

In 1935 a girl who had been betrothed before puberty was repeatedly sent to her husband by her father with presents of food. Each time she refused to stay with her husband, and finally she complained to the Boma that she was being forced to marry. The local court was ordered to try the case and did so. The father was required to return to the husband four cows given for her, and fined three cows.

CASE 42: SUPPORT STRONGER IF PROSPECTIVE HUSBAND
A CHRISTIAN

[About the same time chief was heard to say at court to a christian litigant regarding a girl betrothed to him, but refusing to marry him:] I cannot compel her for you, X, because you are a christian: were you not a christian I would compel her to marry you. [Her father threatened to refuse to receive cattle from anyone else but she stood firm.]

In 1936 we were told that early betrothal and marriage were being abandoned because so many girls refused their husbands when they grew up and village headmen advised against betrothing before puberty. Courts ceased to take cognisance of marriage contracts made on behalf of girls under the age of puberty, and therefore a man who gave more than a single betrothal cow was liable to lose his cattle. By 1955 betrothal before puberty had ceased to be common. The reasons which a girl gave for rejecting a suitor were most often that he was old, harsh, or a polygynist: women sought 'beauty of body', youth, wealth, generosity with food and clothes, and gentleness.

If the husband died the widow was inherited, becoming the wife of the heir who took the dead man's name and social position. Her children inherited as if they were children of the deceased, and the identification of the dead man and his heir was so close the difference in genitors was not treated as important. For this reason we call it levirate.[2] Inheritance was fraternal between a set of full-brothers and, traditionally, also between half-brothers bound by 'milking-each-other's cows', so that only when a man's full and linked half-brothers were dead did the inheritance go to his son. Then exceptions were made, for no son could inherit his own mother or her kinswoman, and if they were still of childbearing age they were allocated to some other man of the lineage. Moreover, if the deceased had many wives they might be divided, some being allocated to one brother of the deceased, some to another. Between 1934 and 1938 argument turned on whether widows had the right to choose which potential heir they would go to, and whether those past childbearing had the right to refuse to be inherited at all, and choose to be 'built for by a son' living in a round house built on the fringe of a son's homestead. If they so chose were the marriage cattle given for them returnable or not? If the widow were young and the sole wife of the deceased there was no question that the heir had the right to claim her. Any children she had borne remained with the heir, except that she could keep a baby until it was weaned. If there were a number of wives agreement might be reached on their division, and a woman past childbearing might be permitted to settle with her son without any demand being made for return of marriage cattle; on the other hand there might be argument about division, or insistence by the heir that he was entitled to the labour of an elderly widow. Among christians the right of *any* widow to choose not to be inherited was supported on the ground that no woman should be forced to marry against her will. There were also difficulties over inheritance since many potential heirs were already married and a christian could not become a polygynist or marry one; but there was still the feeling that the heir was entitled to some compensation for the marriage cattle given for a widow of childbearing age. Variations in the law in time and space, and differences between pagan and christian are discussed later (pp. 145–58). This was a field in which opinions expressed by experienced men differed and one in which the revolutionary idea emerged that a woman with children not yet adult might live alone.

A girl sent to her husband, or a widow inherited by his heir, often found little sympathy if she ran home to her father. As Mwaihojo (147) put it: 'I, the father, would help my son-in-law; I would beat my daughter. If I could not make her go back to him I would return all the cows and then insist on her marrying again to get all the cows from the new husband.' Of 84 widows in the genealogies analysed in table 7,61 (72·6%) were inherited; 4 who were elderly were 'built for' by a son or by the heir; and 19 (22.6%) refused to be inherited and cattle were returned.

Not only were many girls and widows unable to exercise any effective choice of mates: some were later divorced against their will, since a man requiring cattle to pay a fine might be compelled to divorce his wife to recover his marriage cattle though neither he nor she wished for a divorce.

Table 7: Cases of Marriage, Divorce, Levirate, Sororate and Sororal Polygyny Extracted from Genealogies Collected 1934–8

Marriage and divorce	Number	Percentage
Men married	61	—
Men divorced[1]	11	18% of men married
Women married	363	—
Women divorced	34	9·1% of women married
Women divorced before bearing children	14	41% of women divorced

Cases of divorce by generation of men		Marriages	Divorces
Young men	Born 1905+	7	1
Fathers	Born 1875+	32	20
Grandfathers	Born 1845+	17	13
Great-grandfathers	Born 1815+	5	0

Levirate	Number	Percentage
Women widowed	84	100
Levirate[2]	61	72·6
Widows who refused heir, cattle returned	19	22·6
Widow 'built for', living celebate	4	4·8

Extent of polygyny	Number of husbands[3]	Average number of wives
Chiefs	21	11·5
Commoners	40	4

Sororate and sororal polygyny	
Total number of wives	363
Sororate (replacement of a dead sister)[4]	1
Sororal polygyny (junior wife to senior kinswoman)[5]	24

[1] One man was left by 8 wives out of 11, 7 without children. Another man was left by 3 wives out of 6, all 3 without children. Another was left by 5 wives out of 20.

[2] Some women were widowed and passed to an heir more than once. Those who refused the husband's heir were spoken of in KiNyakyusa as 'divorced' but are not here included in the category of women divorced.

[3] Cases included a disproportion of chiefs and senior men.

[4] Probably too low a proportion. One Selya lineage displayed in Appendix IIIa but not included in these calculations showed 2 cases of sororate.

[5] Chief Mwakalukwa (141) married six sets of 'sisters', two of the six including three 'sisters', i.e. eight younger 'sisters' in all.

The traditional ritual celebrated at first menstruation for a Nyakyusa girl was a marriage ritual as well as one marking the change from childhood to womanhood, and the husband played an essential part in it. If the girl were not yet betrothed the full ritual could not be carried out (M. Wilson 1957a: 86–129). It is therefore certain that betrothal before puberty and marriage directly after it was the accepted pattern before 1891 when Europeans settled in the district, as it still was among pagans between 1934 and 1938. The mean age of puberty was about 15 (M. Wilson 1957a: 87; in 1967 the mean age of menarch was calculated as 14·9 years, cf. de Jonge and Sterkenburg 1971: 92). Betrothal from the age of eight or nine was common and it was possible from infancy. Early betrothal of a daughter was favoured by pagan parents since they received a cow from the husband and his help in hoeing. 'A mother would boast to her fellows if she was drinking milk from a daughter's cow;' and early betrothal implied that the manners of both mother and daughter, and the reputation of the lineage, were good. Her father was pleased to establish a marriage bond with a friend's family and if she were betrothed on behalf of a man's young son she would have status as the first wife married and not easily be divorced. Small girls themselves boasted to each other of their 'husbands' saying to those not yet betrothed: 'You *must* be plain,' and one still not betrothed at puberty felt sadly 'on the shelf'. 'See, others are married! Some have children! Why are little ones married and I, the senior, left?' Little girls of eight or nine were self-conscious and coy with visitors, wearing their hair in fancy patterns, and careful to keep themselves clean. But satisfaction at being sought as a wife did not prevent some girls weeping bitterly when the time came to go to their husbands. As one mother put it: 'One girl grieves, and weeps tears, and falls ill. She thinks to herself that work will be heavy at her husband's . . . but another rejoices when she reaches maturity saying "I am going to my husband."' Young men expressed the view that no man in his senses would choose a very young girl if he could find one approaching puberty who was suitable, and could afford to marry her, but girls were scarce and accumulation of marriage cattle slow, so betrothal of a young girl from a suitable family might also be convenient for the groom.

Among pagans, the marriage age of both men and girls had fallen between 1891 and 1934, a period over which the number of cattle in the district was reported by elderly informants to have increased considerably. When war was endemic and cattle raids frequent the older generation of men wished their sons to delay marriage because bachelors were regarded as fiercer fighters then married men; a youth was urged to 'display himself' before he married; when he did marry 'his strength would go'. It was thought particularly bad for the son of a chief to marry too young for then he would 'eat at home, instead of going about with his age-mates and asking for food for all of them. Commoners will always give food to the son of a chief.' Before 1891, we were told, a man lived as an unmarried warrior, raiding, herding and defending his father's cattle, and hoeing until his early 30s. Asagene, a christian with four children, told us in 1937: 'Grown men with spears, young men of my age and Angombwike's (27–30), herded cattle for fear of raids, and boys herded calves nearer the villages. The same individuals used to herd and hoe, taking turns to herd, or hoeing in the afternoon when the cattle were kept by boys near the villages. Marriage was later. I would have been unmarried.' Everyone agreed that delay in marriage for men had been due to the need for warriors, and that the fall in age came with the pacification of the country.

However, delay was also connected with the scarcity of cattle and the desire to establish a herd. An elderly man living near Rungwe put it this way:

'Young men now, if they get one cow say: "A woman!" We kept the cow! If I got one I kept it and it calved and calved again, and again, three times. Then I sought a wife. I married with two and had two cows in the house to milk. But now young men take wives immediately.'

In the 1934–8 period all pagan girls in BuNyakyusa (though not in Ngonde) were betrothed before puberty, and visited and sometimes slept with their husbands. It was agreed that the average age of betrothal and marriage had fallen. When Europeans arrived in 1891 there had existed girls' houses (*isaka*) in which adolescent and younger girls slept, and entertained young men. These disappeared during German times (before 1916). The *isaka* only survived in BuNyakyusa (1934–8) as the hut in which a girl was secluded during her initiation, where her juniors kept her company, and where they were visited by young men. But in Ngonde at the same period *isaka* in which girls slept regularly still existed. About these facts our Nyakyusa informants were agreed, and Bishop Gemeseus was also certain that the marriage age of pagan girls had fallen, though he was careful to point out that there always had been cases of early marriage.

It was also agreed that the marriage age of girls had fallen because brides became scarce: girls nearing puberty who were still unmarried ceased to exist so men betrothed young girls. What there *was* argument about was why brides were so scarce. Some thought it was because cattle had increased in number. Others argued that since peace had come men were marrying younger; others that polygyny had increased. Bishop Gemeseus pointed out that large harems had appeared. These were all relevant factors and it is likely also that the circulation of cattle became more rapid. An elderly Kukwe man living near Rungwe put the cattle argument thus: 'Girls used to reach puberty before betrothal because cattle were few. The enemy, Ngoni, Merere, and others from the north east had finished our stock. There were no cattle. Some men just hoed for a father-in-law and after some time he agreed to the marriage. Cattle increased when Europeans brought peace.'

It was, of course, the gap of 10–15 years in the marriage age of men and women that made polygyny possible.[3] In 1934, out of 3,000 tax payers in Selya 34% of the men were unmarried; 37% monogamists; and 29% polygynists. 70% of the women were in polygynous households.

Most Nyakyusa linked the disappearance of *isaka* with the fall in marriage age, but one old man put the blame for this, as for increase in adultery, on the softness of Europeans. The following statements (recorded by John Mwaikambo in 1937) illustrate the arguments and show how aware Nyakyusa men were of the changes going on:

[Kakune] *Isaka* used to exist. Little girls slept in a round house together with older girls. The older girls met lovers and regularly brought them food. . . . The fathers disciplined their children that they should not work foolishness with boys, but they might enjoy their company without doing wrong. If her fellows saw that one girl lay with a boy they told about it, then the fathers swore at her very much. A special house was not built for the *abasaka* to sleep in but when a man had built three houses one was given to the girls and where the girls slept their neighbours came, so they increased and became many. At that time husbands did not sleep with little girls, because girls who were married at puberty were many . . . The disappearance of the *isaka* and husbands sleeping with little girls began long ago before the war [1914].

[Kilongo and Mwakibwanga:] Long ago girls grew up before marriage, and boys grew up before marrying, because their fathers refused to allow them to marry quickly on account of war. They said strength finishes if a man has a wife . . . Girls grew up before marriage because there was no one to marry them, only a few were married young. When Europeans came war was abandoned and young men, even boys, married girls; then girls who had reached puberty unmarried were finished; all the grown girls were married, and man began marrying little girls.

And also with childbearing, if a woman had a child it grew up before the parents began to have another. If they had another child before an older one could run there would be trouble when they had to flee in war, because it is difficult to carry two children.

Grown girls ceased to exist in the time of the English . . . When the Germans were here there were still many grown girls unmarried.

[Mwampiki] Long ago cattle were few. Many people did not have cattle. Then little by little cattle increased through calving. If a man gave three marriage cattle then, when all had calved three times, all together the cattle were many, and from this they began to increase. Cattle began to be numerous before whites came. *Isaka* began to finish when cattle were numerous and when war ceased. Because when people found they had cattle they married two wives or three. Then grown girls who were unmarried finished. The increase in cattle began before the war [1914].

[Mwakibwanga:] Cattle began to be many long ago before whites came, but *isaka* finished because grown girls finished. This was not on account of cattle but mostly on account of war because, when there was war, many adult men were bachelors. Cattle were numerous in the country and there were also grown girls and *isaka*.

[Salu:] Long ago at the beginning cattle were few, so people did not ask for many marriage cattle, they married with two cows or perhaps three. Then cattle increased and became very many. Europeans found us with many. The custom of *isaka* existed when cattle were there but when Europeans came they pacified the country and we found that many, including youngsters, married women, so grown girls were finished . . . Those of old did not think much about women because war was much and men said: If we marry strength will disappear.

[Nsyani, a great-grandfather with great-grandchildren who are grown up and might almost have children]: Long ago grown girls were numerous. Many people married grown girls and some engaged little girls. It was a very old custom for a husband to sleep with a little girl; our fathers had the custom. He who betrothed a little girl lived with her. And *isaka* also existed very long ago. We found them, we slept with our sisters in *isaka* when we were grown up. The fathers built the *isaka* house. The children of men who built together gathered in one *isaka* house. The *isaka* was abandoned when Europeans came. It was abandoned because we punished girls very much if they did wrong, we bound them with ropes and beat them until they were nearly dead. Then our children really listened to what we said. When Europeans came they said they had forbidden murder. So then we left building *isaka* houses since girls might do as they pleased: we feared to beat them as formerly we punished them. If you only scold them, words alone have no effect.

Nsyani was also certain that polygyny had increased and that large commoner households were new. 'Do you think that formerly there were men with five wives? No! There are many now with six or seven wives.' He could remember one man before Europeans came who had five wives, two with four wives, one with three, many with two. Bishop Gemeseus held that when he arrived (in 1907) important chiefs had no more than six or eight wives, whereas their successors had 15 to 40. This is confirmed by genealogies. Forty wives had borne children to chief Mwaipopo (116) according to reports in Selya. There were five other girls whom he had betrothed young and who had not yet come to live with him. He himself claimed 40 wives living with him at the time of his marriage which we attended. Chief Porokoto (K49) had 15 wives in 1937, and five others had left him; his father Mwakan'ata (K30) had only seven wives according to Bishop Gemeseus. Mwakalukwa (141) had 17 wives in 1934 apart from widows he had inherited. His father Mwamakula I (106) was reported to us as having had five wives, his grandfather six, and his great-grandfather four.[4] These did not include widows inherited. The Kyungu's wives claimed to be eighteen in number in 1937 and said five other wives had left the Kyungu.

Where men marry women much younger than themselves and widows are inherited, polygyny tends to be cumulative, each succeeding heir having more wives than his predecessor. No commoner was found with more than eight wives and the growth of large harems implied increase in the relative wealth and power of chiefs vis-à-vis commoners. In the period 1934–8 the differences in consumption of most chiefs and their people was small: houses, furnishing, and clothing of conservatives like Mwaipopo differed little from that of their people, and the chief's salary was available to buy cattle. The standard of living of the Kyungu in Karonga already differed considerably from that of his people in 1937, but only after 1945 did consumer goods in the form of brick houses with modern furniture, ploughs, jeeps, and clothing for wives become generally important. It was during the middle colonial period, when chiefs drew salaries and remained in office until they were old but had not yet developed new standards of consumption, that large harems developed.

Among christians the pattern was different for all missions forbade a church member to allow his daughter to go to her husband before puberty and the rule was enforced; christians talked much of the advantages of later marriage for girls. Sons of christians, on the other hand, tended to marry younger than their pagan contemporaries for their fathers did not use what cattle they had for additional wives for themselves, and a rich man found it convenient to betroth a young girl for his son and let his cattle increase at the home of the in-laws; they took responsibility for herding and the rich man's stock was distributed. By 1938 it was common for a christian's son to marry in his early twenties.

With the early marriage age of girls premarital pregnancy scarcely existed. In BuNyakyusa we did not meet any unmarried mothers in 1934–8 or even in 1955, though one friend had herself seen 'a child of the long grass', the child of an unmarried girl, and one or two cases were reported in which it was thought that a girl had been deflowered before she went to her husband and not by him. Regular examination of girls by 'mothers' continued and was linked to the handing over of the 'bull of virginity' by the husband. In Karonga, where by 1937 the girls' marriage age was higher, pre-marital pregnancy was known to occur more frequently. It was a terrible insult to call anyone a bastard (*unsigwana*) in KiNyakyusa. 'If you use that word a man will spear you.'

Since girls married so young the only female company young men might legitimately enjoy in the 1934–8 period was that in the initiate's hut, and there all except the initiate herself were below the age of puberty. Instead, love affairs with young married women, particularly those from large harems, preoccupied young men and were a constant topic of scandal. Every wife of a chief was alleged to have a lover. The evidence indicated that during the middle colonial period (1918–1943) there was a lowering of the age of first marriage for men, an increase in polygyny particularly of chiefs, a fall in the marriage age of girls, and acute competition between fathers and sons for wives.

The senior wife (*unkasikulu*) of a commoner differed in status from others. She was the first wife betrothed provided that she was a virgin when she came to her husband. If she were not she was replaced by the next wife betrothed unless her father sent a kinswoman, an *unsakulwa*, who was a virgin, and repaired her sister's error, so that the elder sister's son inherited as senior son. The senior wife alone (among commoners) washed with her husband at the marriage ritual (M. Wilson 1957a: 90, 118); and if she survived her husband she helped to bury him, entering the grave; it was very difficult for him ever to divorce her, particularly if his father provided marriage cattle, and if she left him he was deeply hurt. A Moravian pastor, Kaisi, remarked in 1937 that: 'Even now, if his *first* wife runs off a husband may spear her.' With a chief *two* wives were seniors and washed with their husband at marriage: they were the two selected by the village headmen and married at the 'coming out'. And for each of them a ritual stone was planted celebrating the marriage (M. Wilson 1959:56) provided she was a virgin when married, or supported by an *unsakulwa* who was a virgin.

Each wife had her own round house or a separate room in a long house; fields were assigned to her by her husband and hoed for her; and her sons had a strong claim to cattle coming in for their full-sisters. The eldest son of the senior wife was senior son, irrespective of his date of birth, and lived in expectation of inheriting the bulk of his father's property in due course. With it he inherited authority over and certain responsibilities for junior brothers and sisters, and half-brothers and half-sisters. But during a man's lifetime his cattle were not allocated to houses; even the milk from cows given for her own daughter did not necessarily come to a mother among the Nyakyusa. 'A mother does not have sole right to the milk from her daughter's marriage cattle. They all drink because the mother knows: "I bore this child with my husband's cattle." If she never gets the milk to drink she complains, and some go off home on this account as the mother of An'itike did.' In Ngonde, however, the milk from cows coming in from a daughter went to the girl's own mother, and a boy could not expect to marry with cattle from a half-sister as he might among the Nyakyusa. A case was quoted in Ngonde in which a wife was sworn at by two senior co-wives for using milk from cows which had come for their daughters' marriages, so she begged the use of a cow from her husband's younger brother. Then she was sworn at by the senior wives for wearing clothes which, they claimed, had been obtained with their property. The senior wife of a commoner was entitled to respect from her junior co-wives who avoided the interior of her room and were forbidden to take anything from her loft, or lie on her bed, or use her cooking pots, or address her by name. The junior was expected to use the submissive *taa* in replying to her, and carry small things if they walked together, especially the head-pad which women carried when they went to fetch firewood. The junior might not begin planting any pulse or grain crop or begin reaping before her senior; it was thought that her crop would be small and she would suffer hunger if she did. And the junior was the first to get up when the husband called for water or bananas to be roasted, the senior might follow in a more leisurely way; and it was the senior wife who should divide special food with her co-wives.

In the 1934–8 period among the Nyakyusa, all *abehe*, the ladies of a chief, carried out the normal duties of married woman, weeding and planting and reaping, fetching firewood and water, cooking and brewing, and by all accounts they had done so in pre-colonial times. The wives of the Kyungu also worked in their fields and fetched firewood and water in 1937 when we lived with them, but in earlier times they had been served by slaves and by commoners, for the Kyungu's ladies (*amasano*) had lived in seclusion. They alone of all Nyakyusa–Ngonde women had not laboured to produce their own food and fuel.

Ideally, a husband was obliged to distribute his favours equally, but in every polygynous home there was thought to be a favourite and very often it was this *unkondwe*, not the senior wife, who was given milk, meat, fish, or salt by the husband 'to share with her fellows'. It particularly galled a senior wife to have to ask her junior for salt, because the junior was the favourite and the salt bag was kept in her house. 'She doles it out in tiny quantities,' the seniors complained. Everyone was agreed that jealousy was built into the relationship: 'a man with many wives has thorns within.' 'Is it true,' one man asked 'that the government forbids polygyny among Europeans because European women are so jealous they attack one another with knives?' Suspicion of witchcraft was common enough between co-wives, and the more sophisticated feared sorcery. A young woman on the Lupa who had been the wife of a polygynist explained: 'The real reason a woman dislikes being married by a man with other wives is that she fears the sorcery of her co-wives.'

The attention of the husband was sought by women even more than food and clothes: 'Very many women say they like to be the only wife because then the husband will sleep with them alone.' Once when a wife came to visit us, accompanying her husband, she murmured to me: 'Since I have come here to visit with my husband my friends will get angry and say that I am the favourite and be jealous. They whisper.' And later she boasted: 'I am very much his wife, the favourite. See! He asked me to come today to greet you, my friend.' She was a woman with three children, the eldest boy herding and the youngest still suckling.

Asked about the qualities that made a wife the favourite both men and women spoke about obedience, and diligence and care in cooking. Everyone mentioned cooking. Hospitality to her husband's relations, personal cleanliness, skill in mat-making to provide a good high bed, skill in mudding the house and smearing the floor were also mentioned, and once—only once—amusing conversation. It was agreed that if her cooking were up to it the most recently married wife would get the most attention for a few months, but she did not necessarily oust an established favourite. Sexual attractiveness was rarely admitted to be a factor: 'If she gets up and heats water quickly and cooks, her husband says (to himself): "I love her body."' To mitigate the difficulties of polygyny it was held good to marry an even number of wives so that each might have her 'friend'. The odd-wife-out in a large homestead was likely to be very unhappy.

Conservative pagan men valued polygyny because it provided them with domestic labour, and sons and wives to work in the fields; a variety of sex partners; and a network of affinal links through which they hoped for an increase in wealth in cattle. A rich man who married only one wife was thought mean. He should marry again and distribute his cattle.

If a man with only one wife calls for water there is only one to come; if he builds a house there is only one to fetch reeds and grass; there is only one to weed in his fields and work them. The man with many wives sits on a mat and sends his wives one here, one there, he calls now this one, now that, he is a headman (*ulifumu*). If you only have one servant are you rich? If you have six are you as rich as the man with twenty? No! So it is with our wives. They don't all cook; only the favourite cooks; but they all work fetching water and firewood and so on. Yes, it is not enough to have wives, we must also have cows. The man with no cows only eats vegetables cooked without milk, but a man with cows who has only one wife is called a bachelor, he has to cook for himself, he is not a real person (*akaja umundu*)!

[How does a man with two wives and twenty cows compare with one with six wives and six cows?] Both are rich but the first one lives as a bachelor. Others say he is miserly because he does not like to disperse cattle, he eats alone.

Making a rich man his son-in-law was the way in which a chief bound the wealthy to him and himself benefited from their wealth. 'Sometimes a chief would go to a rich man and say: "I wish to give your son (or you yourself) one of my daughters," and the man agrees, and he gives many, many cows, sometimes 30, sometimes 60. At first he brings 20 cows, perhaps only 10, and the chief agrees to the marriage saying: "Take our daughter." But then, year by year, and one by one, the chief will come and take one cow, and again come, and then take three cows from his son-in-law.' No case was recorded in which more than fifteen cows had been given for a chief's daughter, but the notion was widespread that a chief could milk the rich in this way.

The charge of meanness was constantly brought against wealthy christians who refused to marry again even when pressed by fathers with marriageable daughters to do so. Angombwike said: 'They laugh at us in the villages a great deal. They call us fools and misers and say: "He's a bastard." The fathers in the village came to me and said: "See, your father has many cows and your grandfather before him, and so-and-so of your relatives has many cows; look at all those cows; are you not going to give them to us for our daughters? Are you going to keep them for yourself?" And I said yes. Then they call me a fool, a bastard. . . .' Angombwike's pagan father also pointed out to him the practical advantages of marrying again and distributing his herd: 'See all these cows, if you only marry one woman they will begin to die; many, many will die and they have been saved for you.'

Monogamy was a value introduced by christian missionaries, accepted by the first generation of christians and then maintained, though the issue of baptising a polygynist without requiring him to divorce his wives, or permitting a christian to take a second wife, has been discussed repeatedly in church councils (Wright 1971: 99, 106, 132; Hastings 1973: 22–5, 72–9, 121–2).

Ahombile, an elder at Rungwe, told us in 1936: 'I myself think that monogamy is right for two reasons: first, when God made Adam he did not make many women but one only to live with him; and secondly, if a man has two or more wives he has no peace in his house. Some members of the congregation brought this question up recently saying: "Let each man be allowed to take a helper for his wife, for if my wife goes to visit her relatives I am left a bachelor." We discussed it and we ourselves decided against it, we did not take it to the church assembly. We asked those christians amongst us who had repented as polygynists whether any of them had had peace in their houses before they divorced their additional wives and all without exception said: "No, there was no peace."'

Another argument brought up in 1936 in a church discussion on taking a second wife was: 'When my wife grows old there is no one to fetch firewood and water. I have to fetch firewood myself because she is old.' Where marriage was patrilocal (as among the Mpondo) or uxorical (as among the Bemba) there was a daughter-in-law or a daughter to do the heavy work, but not among the Nyakyusa who were virilocal.

Although land was still plentiful in 1934–8, and additional marriages were the most profitable way in which a wealthy man could lay out his capital in cattle, an appreciable number of men chose to remain monogamous for religious reasons. The rule of monogamy was regarded as the greatest impediment to a man becoming or remaining a christian. It was particularly great if he were the heir in a wealthy family, as Angombwike who is quoted above was. His father and father's sister did their best to dissuade him from being baptised. The christian in greatest difficulty was one whose wife proved sterile for to be condemned to childlessness was felt very hard. The incidence of sterility in 1967 was 6·3% of women (11·6% on the lake shore) (de Jonge and Sterkenburg 1971: 93) and there was no possibility in Nyakyusa society of adoption for no unwanted children existed. One whose wife was indeed lazy about fetching wood and water, and negligent in cooking, was also pitied. It was generally argued that European wives did not work at all but employed servants and therefore they did not understand a Nyakyusa husband's problems. 'Sometimes a man is unlucky in his marriage. His wife just does not cook for him. When he comes home from work he finds she has cooked a little food for herself, none for him. Then he is simply forced to take another wife.' It was very difficult for a single wife to do all that was required of her if her husband wished to entertain friends as a wealthy man should, but one or two men sought to meet this by buying firewood, or hiring an outsider—a Kinga or Safwa youth—to fetch firewood and water and help in cultivation.

The difference in the views of men and women on polygyny was marked. A few women—most often a favourite—defended it on the ground that work was lighter and a woman was free to visit her parents, knowing that her husband would be cared for, or if she were sick she could count on help. 'See, with this wound on my leg, I can't fetch firewood. My friend [co-wife] helps me.' But such help was not always forthcoming. In Ilolo village in 1937 I heard a loud argument and went to investigate. A group of women were weeding beans and some men were shouting at them. It appeared that one wife of a polygynist who had just borne a child and was at her father's, had sent a message to a co-wife asking her to weed the patch belonging to her-who-had-given-birth. The co-wife refused and a neighbour did the work instead. The men were shouting: 'We are shocked, we are shocked!' 'If I had a lot of work to do and was compelled to be away, I would not ask just anyone to do it but my fellow in the house.' Angombwike's comment was: 'It's jealousy.'

A group of abehe (wives of a chief) whom I knew well asked if I knew how many there were of them.

M.W.: Fifteen.
Abehe: Yes, now. We used to be twenty, the others have run away.
M.W.: Why?
Abehe: Because we are many, because of food.
M.W.: We like to be alone.
Abehe: Yes, it's very nice to be alone, the one trouble is the work. You see you hire servants, but we have to do all the work ourselves.

Nevertheless, the great majority of women, and all young women consulted, expressed a preference for being the only wife. In Karonga in 1937, some women were refusing marriage with polygynists partly because, with a money economy such as was already significant there, to be the wife of a polygynist implied poverty. Hence the phrase in the litany of the African National Church which permitted polygyny: 'It is Thy work [God] to give them all new dresses' (M. Wilson 1959:195).

The attraction of churches permitting polygyny did not prove great (M. Wilson 1959: 172, 190) and it was widely accepted in the 1934–8 period that monogamy would spread; even Nyasuru, leader of the African National Church, agreed that it would come. 'We know that our children and grandchildren will have one wife only each. It is a matter of economics, of civilization. Now that wealth has come into the country and women are wearing clothes they are unwilling to share their husband's wealth with another. There is jealousy about clothes. Yes, and about food too.' [And about love?] 'No, no, it is a matter of economics.' The conversation was in KiNyakyusa but the English words 'economics' and 'civilization' were used.

A pagan boy of about twelve or fourteen, grandson of a chief, expressed the new viewpoint when he brought us a gift of Cape gooseberries: [G.W.: You planted them yourself?] 'Yes, I grew them.' [You will sell them to Europeans and buy many cows, and then get many wives!] 'Oh, I do not want more than one wife. You see if you have many wives there is always trouble. If you give a little meat to one then the others complain.' By the period 1965–9, 57% of men in Kyimo village expressed a preference for one wife (Konter 1974b: 101). Of the same sample 90% preferred hired labour to additional wives for labour, and the proportion of polygynists was falling.

The process of marriage

The process of marriage among the Nyakyusa was long drawn out. Negotiations might begin between a man and a friend regarding a marriage between their respective children when the girl was a small child, and the boy in his teens, and the children themselves played no part in the betrothal contract. If the groom were adult and had heard of a suitable girl, he chose a go-between and together they called on a neighbour of the girl's father, asking to be taken to him. If the suit were approved a day was appointed for the formal betrothal. Traditionally, and still in 1934–8, this was the occasion on which, in the presence of the girl's father, the groom thrust his spear into the ground, and the bride was told to pull it out if she agreed to the marriage. Occasionally, it is said, there was more than one suitor, and the girl was told to take the spear of the one she preferred. In Ngonde, in 1937, a hoe rather than a spear was brought and the bride was told to pick it up if she agreed to the marriage. Whichever it was, spear or hoe, the action was binding, and if later the woman sought a divorce her husband reminded her: 'Did you not pick it up yourself?'

Among christians, it was usual by 1934 for a man intending marriage 'to make love to a girl in secret' before he approached her father. This was often a brief and formal procedure in which each party was accompanied by a friend. Mwaikambo described it:

If a man wishes to betroth a girl he begins by seeing her and asking people whether he should marry her or not. If they say he should, he goes with one friend to make love to the girl secretly. If the girl agrees he says to her: 'How about it? Do you agree that we come to your father's? Perhaps you agree in private but when we have come to your father you will say you don't know us?' She replies: 'How could I tell you that you should come if I don't love you [plural], and deceive you?' The friend who accompanies the groom is the go-between who is usually a little older. Then the girls [plural] say: 'Give us something for love.' Then they give them something, or they may not have brought anything. That is how we behave with a sweetheart. On another day they go to the father, stopping first at a neighbour's. They tell him that they seek the child of so and so, this young man [identifying the groom] wants to marry his daughter. Then the neighbour tells the girl that these people have come wishing to marry her. The girl says: 'I love them, they will marry me.' Then the young man gives that neighbour two shillings, and he gives it to the girl. She takes it to her parents, and the young men go home. The neighbour tells the father who has come. If the father does not like them he returns the shillings at once; if he agrees he keeps the shillings and tells them when they should come with a cow to betroth the girl.

'Making love in secret' was spreading among pagans also by 1934 but many informants insisted that a pagan suitor often had not seen the girl he went to betroth before he arrived at her father's house. This can hardly have been so at an earlier period when *isaka* existed.

On the day of betrothal the groomsmen were feasted by the bride's father, and thereafter the mother of the bride 'cooked often for the groom', and he, for his part, came with friends to hoe her fields. They expected a good meal after hoeing. The next stage was either the puberty–marriage ritual described below, which culminated in the bride's 'mothers' taking her to her husband's or, if the bride had not yet reached puberty, a request by the husband that he might 'borrow' (*ukwasima*) her, that is that she might visit him for a few days at a time, and become accustomed to sleeping with him. The groom brought her father a hen—if she was a chief's daughter a cow—and with the father's consent she began sleeping at her husband's house. Full intercourse before puberty was permitted, but a husband was often criticized as 'foolish' if he did in fact penetrate his bride before puberty, because then he had no proof that she had not lain with other men when she finally came to him. It was, however, considered suitable that a girl should 'grow accustomed to her husband' before she grew up, and if it were he who had deflowered her she was still carried in triumph as a virgin in the marriage ritual.

The puberty–marriage ritual began at first menstruation. The bride was secluded with companions slightly younger than herself in a hut in her father's homestead, and a series of eleven rites, all of which involved feasts of some sort, followed. A detailed account of the rites has already been published (M. Wilson 1957a: 86–129): the overt purpose was to ensure the bride's health and fertility; to celebrate her virginity; and to mark her change in status from child to adult, and from a daughter of her father's lineage subject to his shades, to that of a wife in her husband's lineage, for it was her husband's shades who would create a child in her womb and those of her father must 'move aside a little'. The eleven rites of marriage were followed by two more at the birth of the first child.

Enormous quantities of food were prepared by both families and feast followed feast at the home of the bride's father or that of the groom. Talking of their own marriages, people dwelt lovingly on the details—the number of baskets of cooked food and stems of plantains; the bull or calf slaughtered; the number and size of flasks and calabashes of milk and pots of beer. Relatives and neighbours were asked to help to prepare food and the importance of reciprocity was recognized: 'We cook. I think that I also will be in trouble if, sometime, neighbours don't help me; there would be no food if they cooked nothing.' To be recognized as 'the child of a rich man' was the ambition of both bride and groom, and the prestige of giving, and of providing lavish hospitality was great. Parties of women moved back and forth carrying food for feasts. We ourselves saw 70 young men who had come to perform a wedding dance (M. Wilson 1957a: 92, Pl. 6) provided with fifteen large baskets of food, 7 calabashes of milk, and 3 pots of beer. And at the *ukukwa* of a chief's daughter 46 dishes of food and 4 flasks or calabashes of thick milk were provided for the groom's party of 59. The food included rice, meat (a bull had been killed), thick porridge, and sweet potatoes. Three pots of beer were reserved for the older men. Eleven women took food to the groom's father, carrying 4 pots of beer, 3 loads of firewood, 2 baskets of flour, and 2 baskets with milk flasks. A line of 'mothers' each carrying a basket with food or beer, or a great log of wood, on her head, and walking purposefully and proudly, was very visible. Paths ran through villages and a party was always noted, and its identity and destination commented upon. Each host spoke disparagingly of his own offering but hoped that he might have provided more than his guests could consume. A guest who thought the hospitality poor might express disappointment, and families regarded as mean were laughed at. 'Young people warn one another: "Don't marry into such and such a family, they don't cook *anything*."'

The greatest occasion was the *ukukwa* when the groom and his companions brought the bulk of the marriage cattle, and it was only then that the total number of cattle to be brought was stated. The go-between of the father told the go-between of the husband how many cattle were still to come and when the bride might go to her husband. 'If I marry the daughter of a chief, I betroth her with three cows, and at the *ukukwa* I bring eight, then they will say: "We expect twenty. You have brought eleven, nine remain, but when you bring two more cows and a bull, fourteen in all, you can go with your wife. Six will remain." When I have given twenty then he cannot claim others, no, not even a chief. Even if hunger takes him he cannot claim another, but perhaps I, in kindness, may give him another; and if the mother of my wife dies then, even though I have finished bringing marriage cattle, I take another cow to the funeral, and if my father-in-law dies also another, so that altogether there are 22. Since I am the son-in-law of a chief I cannot refuse to take a cow to the funeral. But later, if my wife leaves me, then I claim all 22.' A man could not argue about the number of cattle named by the bride's father. The go-between might protest, 'We are poor,' and the cattle might be slow in coming or small in size, but the groom had to accept the number named, and often he speculated anxiously beforehand on what precisely it was likely to be.

The bride's family watched with excitement to see the quality of cattle brought and her father complained if he thought them inadequate. In 1935 Mwaipopo, the chief, arrived with a party of 80 men and women to *ukukwa* his forty-first wife. They were driving 14 cows, mostly full-grown, and decked with bells. The women at the bride's home called the triumphant *akalulu* and marvelled at 'the great number of cows in Mwaipopo's country'. No one questioned their quality. But in Ilolo village at one *ukukwa* noted, the women's comments were derogatory: 'How many [cattle] are there?' 'There are none.' 'Mother, mother; they are tiny ones,' 'Only a bull,' 'Little tinies (*akapikipiki*).' The women indoors pressed outside to see for themselves. One walked to and fro shouting 'They bring us only a bull. . . . They bring sheep.' Later a friend, Esther, whispered to the bride, 'They are poor, they are wearing bedraggled clothes.' Bride (with feeling): 'I agree *very* much.' On this occasion and repeatedly, at various marriages, the bride and her attendants refused gifts offered saying they were insultingly small. Sometimes a larger gift was produced and accepted, sometimes the girls concerned were left without anything.

The bride mentioned above, was a daughter of Nsajigwa, younger full-brother of Porokoto the chief (K49). Negotiations were opened with a gift of two shillings from the groom, handed to the bride as 'the spear', which she received and which was passed on to the chief. She was betrothed in June 1937 with one cow and 30s; in July a gift of food, beer, meat, and firewood was sent to her father for the *ukusumbulela* feast, and the marriage followed in November when a cow, heifer, bull, and 40s ('three cows and a bull') were handed over as *ukukwa*. The groom's go-between was told to bring one more cow, 'a big one', and undertook to do so when a cow owing from elsewhere was paid to the groom's family. Syungu, the senior wife of the lineage (see M. Wilson 1957a: table e, Genealogy of Mwasalemba) arrived at the marriage feast with 35 other women carrying food to add to that prepared by Porokoto's wives and neighbours. The bull brought by the groomsmen was killed for the feast and the meat divided according to age-villages. The groom was accompanied by 80 young men and 32 women. After the feast nine loads of food (including a flask of thick milk and a leg and the hump of the bull killed), four pots of beer, and two logs of firewood were carried to the groom's father's house, and the women who carried it were given 2s 40c there. The marriage cattle were divided by the chief who allocated one large cow to his senior half-brother Mwasakalija I (Mwasalemba); 40s to this man's senior son, Losi; the heifer to Mwasakalija II (Mwakilema); and the betrothal cow and 'calf' (30s) to himself. The father of the bride, Nsajigwa, got none.

A direct connection was made between receiving marriage cattle and sending gifts of food to the groom's father. 'We cook food and send it to rejoice a man's heart, so that he says to himself "I have not thrown away my cattle, see he cooks food for me, he is my kinsman."'

Cattle were the most important property to pass at a marriage but never the only property. Chickens, bark-cloth, hoes, and spears and, by 1934, cash were all suitable gifts for the groom to bring. Traditionally, he took a chicken or a bark-cloth to his bride's father when she reached puberty, and a cock or hen (according to the sex of the child) when she bore her first child, and a hoe before she returned from her father's. A chicken and a hoe or food were also suitable as gifts to her 'mothers' when they brought the bride to him, and she should come with household equipment: cooking pots, hearth bricks, ointment, firewood, and above all mats for her husband's bed, as well as a pot or two of beer and a calabash of milk. At the marriage of a chief on the lake plain in 1934, forty mats were brought by his bride and a fine-woven mat represented a month's work for a skilled woman. Each bride was required to take her husband at least one mat made during her seclusion; the onus of providing her with an adequate number lay on her mother, but she (the mother) could expect help from her husband's sister and sons' wives. The importance of mats was reflected in the remarks of Mwakelebeja who had noted a fine mat (the gift of a chief) hanging on our wall:

Mats are also wealth. . . . If Mwaihojo [147] insults me I take my cows and my wives and move to Mwaipopo's or Mwangomo's [124] country, the cows in front and the wives behind carrying mats, and then people are in awe and run away saying: 'This man is impressive (*nsisya*), see his cattle and mats!'

The theme of a man moving with his household following recurs in myth and folktales (M. Wilson 1959: 9) and, indeed, a line of women walking with their household property or with gifts on their heads, and boys driving stock ahead of them, is as obvious a demonstration of wealth and status as the publication of a will, or wedding pictures on the social page. One day in Ilolo village twenty women passed, eighteen with baskets of food and two with logs of firewood. A young man followed behind. We were told:

The young man is going to visit his sister's husband; it is to enter manhood, very wise, he has called all in his village to cook. It is the custom of a rich man, a wealthy man, one whose children are not quickly married because all know that he is wealthy [and the number of cattle asked will be high]. His brother-in-law will not be taken by surprise — his wife will have spoken in secret saying: 'It seems that my brother is cooking food.' He seeks a bull and hides it in the house to give them, because they ought to eat there. He rejoices saying: 'I have not married in poverty, but in wealth.' And the bride's brother says: 'I send food because I have eaten his cattle.' [But in the evening the party returned very dissatisfied. They had been given only a goat to eat and a gift of 1s 50c. The comment was 'That is not a proper way to marry a woman.']

Feasts were carefully planned.

When a woman's first child is born she goes to her mother; later I, the husband, visit and give a hoe or perhaps 4s, and the mothers say: 'We will bring the child back to you.' I say: 'Wait a little, I have not food ready yet.' And then I ask my father to help me, perhaps with milk, and I ask my mother to cook food, and the food will be sent to my house, and I buy a small bull for 8s and my wife's mothers come with food and beer, bringing my wife and child, and people will say: 'A . . . has cooked much food!' [smiling broadly]. And I send milk and beer to my father, and he will call his friends to eat saying, 'Our child at X has remembered us.'

Because visible property carried such prestige, Nyakyusa fathers preferred to receive cattle rather than cash at the marriage of a daughter, but many grooms wished to give money for cattle were liable to die, and a cow that died had to be replaced if it had not calved after being handed over. In the 1934–8 period the marriage transaction was still reckoned in cattle in the Rungwe valley, and only precise questions showed whether some cows have been replaced by shillings. 'Ambokile gave two cows for marriage, one 40s and one 30s, and then, later five cows. The first two were in money the other five were cows.' 'Ambilikile gave four cows to *ukukwa* in money, three of 40s each and one of 30s, all together 150s. But he was replacing cows which had died. Initially he gave seven cows and no money, but four had died.'

Before 1938 shillings in place of marriage cattle were not readily accepted within BuNyakyusa, but such substitution was common in Ngonde. It was acceptable everywhere for the groom to give shillings or cents in place of a hen, a hoe, or bark-cloth to the bride herself, or her maids, or mothers, or the doctor who had looked after her as a child and who accompanied the mothers taking her to her husband. Gifts given through the go-between to the bride's father might be claimed back in case of divorce, even if in cash as, for example, 2s in place of a hoe, but most small gifts were not recoverable, for the handing over was not formally witnessed.

The exchange of gifts between *abako* (affines) did not cease with the birth of a child. Son-in-law and father-in-law sought help from each other in the provision of feasts; and gave help in cultivation. A son-in-law was obliged to bring a cow to kill at the funeral of father- or mother-in-law if he possibly could, and if his child died and its mother visited her home, her father should send a gift of beer when she returned. Should his wife leave him but the quarrel be patched up, the husband should take a calf to his father-in-law to re-establish friendship.

As already noted, one overt purpose of the puberty ritual was fertility, and the handing over of marriage cattle and the 'bull of puberty' given for a virgin were explicitly sanctioned by the fear that if they were not given the bride would not bear a child. Successful bearing and raising of children was also thought to depend upon the observance of certain rules, notably a separation of the sexual life of parents and children, and the spacing of pregnancies. It was forbidden for a mother to conceive again after the marriage of her eldest son, and she and her husband should sleep apart, or at least practise *coitus interruptus* after the first menstruation of her eldest daughter, until that daughter had lain with her husband (M. Wilson 1957a: 103, 115–6, 137). Neglect of these taboos might mean sterility for son or daughter. And if births were not spaced it was believed that the health of the older child would suffer. Nsajigwa, an elderly christian man explained: 'Formerly it was taboo to make a woman pregnant before her previous child was four or five years old. It was a great case with her husband's sister. The child must know how to run alone before a younger brother was born. We said: "How can the women carry two children?" Now she becomes pregnant again when the elder is two. It was said of those who bore again before the elder could run: "They kill the [elder] child."'

Arani, the senior wife of the chief Porokoto, confirmed all this: 'There should be four years between the birth of children. . . . But you Europeans have a child every year, we see.' Everyone was agreed that the traditional spacing of about four years between births (few put it as high as Nsajigwa) was required because if raiders came and the mother had to flee she could not carry two children. Once the country was pacified such a wide gap between births was no longer insisted upon but anything under two years was thought most improper, and a three-year gap was thought right. 'We all say a woman should not bear again for three years.' One case was quoted of a woman beaten to death by her husband because she refused to sleep with him on the ground that she had a young child. He was drunk and she urged him to sleep with his other wife saying: 'See, you have come from beer, you will make me pragnant.' He gave himself up to the British authorities. And a certain christian woman was known to have quarrelled repeatedly with her husband because she wished to space her children more widely than he permitted. He insisted on weaning each child when it was a year old and his wife soon became pregnant again. The welfare of the children was the explicit reason for spacing, and parents who broke the taboos were thought negligent (M. Wilson 1957a: 130–1). The husband's sister had the right to say when a child might be weaned, and by implication another conceived. In a polygynous family a nursing mother slept apart; in a monogamous family *coitus interruptus* was practised.

The demographic implications of these rules were important. If a woman bore her first son at sixteen and he did not marry until thirty, then she was likely to reach the menopause about the time he married, but if he married young then she must live apart from her husband. With a four-year spacing of births she was unlikely to bear more than eight children. As many children as possible were desired, and six were regarded as a quiverful, but such small samples as were collected suggest that, even where medical services were available, more than a fifth of the children born died under one year, and a woman on the Nyakyusa plain who bore more than two children who survived to marry was fortunate (p. 84 n.11).

Husband and wife

A wife's duties to her husband were carefully taught her by her mothers at the conclusion of the puberty–marriage ritual. She must cook and brew beer, fetch water and firewood, clean the house and byre, mud the walls and floor, work in the fields, and make bark-cloth and mats. Cooking was the primary duty of a wife, closely identified with sexual intercourse, and the most conspicuous activity of the favourite. 'The beloved' was not only diligent in cooking, but her husband ate her food, even though the other wives had cooked also. Cooking required fuel. The bride and each of her companions fetched firewood during their seclusion and placed their bundles on the rafters of the house they occupied, for a good housekeeper must always have a supply of firewood in her loft. Some of the smaller companions, perhaps nine or ten years old, brought only little bundles from the forest, but this was important. We were told: 'It's the wisdom of learning as you learn to read; fetching wood is to teach her to do this, to cut firewood at her husband's.' Fetching firewood was a woman's heaviest job in BuNyakyusa: a good housekeeper went every third day, spending perhaps five hours, walking to the forest, cutting the wood, and bringing it back. If she lived far from the forest it took longer, and for some a shorter time. Only in emergency, if rain was continuous or she were ill, did she deplete the supply in her loft, but since the rainfall in BuNyakyusa is over 100 inches a year she might require to use dry wood from the loft and replace it with wet wood. When a bride was brought to her husband she brought at least one heavy log with her. This remained in her loft as 'firewood of shades'. 'Women always keep one piece of firewood for the shades—her fathers-in-law—to see when they come to look. It belongs to the shades and people say that the shades use it when they want to warm themselves at the fire. This piece of firewood goes with a woman when she dies. It is burnt at her funeral for light at night, or for cooking.' The importance of this duty was also reflected in the stock complaint of her husband if a woman were negligent over fuel: he would say: 'I have wasted my cattle.' With expanding settlement and continuous cutting wood grew scarcer and scarcer; only in new settlements in the forest was it close at hand. In contrast to wood, fetching water was a relatively light duty in BuNyakyusa compared to elsewhere in

Africa; few homesteads were more than a quarter of a mile from a stream and many within a hundred yards.

A wife made the little mud bricks which were packed between the bamboo walls of houses in herring-bone patterns; she mudded the interior walls, and pounded and smeared the floor with mud and cow-dung until it was hard and shining. On the walls inside there might be intricate and lovely patterns made with fingers in the mud (M. Wilson 1964: figs 4a and b). The importance of this was reflected in discussion of qualities desired in a wife. Dung was removed from the byre every day for cattle were stalled in a long house in which the herd-boys slept, and cleaning the byre was the job of women, not of the herd-boys. As a wealthy chief explained: 'A man is always angry if dung remains in the house,' and cleaning the byre was a common point of friction where a man had only one wife and many cattle. When floors were well pounded and smeared, and dung removed, it was easy to sweep a house clean, and a good housewife was *umwifyusi*, clean in the house, clean in cooking, and clean in her person.

In the 1934-8 period each married woman had land allocated to her which her husband, working with his young sons, was required to hoe, or arrange to be hoed, while she planted, weeded, and reaped with her unmarried daughters. She was given certain ridges—a patch for each type of crop—and a section of the banana plantation. She stored and controlled most of the produce, using it to provide food for her husband and children, and for her husband's guests, and feasts. She could entertain her kin and friends as well as his. Only millet, rice, and coffee were exclusively men's crops, and stored and distributed or sold by a man, though his wives reaped and washed the millet, and helped to reap the rice and coffee. A polygynist might also have 'tax plots' (*busongo*) of beans, bananas, groundnuts, maize, or cassava to sell to pay his tax, or to buy himself a cloth, a hoe, or salt, or use to provide gifts for a daughter whose own mother was dead or divorced. A husband could not sell maize, beans, groundnuts, sweet potatoes, or bananas from his wives' plots, though he might ask them for help with his tax (G. Wilson 1938), and for a woman to take millet, all of which belonged to her husband, in his absence was theft: in one such case a cow was claimed from her father as fine. Though in a polygynous family the rights of each wife were clearly defined, in a monogamous family they were more uncertain for monogamists did not establish tax plots and respective rights of disposal of husband and wife were less clear (Konter 1971:27-8; 1974b:119, 132).

If a wife were divorced she lost her land, and if a widow moved from her late husband's homestead she did so also, but this was not important when land was plentiful and her new husband or her father could provide her with fields. In 1954-5 there was a rush to secure rice land, men from hill chiefdoms seeking land on the plain. A law was passed limiting rice land to one field for each individual, but men might secure a field for each wife as well as one for themselves so, for a time, many rice lands were held by women, and each wife had the right to dispose of the crop from her own field. Land generally, but especially rice land, became an important part of a son's inheritance, each eldest son inheriting his mother's land: only in a few cases when she had no son, did a mother's land go to a daughter.

The fact that a woman lost her land-rights if she were divorced was crucial to women by the 1965–9 period. As Dr Konter (1974b (early draft): 193,202) put it, a woman 'does not really possess the field but may use it and pass it on to her own children so long as the marriage remains intact. . . . A husband remains the owner of a field which he has given to his wife.' But a widow retained her field if she stayed in her late husband's homestead, and by 1965–9 between 3·9% and 5·9% of the 'farms' in villages investigated were held by widows (Konter 1974b: 184).

Up to 1938 millet was exclusively a man's crop 'because it is important: it may be sold for a cow.' A young man's rights of disposal over what he grew were limited by his obligations to his father, while the rights of an older man who was a senior son were unfettered. In the mid 1940s, as men returned from the army, a revolution took place: women began growing millet to make beer for sale. Women were urged by husbands and sons to cover themselves, and told to earn clothes for themselves by hoeing for millet and brewing beer. During the 1930s scarcely any Nyakyusa women hoed. Pagan women never considered doing so and, at Kabembe mission in conservative Selya, christian women told me: 'The Kinga women hoe but we do not know how to hoe. If we have no husband we just starve.' By 1938 three christian widows living near Rungwe mission (the most sophisticated part of BuNyakyusa) had begun, but others commiserated with them and felt it unreasonable that any woman should be required to do this. In Ngonde the practice of women hoeing was already general—even the ladies of the Kyungu (but not his senior wife) hoed. The ladies told me: 'Women here used not to hoe; men hoed. Before the war (1914–18) women did little hoeing, but now we hoe for all kinds of food including rice and millet. Women began when food was short because their husbands were dead or lazy. Still, in the hills, it is men only who hoe. We don't like doing it: we are driven by hunger.'

By 1955 in Selya, married women whose husbands or grown sons were at home hoed for millet with which they brewed beer for sale: they still expected the deep-ridged fields on which staple vegetables were grown to be hoed by men. But throughout the Rungwe valley widows and grass-widows whose husbands were migrant labourers, hoed for food for themselves and their children. Hoeing implied using a long-handled iron hoe—a man's tool— whereas women had used only a short-handled wooden hoe for weeding and planting. By 1955 women around Rungwe mission not only hoed but many pruned bananas, using the bill-hook, also a symbol of a man's duties.

To the Nyakyusa, in the 1934–8 period, mats were 'impressive' whether made of fine grass in traditional style or of palm-leaf in a new style learnt from Swahili women. They were an important part of the outfit of a bride—a wealthy man's bed was built up with a hundred mats or more—and they were used as gifts. The principal crafts of Nyakyusa women were bark-cloth-making and mat-making (M. Wilson 1964: Pl. III, V, figs 4, 7), and these also were practised during the seclusion at puberty, the bride and her companions making and decorating their own bark-cloth belts, and she making at least one mat for her marriage outfit.

Dress commonly reflects status as Thomas Carlyle and Virginia Woolf were at pains to show, and styles felt to be appropriate are often enforced by law.[5] Wearing cloth had been a mark of status among the Ngonde from the time of the first Kyungu and a gift of cloth at a funeral was only less important among them and the Nyakyusa than the gift of a cow for the feast. It was therefore in conformity with the relative status of men and women that, as trade cloth became available, it was worn by men, rather than women. From the beginning of the colonial period men spent their first earnings on cloth (Ballantyne and Shepherd 1968: 250) and they were still doing so in the 1934–8 period. The fringed black alpaca shawl, worn by the wives of early Moravian missionaries in Africa, caught people's fancy and became part of the formal dress of christian women among the Xhosa (M. Wilson 1972b: 196), but was worn by men among the Nyakyusa. This was not the only style borrowed by Nyakyusa men from foreign women. Mrs D. R. MacKenzie related with amusement (personal communication 1933) how, about 1920, she had distributed coat-dresses to the women of her congregation at Kyimbila, the gift of a women's committee in Edinburgh, to be worn in church in place of the exiguous bark-cloth dress. The following Sunday the women filed in still in their bark-cloth; their husbands followed swaggering in the coat-dresses which somewhat resembled the Swahili *khansu*, familiar on the coast. Similarly, wire waist-rings were worn by men before 1914 as Fülleborn's (1906:Pl. 66, 67, 70) photographs show: by 1925 they were also worn by women, and by 1934 almost exclusively by women. MacKenzie wrote in 1925: 'men of social position are known by the number of *manyeta* . . . which they wear: one for a man or woman just "above the common", six or seven for a man of high standing' (MacKenzie 1925:29). In 1936 we saw one elderly male dancer wearing nine waist-rings but he was exceptional, whereas favourite wives of wealthy men or women doctors were expected to dress in this fashion (M. Wilson 1951a: Pl. XIII; 1964: Pl. IVa).

After Independence dress remained important as a symbol of status and respect: short skirts for girls and long hair for men were taken both as a challenge to authority and 'indecent' in Malawi; the absence of collars, ties, and suits as an appropriate expression of the egalitarian values of Tanzania, as well as a suitable adaptation to the climate; the exiguous body covering once generally acceptable among Nyakyusa–Ngonde was felt no longer tolerable there, though acceptable on the beaches of Europe and America. The passion of feeling about 'appropriate' dress reflects radical differences in values; the conflict between an egalitarian and a hierarchical view of society; conflicting ideas about the proper relationships between men and women, young and old; and conflicting ideas about how 'decency' is expressed.

From 1934–55 pots and baskets were bought from peripheral groups—Kisi and Ndali—or from outsiders. Women earned a little cash by selling chickens (which were women's property) and small quantities of food either to neighbours, or on the market in Tukuyu or Karonga, but up to 1955 I heard of none who regularly practised as traders, except for the wife of a sophisticated man at Rungwe, who served in his shop. Up to 1955 the one specialist occupation of pagan women, which was highly regarded, was that of doctor (*inganga*) or priest (*unyago*). The doctor knew medicines for cure or protection, the priest the right procedure and medicines in celebrating one or more of the rituals of kinship. Medicines were often learnt from kinsmen but might also be bought, and there was no sharp division between those used by a man and those used by a woman, or indeed between the function of doctor and priest. Lyandeleko, a famous woman doctor, had medicines believed to cure sterility learnt from her husband, who came from a family famous as doctors, and medicine for the twin ritual learnt from her own father. She also had medicines for childrens' diseases. Another woman doctor with twin medicine was a catechumen in 1938 and she was teaching the medicine to her sister. A woman who worked in this way controlled her own earnings, and any cattle she acquired were the inheritance of her youngest son, quite separate from property inherited by her eldest son from his father.

Attending rituals occupied considerable time. It was an outing for women, an occasion for meeting kinsfolk and friends, and legitimately leaving household duties and cultivation for a day; it was an obligation, for failure to mourn or rejoice with kinsfolk was at best ill-mannered, at worst likely to lead to a charge of practising witchcraft; and it was often thought to be a condition of children's health, for kinsmen were 'members one of another' to the point that failure of a brother's wife to take her children to be treated, when one brother of a set had begotten twins, was thought liable to lead to sickness, perhaps death, of the children; failure of a woman to take her children to her father's funeral ritual was thought likely to cause them to go mad or fall ill. Children, in particular, were mostly carefully treated in ritual for they were not among those who had been through such rituals before and were thought to be in greatest danger. At any ritual there were commonly more women and children present than men, perhaps because of concern for children, or a greater faith among women in the efficacy of rituals, or enjoyment of the outing, or all three reasons at once. Women were even called to and attended rituals for children by a husband from whom they were divorced; the mother of a nubile girl was called by the girl's father, the chief Mwaihojo (147), to her puberty ritual, though the mother had been divorced from Mwaihojo, and the cattle returned, some years previously; she had run off with his cross-cousin (*untani*). Visiting home—her father's house—was an important right to a married woman enjoyed after the birth of each child if her own mother were alive and still married to her father, but particularly important after the birth of the first child when she might expect to spend about a month, until her father, having received a cow or other gift from her husband, sent her back to him with gifts of beer and food.

Women participated fully in rituals of kinship, and might be the officiants, directing proceedings and providing the medicines used but, except for the senior wives of chiefs, priests, and village headmen, women had almost no part in the traditional communal rituals, and they scarcely figured in mythology. Only she-who-taught-cooking was a heroine in her own right: the other women mentioned were *wives* of the Lwembe or his successors (M. Wilson 1959: 14–15), whose names were remembered because their sons were distinguished by them, since a son took his name from his mother with a male prefix.

A husband's duties consisted first in supervision of the cattle, though he expected to have sons to herd and milk for him and if he lacked a son himself but had cattle, he would try to persuade some younger brother or other relative to live with him. Little boys slept in the byre with the cattle; those of more than ten or eleven years old in a nearby age-village returning to their mothers for food, and to help their father with the cattle, and later with hoeing. Sheep were very few, and goats never seen at all; chickens belonged to women; so cattle were the only stock with which men were generally concerned.

Secondly, a man hoed and pruned bananas. His primary responsibility was to hoe for his wives, but he also hoed for his in-laws, especially during the betrothal period, and until his marriage he helped his father. When his father died, if his mother were past childbearing and not inherited, she might elect to live near him and then he had the responsibility of hoeing a field for her as he would for a wife. A man also built the solid round and long houses of bamboo, and thatched them, while the women packed mud bricks in the gaps between bamboos, plastered, and fetched thatch. If a man failed to hoe or build a house (or at least a room in a long house) for each wife, she had grounds for complaint, even for divorce. He also hoed millet and perhaps rice, and his own *ubusungu* plots which all the wives together should weed and reap, and in the hills he planted and tended coffee in the shade of the bananas. The 'dignity of the homestead' (M. Wilson 1951a:78) added to the owner's prestige and a man took pains to shelter seedlings of indigenous shade or fruit trees like *chorophora excelsa* or *trichillia supp.* or plant exotics begged or lifted from European settlements. It was his duty also, with the help of young sons, to weed and sweep the open court between the houses, for that was the burial ground, and there he might be 'sweeping his father's grave'. Dr Kerr-Cross (1890: 283) noted small boys sweeping in 1888, and it was a common sight in the 1930s.

The most important specialists were smiths, diviners, and doctors each of whom learnt their craft from an older man who was skilled and who might be a relative but was not necessarily one. Mwakyonde, the second heir of a chief, who 'came out' as a chief but lost his small country in war to his senior brother Mwaihojo, became famous as a doctor. He had learnt four types of medicines from his mother's father, paying him a hen, not the usual cow, because he was his grandfather. Two medicines he learned by exchanging the secret for knowledge of one of his own. Only the offices of rainmaker or priest of a grove were necessarily hereditary, passing like cattle from elder to younger brother and on to the senior son of the eldest brother (M. Wilson 1959: 5). Lesser crafts included carving stools and decorating milk flasks (M. Wilson 1964: figs 2–5, Pl. VII); these a man learnt by watching someone skilled. Small traders, mostly dependent upon Indian-owned stores and holding 'hawkers' licences', were spread through the country by 1934; they bought small quantities of produce and sold salt, paraffin, matches, and cloth. There were also a small number of clerks, school teachers, and preachers in government or mission employment, domestic servants, and a handful of labourers on a tea estate.

Besides caring for his herd, hoeing, building, and somehow earning enough cash to pay his tax, an adult man was concerned with the administration of the family estate, providing marriage and funeral cattle for dependents, claiming cattle due to him, organizing rituals and feasts, enhancing his prestige by showing generosity but cannily laying out whatever wealth he had to bring the maximum return. He was also expected to attend court and there learn the law and participate in the administration of it. Young men who did not attend court were reprimanded by their seniors, on the ground that they would remain ignorant.

The passage of cattle gave a Nyakyusa husband exclusive sexual rights over his wife, and rights over any children conceived while she remained married to him, irrespective of who the genitor might be. A genitor had no rights unless he were also a husband recognized through his acceptance by the woman's father as a son-in-law. In 'cock marriage' acceptance had followed a period of service to the father-in-law; by 1934 acceptance was dependent upon the passage of cattle. Occasionally and privately, an ageing husband might grant right of access to a wife to a brother who was to be his heir, or even to a son, but by all accounts this was uncommon. There was no recognition of lovers as among the Gogo (Rigby 1969: 207–8), though in popular belief every wife of a chief, living in a large harem, had a lover with whom she slept. 'Everyone says so and knows it. Only some get caught but all have lovers; they practise *coitus interruptus*.' There were mystical sanctions against adultery: if a wife were unfaithful, the husband feared weariness and diarrhoea, though not if the lover practised *coitus interruptus*; the wife also feared a prolonged labour if she became pregnant and some husbands used medicines which they believed would cause venereal disease to any man who lay with their wives.

A woman had no exclusive sexual rights; polygyny was tradionally approved; but it was thought that adultery by the husband during his wife's pregnancy might injure her. They were mystically linked during pregnancy and, immediately after the birth of a child, the husband observed some of the same avoidances as his wife. His life during war and hunting was also thought to depend upon her behaviour; if she were unfaithful he would be killed in battle along with her lover (M. Wilson 1957a:132–8). Wives often complained of sexual neglect by their husbands, giving that as their reason for seeking divorce and, indeed, it was commonly said that the way in which a man rid himself of a wife chosen by his father and married with his father's cattle, was to stop sleeping with her. He could not initiate a divorce without insulting his father but if she left him then he could claim his cattle. He always denied that he had neglected her. Husband and wife also shared obligations to observe taboos during menstruation and to space their children, the health of husband, wife, or child being thought to depend upon this.

There was a premise of inequality between men and women. Nyakyusa women were expected to observe a pattern of deference, obedience, and service much like that of a son to his father, but continued through life, and transferred from father to husband. A pagan father actually said to his daughter at her marriage: 'Fear and respect your husband, he is your father.' The maturity of sons was recognized at the 'coming out', but the maturity of women was never recognized and they were expected to behave as juniors towards men all their lives, stooping to greet (M. Wilson 1951a: Pl. IX), answering with the submissive *taa*, obeying orders without question, not answering back. In the 1934–8 period a woman always stooped to greet an adult man, even one younger than herself, and to greet an older woman, but not one younger than herself. A young man stooped to greet a man of his father's generation whether standing or sitting, or a contemporary who was seated, but not a man younger than himself. He would also stoop to greet a woman of his mother's generation related to him. Great stress was laid on greeting people properly: 'Mothers teach their children to stoop to greet elders. Other people blame the parents if children are rude.' For a woman, stooping to greet implied sitting and bending her head, whereas a man squatted, but did not sit down. A wife was always expected to stoop to greet her husband; she never ate with him, and they never openly enjoyed each other's company. Two phrases were revealing: Kasitile [a man] addressing his shades in a ritual expressed his submission to them saying, 'I, your wife, have done wrong . . . I am a woman . . .' (M. Wilson 1959:134); and a young man, discussing the duties of men and women, remarked: 'We are the women of Europeans.'

Men argued that the passage of cattle gave a husband authority over his wife: he could exact labour, he could beat her, if she neglected her work. The following conversation took place in 1936 between four elderly pagan men, Mwambuputa, Nsusa, Mwakwega, and another, and Godfrey Wilson over beer:

G.W.: Why do you not enjoy the company of your wives?
Elder: They quarrel with me when guests are present.
Another elder: That is very bad.
Another elder: Why do they argue when we tell them to do things? It's all very well for you, Mwaipaja [G.W.]. Kagile [M.W.] does no work. *We* are all your wives, but we have to tell our wives to do things and they are apt to refuse. Then we must be harsh.
G.W. Some Europeans are poor and their wives work for them.
Elder: How many wives have you?
G.W. One.
Elder: Exactly! If I tell one wife I'm hungry she will say: 'My friend is cooking for you' and the other says the same. If there is only one wife you may be kin (*bakamu*) indeed, but not with two.

The women's view, expressed to M.W., was different: 'If you are tired when you come in from weeding or fetching firewood, and sit down, your husband shouts at you: "Get on, you lazy thing, and cook for me."' The typical complaint of a dissatisfied wife was: 'He is always beating me and shouting at me,' or 'One is the favourite, and another also loved, but the others are just rubbish, they are beaten much and can do nothing right.' Indeed, women said: 'a husband beats his wife even if he loves her,' and an elderly chief's wife, asked why some wives had left, replied that all had 'run away from the stick'. There was real fear of physical injury, and neighbours often intervened. A wife might flee to her father; he sought evidence from neighbours; and if he were satisfied that the husband were indeed harsh he might beat his son-in-law (as shown in case 29) or return his cattle and demand a divorce saying: 'He's just rubbish, he's not my child, how can there be kinship?' Or simply: 'You are no longer my son-in-law.' He might also bring a law-suit for damages. In one case a husband who had knocked out his wife's tooth was brought to court by her father and fined a cow which went to her father. She had fled to her father and remained with him until the fine was paid. Her husband had complained of her cooking. In another case the husband was fined two cows for assaulting his wife. On the other hand, a wife was told that it was her duty to 'nourish her father' and stay married, not compelling him to return marriage cattle, and the threat always was that her father might use the terrible phrase 'she is not my child' (*akaja mwanangu*) and refuse to receive cattle again on her behalf, something very shameful and mystically dangerous. Formerly, according to the chief, Koroso (173):

If a woman did wrong at her husband's the husband took her to the go-between, who went with her to her father's neighbours, and said: 'Your child does not listen to her husband: she said this and that.' (The husband himself did not go). So the neighbours told the father, who replied: 'Indeed my child is bad.' Then he was covered with shame and said: 'Indeed this child has done wrong.' He returned all the cattle and their progeny, but if perhaps he wished her to return to her husband then he sent her back with a cow, a calf from one of those brought by her husband for the marriage.
G.W.: Fathers agreed in such cases to return all the cattle?
Koroso: They agreed.
G.W.: What was it that compelled them to do so? Now they refuse.
Koroso: Shame compelled them. Shame was strong formerly, now it has disappeared. They were covered with shame saying, 'My child has done wrong, she has rotted.' They compared and said 'Everything in my house is bad.'

A wife might also be sent home to seek a replacement if she broke a calabash or, in modern times, a china plate, but it seemed that accidental breakage was overlooked and distinguished from breaking 'on account of pride'. Pride (*amatingo*) and shame (*isoni*) were what mattered, and shame might compel behaviour not required by law. After the conversation quoted above, chief Koroso volunteered: 'And if a girl was not fathered by her own father but was illegitimate, then her father refused to receive cattle: he said, "The child was not mine but another's." My father, Mwakalinga [142], told me before he died that so and so, one of my half-sisters, was not begotten by him. He said, "Don't ever receive cattle for her." So I refused to receive them. . . . No, she was not married "cock fashion" because my father, Mwakalukwa [141], received them. He said: "I don't know, but she is our child." Formerly shame was strong, but now it is not there, fathers claim for cattle.' There was a similar contradiction between the theory that the child of a married woman should be treated as the child of the *pater* in ritual, and the actual practice when it came to giving an infant the *ikipiki* medicine which symbolized 'the blood of the lineage' (M. Wilson 1957a: 147–9).

Authority was conceived as having a mystical dimension, and if a wife were disrespectful to her husband or his parents she feared sterility, or sickly children. 'It is said that when a wife has sworn at her husband in secret, her child grows thin. Or perhaps if she has sworn at him openly, or at her mother-in-law or father-in-law, or her husband's father's sister, then, when her own

138 FOR MEN AND ELDERS

mothers come to see her they are shocked (M. Wilson 1957a:188–9). They say: "Why is this child [their grandchild] so thin?" She replies: "I don't know." Mothers: "You have sworn at your husband." "No". They beat her and beat her and tell her to admit it. At length she confesses: "Indeed, I did swear at my husband". Then they take the child to a doctor to get medicine. That is *ingoto*.'

A husband was said to mutter (*ukwibunesia*) to his shades if his wife were proud or 'whispered to people' (saying he is a fool) or abused his married daughters when they came home to visit, or grudged them food. And if she quarrelled with her husband while she was brewing beer she feared lest the beer go sour (M. Wilson 1957a: 217).

A wife held no communication with her husband's shades (though she provided them with firewood) and at her husband's there were no shades of her own lineage; she exercised no legitimate mystical power over her husband; her weapon was witchcraft. Men indeed feared the witchcraft of a discontented wife, as Kasitile made clear when he was ailing (M. Wilson 1959:126–7; 1951a:203). Women's mystical power was almost always spoken of as evil: there were many witches, no *abamanga* (strong ones exercising power for good) among women (M. Wilson 1951a: 96–9). One case only was quoted in which the anger of a wife was spoken of as though justified. The case was reported by the sister's son of the man concerned in 1935.

CASE 43: AN ANGRY WIFE SPOILS THE FISHING

Kalindo fished and caught two fish. He gave one to each of two wives. His third wife was absent. When she returned she was angry saying: 'They grudge me food.' Kalindo found no fish in his traps for a long time and he went to enquire the cause of a diviner. The diviner said his third wife was angry. She had not prayed, but the shades of her husband were angry also and had stopped fish entering his traps. So Kalindo told his wife that the divination had caught her, and asked: 'Were you angry?' She admitted she had been but said she was now satisfied. Kalindo took his calabash of water and prayed with water in the evening in the banana grove. Next morning he found his traps full of fish.

The fact that a woman's legitimate mystical power was felt to be much less than that of a man was apparent in the interpretations of misfortune: it was the danger of a father's anger that was constantly mentioned, rather than that of a mother, but Kasitile, when he was ill, spoke on one occasion of his deceased *mother* being angry because she had not found beer at the back of the house and 'for a chief there should always be beer in the house'.

At all feasts and rituals, indeed on all public occasions, and usually within the family, men and women sat apart, and food was allocated to them separately. When men sat drinking a woman was at hand to provide the hot water required, and she who had brewed, as well as other women, might be called individually to come and taste the beer, but they sipped and left; they did not remain to keep the men company. In the rituals of kinship the opposition of lineages, of villages, and of chiefdoms was expressed; in the communal rituals, that of generations, of villages, and of chiefdoms. I saw no ritualized expression of opposition between men and women: their difference and separation was taken for granted. Opposition was taken for granted also; 'the war of the mats' was a phrase that came readily to the tongue; but it was not dramatized. Both antagonism and affection between husbands and wives were constantly visible, and they were intertwined. We knew two elderly couples, both pagan, who were evidently deeply attached to one another and who spoke familiarly together, but they were noticeably different from most married couples, and in both cases there were other wives, unloved and distant from their husbands. A close relationship depended on the favour of the husband and this a senior wife might lose to a new co-wife.

In BuNyakyusa, in 1934-8, there was no category of women living independently, except for the prostitutes who had begun to appear on the Lupa gold-fields. The wives and daughters of chiefs were recognized by special terms, more marriage cattle were given for them than for commoners, and higher fines in case of adultery, but they lived like ordinary women, fetching wood and water and cultivating, and subject to their husbands. The two senior wives of a chief, or one senior wife of a commoner, took precedence in ritual but had little practical authority. There were no women chiefs as among the nearby Nyamwanga or Bemba, no women who established their own homesteads and married 'wives' as among the Nuer. The only situation in which a woman was socially a man was as 'father's sister', when she exercised power in the distribution of inheritance and was given due respect; she was even thought to be able to stop conception in her brother's daughter, and might, in rare circumstances, claim a cow at that daughter's marriage. But a father's sister was also a wife, and most of the time her duties as a wife overshadowed her rights as a father's sister. One single case was reported in which a woman had inherited cattle because no man in the lineage remained alive.

An elderly pagan woman might be built for by a son, even (we were told) before Europeans arrived, but she occupied nothing like the position in the homestead that the mother of an Mpondo head of the homestead occupied: she did not organize the women's work in the way in which an Mpondo mistress (*inkosikazi*) did. Indeed it seemed as if there were no mistress in a Nyakyusa home unless a senior wife were a woman of outstanding personality; usually all the women were the wives of one man and there was bitter competition between them for his favour. Furthermore, co-wives lived close to one another, the young ones often occupying separate rooms in one long house (LeVine 1962). The role of supervisor of young wives filled by a mother-in-law where there is patrilocal marriage (in the homestead of the husband's father) (Hunter 1936:18, 24, 35–41, 45) and by a mother or elder sister where there is uxorilocal marriage (Richards 1939: 114–7) was not filled and, if a young woman were idle and her work neglected, the conflict came directly with her husband. Points of friction vary with the society: among the Nyakyusa there were few witch-like mothers-in-law, or elder sisters, but much quarrelling between wives and husbands over the wives' work, and jealousy between co-wives (M. Wilson 1951b: 307–13).

In the 1934–8 period many Nyakyusa women did not accept the place which conservative men assigned to them. They had glimpsed another sort of relationship among Europeans who lived in the district, and the courts supported a girl refusing to marry a man chosen for her as a child by her father, or a widow refusing to be inherited. Christians taught that monogamy was right, polygyny wrong, and that the bond of marriage should be love between husband and wife. Inequality between men and women was not challenged either by the courts or the missions: indeed some European missionaries, as well as some christian Nyakyusa men, were critical of the 'pride' (*amatingo*) of christian girls which caused some young men, themselves christian, to prefer to marry pagan girls; but christian women read the gospels, which are full of revolutionary ideas; they were accepted as full members of the church; the Moravians ordained women as well as men, as elders of the church. The yeast was at work.

Stability of marriage

The aspect of Nyakyusa marriage about which information is most inadequate is stability. During the 1930s divorce was frequent but we lack any adequate statistics. 'Formerly making love was small because men feared to die.' The chief Mwaipopo said: 'If a man came [to seduce my wife], even my son, I would spear him. Now there is a big case because it is Europen times. The adulterer says to himself: "They won't do anything because there are Europeans."' Mwaipopo and Kasitile together insisted that: 'In the old days a man would not go to a friend's wife. Now my son will come even to my own wife.' The chief Porokoto and six elderly men agreed that 'some did run off even in the old days' but they were sure that divorce had greatly increased. Chief Koroso, on the lake plain, explained that certain women had been recognized as runaways and 'a wise man did not marry a runaway, only a man without wisdom did so.' There were men still living who had refused women because they were runaways. Charsley has questioned whether marriage was indeed stable at an earlier period and he quotes the missionary, C. Schumann, writing in 1916, to the effect that 'few women of thirty were still with their first husbands, and very often a woman was currently married to her fifth or sixth husband, occasionally up to a twentieth husband.'[6] In the Nyakyusa view the increase in divorce began when European rule was established, about 1893. Without statistics it is impossible to demonstrate what change, if any, has taken place. What is certain is that in the 1934–8 period elderly chiefs who regularly sat in court were convinced that divorce had increased since they were young. It is also certain that both young and old thought marriage ought to be stable, and the increase in adultery fines in 1935 was agreed upon in the hope that adultery and divorce would diminish. A girl was admonished at the puberty–marriage ritual to 'stay with her husband' and the mothers sang, 'Let us go forever and never return' (M. Wilson 1957a: 90). At betrothal the groom thrust a spear into the ground in the courtyard of the bride's home. She plucked it out and handed it to her father in token of her consent to the marriage. It meant: 'With this spear you may slay me if I run away from my husband' (M. Wilson 1957a:74, 79, 117).

A continuing alliance between lineages was greatly valued and christian opposition to compelling a widow to be inherited or sending a girl to replace a dead wife was criticized because it broke this alliance. A man who ran off with women was said to 'waste his property' and a woman with the reputation of being a runaway (*mbeti*) was despised. If her father refused to receive cattle for her she was deeply shamed. Property overshadowed love in marriage but did not bind it; many men were prevented from marrying through lack of cattle but women were not content to remain with a man who was rich if they preferred someone else. It was recognized among women that one who ran away from her husband after she had borne several children might have difficulty in remarrying, and a high proportion of the divorces were of women recently married. After the increase in the adultery fine in 1935 a woman seeking divorce might leave her husband but conceal the fact that she had a lover so that he might not be fined. If her father, also fearing lest he be held responsible for the fine, refused to receive her she had no choice but to live at the chief's court 'looking for her cows', that is, for an offer of marriage. The lover might be ready to marry her, but he would delay, if he could, until a divorce was granted and he could marry her without incurring a fine. Large harems, the absence of unmarried girls, and the presence of many lusty bachelors created a situation in the 1934–8 period in which adultery, often though not necessarily followed by divorce, was taken for granted. By 1967, 29% of marriages ended in divorce (de Jonge and Sterkenburg 1971 : 105) but the number of divorce cases coming before the courts had fallen.

NOTES

[1] From the time a cow was handed over for betrothal the bride was referred to as a 'wife' (*unkasi*), the groom as her 'husband' (*undume*).

[2] The levirate is distinguished from widow inheritance by the fact that under the levirate any children borne by a widow are legally children of the deceased. The legal status of children of the heir in Nyakyusa law was clear since the deceased and his heir were one; a more difficult issue was the legal status of children borne by widows inherited by other kinsmen of the deceased. These were spoken of *both* as children of the deceased and of the man who had inherited their mother. If a widow were 'divorced' and cattle returned, and she remarried, any children she then bore were legally children of her new husband.

[3] Seven years' difference in the marriage age between the sexes allows 20% of the married men to have two wives (Sonnabend 1934: 319–21). The age difference at first marriage in BuNyakyusa ranged between 10 and 15 years in 1934, but had fallen by 1955 (M. Wilson 1959: 208). It was eleven years in 1967 (de Jonge and Sterkenburg 1971: 103–4).

[4] The evidence of Bishop Gemeseus can be taken as exact. Evidence from genealogies is more doubtful for, though we sought to record all wives, some junior wives, particularly younger sisters who formed part of the 'house' of a senior wife, may have been omitted. Giraud (1890: 188) reported that Mwamakula (106) had 50 wives in 1883, but he merely estimated the number of women, claiming to be 'wives' of the chief, who called on him for gifts.

[5] Thomas Carlyle, *Sartor Resartus*, 1833; Virginia Woolf, *Three Guineas*, 1938. Even when sumptuary laws disappeared in Europe, America, and at the Cape, laws prohibiting nudity and transvestism remained.

[6] Charsley 1969: 53, paraphrasing C. Schumann, *25 Jahre Berliner Mission in Deutsch Ostafrika*, 1916, p. 22. Perhaps Schumann mistook the 'runaways' to whom Koroso referred as representing the norm, as if Hollywood stars were taken as the norm for the United States.

Chapter 7

DIVERSITY FURTHER EXAMINED

DIVERSITY is the genesis of change, hence particular attention is given to differences which were apparent among the Nyakyusa–Ngonde people. The argument of this chapter is that the diversity of the pre-colonial period was first and foremost local: it was linked to ecology and peculiarities of local history, and was nourished by isolation. It did not involve change until, and in so far as, once isolated communities began to interact; then, immediately, they began to influence one another, compelling adjustment of differences. New local differences began to emerge, again related to isolation and peculiarities of external contact. Apart from local differences, there were also widespread differences between chiefs and commoners, cattle-owners and poor men, dating back perhaps to the 15th century, which were reflected in forms of marriage. The preference for marriage with cattle, as opposed to marriage by service, had spread through the Rungwe valley and over the Ngonde plain. Throughout the colonial period, new variations emerged in the political and economic field, but the major differences were between pagan and christian, between those who had some school education and those who had none. Such differences appeared most conspicuously in the changing relationships between husband and wife, and in a lesser degree in changing relationships between parents and children. Differences in the behaviour of successive generations, in the accepted values of successive periods of time, are the substance of social change, and these are recorded so far as evidence exists.

Local differences dating from pre-colonial times

The Nyakyusa–Ngonde people spoke one language distinct from that of their neighbours, the Kinga, the Nyiha–Safwa (including Lambya and Malila), the Sangu, the Tumbuka (including Henga), and the Iwa–Nyamwanga (see map 2 and M. Wilson 1958; B. Brock 1966). They were not mutually intelligible with any of these neighbours though KiKinga was said to be 'a very easy language' for a Nyakyusa to learn. The Nyakyusa shared a common ritual with the Kinga and depended upon them for hoes and salt, but they only began to intermarry 'in European times'. In 1934 unoccupied belts of country still separated Nyakyusa–Ngonde from their neighbours, except in the extreme south where Ngonde-speakers mingled with Henga on the Rukuru river. In the fragmented population of the Corridor area the Nyakyusa–Ngonde, who numbered about 135,000 in 1931 and 292,000 in 1950, spread over an area approaching 5,000 square miles, were the largest 'people' speaking one language.

Within this language group there were peoples speaking seven main dialects: the Nyakyusa proper who included the people of the lake plain and

Masoko; the people of Selya in the middle region; the Kukwe of the hills; the
Ngonde south of the Songwe in what was then Nyasaland (now Malawi); the
Ndali[1] in the hills to the west; the Sukwa resembling the Ndali and also in the
western hills but south of the Songwe; and the Saku on the eastern corner of
the plain close to the Livingstone mountains (see map 3). Besides these, there
were small groups of early inhabitants not fully absorbed by invading
Nyakyusa–Ngonde, who also differed in dialect and custom. These included
Penja, Lugulu, and Nyiha in the hills north of the Songwe, the Kisi where the
lake, the plain, and the Livingstone mountains meet, Wenya, Fungwe, and
Tambo on the western border of Ngonde. In the 1934–8 period the Penja
were remembered as a people who did not traditionally bury their dead; the
Lugulu still celebrated a ritual of vituperation which shocked their Kukwe
neighbours; the Kisi were famed as potters, exploiting a seam of good pot-clay
in their narrow strip of territory between the lake and the mountains; Wenya
were Tumbuka-speakers like the Henga. In phonetics, vocabulary, and
syntax the seven dialects differed sufficiently to be easily identifiable by
Nyakyusa–Ngonde speakers—even we ourselves were quickly recognized as
having learnt to speak in Selya, though we had lived nearly as long in
BuKukwe. Kerr-Cross (1890: 284; 1895: 112–3) identified five main dialects
in 1888 and 1893;[1] in the 1934–8 period books in KyaNgonde and the
KiNyakyusa of Selya were used on both sides of the Songwe, on the plain and
in the hills (including Ndali) though Ngonde, Nyakyusa, and Kukwe each
preferred books in their own dialect; and in 1970 dialect differences were still
causing difficulties in a revision of the translation of the Bible (Rev. Tom Price
personal communication). Bitter argument over which dialect, or what
combination of dialects, should become the written form, has repeatedly
occurred in Africa and those peoples, like the British, whose written language
quickly stabilized in one form, like 'the King's English', were fortunate.

Differences in Nyakyusa–Ngonde dialects coincided in some measure with
differences in economy, related to differences in altitude, rainfall, and
accessibility, and these in turn with differences in political structure, law,
ritual, and convention. The ritual followed by any family depended upon its
origin. The charter was family custom, and wife and children followed the
custom of husband and father. When a daughter married, she then followed the
custom of her husband except when she returned to celebrate rituals in her
own lineage. In theory every family continued to follow lineage tradition; in
fact local differences were recognized and practice tended to be assimilated to
the area in which a family lived. Local differences in crops were recognized as
one source of differences in ritual, for staple foods were the symbols used, and
the staple varied with the altitude (M. Wilson 1957a: 11–12). Differences in
ritual were recognized between people of Selya and the Nyakyusa proper
(whose rituals were almost identical) and the Kukwe, the Ngonde, the
Lugulu, the Ndali, the Kisi, and the Penja. It was the function of the officiant
in a ritual to direct details of form, and a family sought an officiant who knew
their ritual, but assimilation to an area of long residence was manifest. We
knew intimately a family descended from a Sangu doctor who had lived for
three generations in Selya. They all spoke KiNyakyusa not KiSangu, and

their rituals approximated to those of Selya. Differences such as those between Selya and BuKukwe (M. Wilson 1957a: 37–129) were tolerated even when celebrated by a Kukwe family living in Selya, but any extreme divergence, such as the Lugulu rite of mutual vituperation between in-laws (M. Wilson 1957a: 149–51), aroused the shocked amusement of Nyakyusa proper, Selya, and Kukwe, and ridicule tends to extinguish an eccentricity.

As has been shown, in Ngonde there developed a kingdom, as opposed to the small independent chiefdoms of the Nyakyusa plain and the hills. We argue that this was dependent on the growth of trade in Ngonde but not in the Rungwe valley, and that trade turned on geography. In Ngonde alone there was slavery in the form of debt-slaves, kinsmen of criminals, and war-captives. Ndali and Sukwa differed from Nyakyusa proper, Selya, Kukwe, Saku and Ngonde in that they did not have a ramifying lineage of chiefs or a system of age-villages; a man built his house near his father and brought his bride there. The Ndali required less strict avoidance of father-in-law and less rigid limitation on childbearing after the marriage of a son. There were also differences in the death-ritual and the rules of marriage. But in language and economy Ndali were very close to Nyakyusa in the 1934–8 period, and had been close when Kerr-Cross travelled through in 1893 (Kerr-Cross 1895: 113, 120–1). BuNdali and Misuku were particularly isolated, cut off by great rivers, hills, and marshes, and their most striking peculiarities, the absence of chiefs of a hero's lineage, and of age-villages, may be attributed to their isolation.

The Kingdom of Ngonde included a larger population and maintained much wider trade contacts than any Nyakyusa chiefdom. The political structure was more complex. Tribute came to the Kyungu from different ecological areas: fish from the lakeshore, beans from the hills, bananas and millet from lower and higher altitudes. Five languages, not mutually intelligible (Nyakyusa–Ngonde, Tumbuka, Nyiha, Iwa-Nyamwanga and Bisa) were spoken within the area over which the Kyungu once claimed suzerainty, and traders visiting from the coast spoke a sixth, Swahili.

According to oral tradition there have been three layers of population in the Rungwe valley: pygmy hunters in what were once extensive forests; hunters and cultivators like Penja, Safwa, and Nyiha; and incoming chiefs who brought cattle and iron. It is likely that the proportion of invaders of the royal lines of Lwembe, Mwakilembe, and Kyungu in any local population varied: the 'sons of Lwembe' and of Mwakilembe increased, and their descendants were many in Masoko, the lake plain, Selya, and BuKukwe; but for some generations younger sons of a reigning Kyungu were strangled at birth and his lineage spread more slowly (G. Wilson 1939: 13–17). Descendants of the famous heroes never moved into Ndali and Misuku. The distribution of age-villages suggests that this institution was first established by incoming chiefs. It existed neither among the Ndali, nor among the early inhabitants of the Rungwe valley, the Penja, nor among the neighbouring Safwa, Nyiha, Kisi, or Kinga (M. Wilson 1958: *passim*). Age-villages developed furthest in those areas where the incoming chiefs were strongly established; and in the 1930s Nyakyusa colonists were introducing them into

Mbeya district where they settled among Safwa and Nyiha.

Interaction between early inhabitants and the descendants of the heroes probably continued over 500 years, and the growth of divergent dialects was fostered by isolation within the Nyakyusa–Ngonde area itself. The absence of any centralized political structure north of the Songwe, and the rivers, marshes, and sharp differences in altitude, with corresponding differences in disease patterns, made trade hazardous. A man from the hot, marshy plain (1200 ft.–1500 ft. in altitude), who travelled in the cold regions over 6000 ft. was likely to fall ill of malaria, and one from the mountains who visited the plain also fell ill. When the German missionaries first settled in 1891 the hills were reported to be free of malaria, and hill villages only became infected as movement within the Nyakyusa-speaking area increased. Certain illnesses, believed to be hereditary, were thought characteristic of particular groups, and rituals were celebrated and medicines drunk to prevent their occurrence.

The differing effects of accessibility and isolation and differing influences from outside, continued during the colonial period. When once isolated communities began to interact the diversity between them created change. This was apparent in speech as each dialect was modified by interaction with others; it was evident in ritual; it was evident in marriage relationships. It is possible to trace and date certain changes beginning in Ngonde, spreading to the Rungwe area, and still later to Selya. Already in 1938 the influence of Swahili on KiNyakyusa was evident, modifying among other words, the terms for in-laws: it had much less influence on KyaNgonde, but from Karonga there crept into KiNyakyusa certain terms, perhaps of Tumbuka origin, which were recognized as 'coming from Nyasaland'.

Diversities become conflict the moment that one party insists that their way of speech or behaviour is correct and the other wrong. Conflict compels change (G. and M. Wilson 1945: 84, 126–36, 152–7).

Differences linked to wealth
Widespread differences in the forms of marriage existed in the nineteenth century in the Nyakyusa–Ngonde area that were linked to wealth, rather than locality. Cock marriage had been common as the poor man's form throughout the area before 1891, but by 1934 it only survived among neighbours of the Nyakyusa–Ngonde, not among themselves. Slavery had existed before 1895 in Ngonde alone, and therefore slave marriage was localized, but it was a form enjoyed only by the rich, and clients of the Kyungu. One of the gifts that had been dispensed by the Kyungu were slaves, and a slave girl might be given to a commoner who lacked a wife. If she bore daughters who married, the cattle for the first two went to the Kyungu, whom they called 'grandfather'; only if a third daughter married might the cattle go to her father. Or a slave girl might be married by the Kyungu himself. If a woman slave were married to a man slave the cattle from any daughters she bore came to her master, who replaced her father as the owner of her reproductive capacities. Genealogies collected in Ngonde revealed occasional slave marriages, but it is unlikely that they were ever numerous.

As noted earlier (p. 38) widows in wealthy families might be divided between several heirs, and this gave them some opportunity of choice not exercised by the single widow of a poor man. How far a widow had the right of choice in traditional law was a matter of dispute among pagans. In 1935 Ntulanongwa, a pagan, said: 'When a man has died they do not necessarily choose the senior son to be the sole heir; they say the widows shall be divided. If a man has five sons they call all the widows and sons and tell each widow to choose whom she likes. If the senior son is not chosen the chief pacifies him saying: "It's all right, because the younger brothers are your children, it's better than the women running off with others." The inheritance is allocated by the chief and his senior men. People fear lest, if they give all the widows to one man, he will be harsh and the women will stray. This custom still exists.

CASE 44: CHOICE BY SIX WIDOWS
Mbetwa died and left five sons. There were six widows. The chief called the village headman and other senior men and said: 'Let each widow choose whom she loves.' When they had chosen an old woman was left, so they told her to go with the senior son.

CASE 45: AN UNPOPULAR HEIR
My father-in-law, Mbile, left six widows, three young and three old whom he had inherited. Mbile had no grown son, but there was a son A, of his elder brother, and a son B, of his younger brother. Mbile and his brothers were sons of one mother and one father. B the son of the younger brother had already inherited two widows [from his own father] but they were old, and when Mbile died B said: 'I will inherit', but A, the son of the elder brother, said: 'I will inherit because I am the senior.' Then they fought, and the elders said: 'Since you fight over Mbile's inheritance you must divide the wives.' The women loved B, the junior brother, and ran off with him. He left the old wives of Mbile and those inherited from his own father. Then A, the son of the senior brother, took out a summons from Mwangoka's court. He asked: 'Why does my child run off with the inheritance?' Messengers from Mwangoka's court went to seize B, the son of the younger brother; he had fled with the women. Mwangoka's court messengers caught two of the women and gave them to A, the son of the senior, but one was left to B, the junior son who had run off with all three. The court gave her to B saying: 'You were all his children.' And to A, the son of the senior brother, it said: 'You must build for them all, your mothers, and the widows of your father's younger brother.' But the young widows refused to be inherited by A to whom the court gave them, and they left and married others, and he gained cattle. This was about five years ago [1930]. Now A, the son of the eldest brother, has all the old women, and from the young ones he has gained only cattle. The young men, A and B, have 'divorced' one another, they have broken the kinship and each is a stranger to the other.

CASE 46: THE WIDOW WHO INHERITED
A widow—a pagan—from a pagan family, though she had no son, inherited her husband's cattle. No men at all remained in the lineage of her husband, nor any mother's brother's son. [No other comparable case was traced.]

These examples show that variations in the application of traditional law existed, other than differences locally rooted and recognized as linked to dialect.

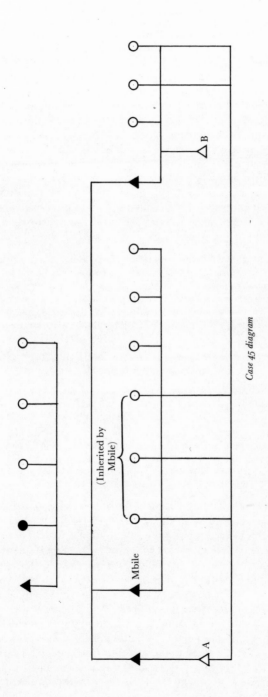

Case 45 diagram

Differences in pagan and christian marriage

New ideals of marriage arrived with christian missionaries, notably the idea
that a marriage was primarily an agreement between two individuals rather
than two lineages, and that the bond should be love rather than cattle. As
already noted (p. 21) the first Moravian missionaries opposed giving cattle at
marriage at all, and Fibombe, one of the first converts at Rungwe, refused
cattle offered for his sister who married in Mwakalili in 1898. A generation
later in Ngonde, an ordained minister refused cattle for his daughter in the
same way, but Nyakyusa and Ngonde christians generally did not accept such
a change in marriage law, nor did missionaries, other than the first generation
of Moravians, press it: in Rungwe christians gave marriage cattle from 1904
onward. Christian women expressed astonishment that any society could exist
in which marriage cattle were not given: they said that 'in BuNyakyusa a son-
in-law would not respect his parents-in-law if he did not give cattle; he would
just take one woman and then another.' And a young christian man explained
the obligation to give some recompense to a father thus:

We comfort the father because he has nourished his daughter. The father asks 'What
do I profit from having a child?' He has fed her and paid a doctor when she was ill. So
the young man comforts him saying: 'I shall go to the coast and return shillings in
recompense for your trouble.' The girl does not work at her father's but at her
husband's, hence we give marriage cattle. It is bad because pagans say: 'I have bought
the woman, if I beat her she is mine, if I kill her she is mine,' but we [christians] do not
speak so.

Isakwisa, a middle-aged christian man living near Rungwe mission
expressed a view general among christians. He said:

With us if you do not give marriage cattle for a woman she will be proud. She has too
much freedom. She goes about anywhere. If she goes to sleep across the river she says:
'I do no wrong because you did not give marriage cattle for me.' We give marriage
cattle to bind women that they may not be proud; they are like prostitutes if the
husbands do not give cattle. If I fetch her back from sleeping with another she says: 'I
like to love everywhere.' And all laugh and say: 'What sort of wife is she? How many
cattle did you give?' But if you have given cattle men say: 'Yes, indeed, she is the wife
of so-and-so, he has given marriage cattle.'

As among the pagans, the right of the bride's father to name the number of
the marriage cattle to be given was acknowledged: 'We look to the father of
the girl; when he has spoken that's all,' but once he had named the number
required he could not later alter that number; the most he could so would be
to beg the loan of a cow which would be returned. Fixing the number occurred
not at the time of betrothal, but later at the *ukukwa* (p. 125) and a groom was
often in acute anxiety as to what the number would be. He got some
indication by discovering the number asked for the bride's sisters or half-
sisters, and could expect that more would be required for eldest and youngest
sisters than for middle sisters. The Berlin missionaries recommended limiting
the number of cattle given to three or four (the general pattern in the period
before the 1914–18 war to which later Berlin missionaries looked back as an
ideal of mission achievement) and a Berlin convert remarked: 'We Berliners

laugh at the Moravians for giving so many cows. We try to give three or four only, but if a christian marries the daughter of a pagan he wants ten cows because he says: "This christian will not marry other women."' The speaker in fact had given eight cows for his wife who was the daughter of a christian.

Some Nyakyusa converts argued that if a large number of marriage cattle were given the wife became a 'slave' (untumwa) to her husband; others disagreed, arguing, as did pagans, that a substantial number of cattle were necessary to 'bind the marriage'. A Nyakyusa pastor put the dilemma: 'We fear the slavery of women. Love ought to be the most important thing in marriage, but now it's cows. We christians say to a wife: "My dear, these cattle don't matter, no one has bought you."' And an elder expressed much the same view: 'I myself do not like many marriage cattle. Cattle bind the girl so that she becomes like a slave. If the husband beats her she thinks "I am caught by the cattle, if there were no cattle I would leave."' [Don't you think it good that marriage should be bound?] 'I don't much like cattle, I like the love of christians.'

The number of cattle given at marriage by both pagans and christians increased from the 1890s onward, and christians were reputed to have begun the demand for larger numbers. The chief Porokoto said in 1936: 'The custom of giving many cattle in marriage came from christians, because they marry only one wife. A christian says: "I want eight cattle for my daughter for I gave many cattle for her mother."' It was clear that christians in BuNyakyusa were usually in the van of any change—they were the radicals of the period 1891–1955—but it also seemed that they were claiming the privileges of an elite. For as long as tradition reached back, chiefs had asked more cattle for their daughters and given more for wives than commoners, and christians with some education, who thought well of themselves, began to ask for more than the usual number of cattle for their daughters. 'They compare their wisdom with that of pagans and think they surpass them. The pagans fear the chiefs, they fear to surpass the chiefs and headmen. If an ordinary man asks many cattle his fellows will be much astonished, then he fears. A christian asks many cattle for his daughter, thinking of her cleanliness and wisdom, and skill in cooking. He brought her up well as a child, and she has the new wisdom.' This was the statement of a leading christian, one of the best educated men of the district, and it was clear that what limited a pagan father's demands was public opinion, for if his neighbours were 'astonished' he feared lest he or his family fall ill from 'the breath of men'.

Many pagans conceded privilege to christians because of their education and knowledge of new ways. But christians were also criticized by pagans for meanness, for 'keeping cows for themselves' because they refused to marry additional wives. A pagan father might ask more cattle from a christian suitor than from a pagan one 'because he says: "A christian will not take another of my daughters."' The expectation and hope that a rich suitor might eventually marry not one daughter but two or even three was always in a father's mind. Others held that a pagan father asked more cattle only if a suitor were rich, and christians were often rich.

In BuNyakyusa before 1914, it had been customary for the missionary to refuse to celebrate a marriage until all the cattle had been handed over. It was argued that this rule diminished disputes later, and it is likely that it was supported by Berlin and Moravian missionaries with experience in South Africa where the influential Natal Code contained such a provision, but in Ngonde, where a Scottish mission operated, the church took no cognisance of marriage cattle, and Scottish missionaries who worked in BuNyakyusa after 1920 continued this policy. Bishop Gemeseus (personal communication November 1937) explained: 'Before the war a couple was never allowed to marry until all the marriage cattle had been handed over, but when we came back after the war I was told that MacKenzie [Rev. D. R. MacKenzie was in BuNyakyusa 1920–5] never troubled over cattle so I, also, stopped asking about them.' But a father was careful to notify the church elders at the time of the wedding if marriage cattle were outstanding, so that they might be witnesses if any dispute arose.

Christians did not bring cows to kill at funerals since these were believed to 'accompany' the deceased to the world of the shades, and were classed by some as an 'offering to idols', but nothing precluded a christian from bringing another cow to his father-in-law after the birth of a child. In case of the death of a wife, christians were the first to modify the traditional law that all the marriage cattle were reclaimable. Death was due to God, they argued, and some did not ask for the return of marriage cattle, though others did so. The 1935 decision of the courts that the cattle be divided, the father keeping half and returning half was a compromise felt to be equitable. A christian widow could not become the wife of an heir who was already married and remain a christian and, even though an heir were single, she had the right to refuse him, church and courts supporting her in this, but the marriage cattle had to be returned. The most that could be expected of a christian heir was that he would not press for their quick return. 'A christian heir would not wait more than a year for cattle; then he would claim them. If a widow mourned for two years that would be a very long time.' Widows were expected to remarry and so enable their fathers to return marriage cattle to the heir, but in 1938 there were three widows living at Rungwe who had not remarried and one of them was classed as 'young' as she had borne only two children. All three hoed for themselves and they were regarded as a sign of new times.

CASE 47: CHRISTIAN COMPELLED TO DIVORCE TO PAY DEBT

Mbukigwe [a christian], was forced to divorce his wife to pay the debt incurred when his pagan sister left her husband. Cattle which Mbukigwe had given to his father-in-law were seized by court messengers and his wife left him. [No comparable case involving a christian was traced.]

CASE 48: WOMAN REFUSES TO BE DIVORCED TO PAY DEBT

A married Maria, daughter of N, a christian. The younger brother of A was a thief and court messengers came to A for cattle, and from him went to his father-in-law N. They took four of the five marriage cattle A had given, and N said: 'Only one cow is left, Maria must leave her husband'.
Maria: 'Shall I be able to bring my child to you?'

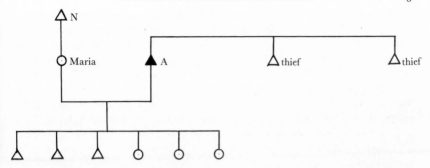

N: 'Even if A earns more cattle they will be taken.' [Two younger brothers of A were known as thieves.]

Maria: 'No, I shall not leave because I have borne three children. Will you not gain, father?'

The elders of the congregation said she should leave her husband, but the missionary disagreed, and, finally, the elders agreed with him and N accepted the decision. A traded salt and cloths and sent cattle quickly to N. Maria said to her father 'See! Have you not gained?' N: 'I agree, my child.'

A sold honey and gave another cow, and before he died in 1934 he had completed giving marriage cattle. Maria bore six children. A's younger brother wished to inherit her on A's death, but Maria refused. Her eldest son was 18 so he built for her.

Christians were in no way freed from obligations for debts incurred by pagan kin. For example, the christian son-in-law of Fibombe had a pagan younger brother who eloped with a woman and was fined. The son-in-law, forced to help his brother, begged one cow from Fibombe.

Two cases were noted in which christian women wished to leave their husbands but did not do so because it would have created great difficulties for their families to return the marriage cattle. In a third case a christian girl in Ngonde gave the missionary concerned the impression that she went most reluctantly as the replacement for a sister who had died, but asked directly she replied: 'Yes, I will be married.' Again, in this case, the return of cattle would have been exceedingly difficult. She was the only daughter and several brothers were waiting to marry.

CASE 49: CHRISTIAN FATHER REFUSES CATTLE FOR RUNAWAY DAUGHTER

A christian, a classificatory father, refused to receive cattle a second time for a brother's daughter who had run away from her christian husband with a lover, and so shamed her. The lover paid damages to the husband and the 'father' returned the marriage cattle to him.

A customary form for christian marriage had been well established in BuNyakyusa by 1934. Agreement of the bride's father was still the first condition for christians as for pagans. There was a formal betrothal much like that of the pagans but a strong preference for betrothal to a 'grown girl' (one approaching puberty) and if she were over twelve years old, it was expected that the groom should have 'made love to her' and sought her consent before approaching her father. It was also expected that he send her presents of cloths since christian girls were required to wear cloth, unlike pagan girls who wore bark-cloth belts which they made for themselves. And the groom was required to hoe for the bride's mother, or if he were in employment provide 10s a year to pay a substitute, and he was also expected to give her small presents of salt, and to give cents to her father's sisters when they asked for something. Celebration of the puberty ritual was forbidden to christians, but feasts were exchanged at the handing over of marriage cattle (*ukukwa*), and again when the marriage was registered, and blessed by the church.

The examination of a bride to prove her virginity continued among christians and the 'bull of puberty' was claimed if she were a virgin, but the bull was not necessarily killed and eaten, and there was no placing of meat in the banana grove for the shades, as there was among pagans. Instead 30s (the price of a bull in 1934–8) might be given to her father and part of it distributed to the 'mothers'. Behind this was the conviction of many that, in the christian community, fertility did not depend upon the goodwill of the father and his shades but on God. Christians said that among pagans strength came from the shades and 'the bull of puberty is very important . . . the father and mother eat the ritual piece together.' Some christians were prepared to concede that if a pagan father and brothers said of a pagan girl: 'She is not our child' she really would fall ill or fail to conceive, but it was otherwise, they thought, in christian families. 'It is God who gives power to bear and beget children,' and they quoted the case of Elizabeth in St. Luke's Gospel, and Hannah in the first book of Samuel (Luke, 5–25, 57–8; Samuel I, 1–20).

Elopements occurred, and so long as both parties were unmarried the church would try to persuade the girl's father to accept a marriage, but if the bride did not bear a child or quarrelling began, then the opposition of the parents was likely to be cited as a cause of misfortune. The following case illustrates this:

CASE 50: ANGER OF PARENTS CREATES TROUBLE
IN MARRIAGE

A, a teacher at Rungwe, wished to marry B whose father and father's brother were both christians. Her own father agreed to the marriage but his younger brother objected, saying that the groom's lineage was very bad, they were very harsh and cunning. He said that if she married that man then no cow of his would be accepted by him. The girl loved A and they were married, but she did not conceive, and their household did not flourish. She was constantly beaten with a stick. She wished to leave her husband but her fathers did not agree saying 'You yourself chose him.' [The crux lay in the comment of the narrator:] This is often seen. There are many cases. Trouble comes from the anger of parents.

CASE 51: FEAR LEST ANGER OF CONGREGATION
PREVENT CONCEPTION

[One case was recorded in which the groom brought a goat for the congregation to feast upon because his wife had not conceived and he feared lest their anger had prevented conception (Hunter 1937: 275–6). The narrator commented:] They do not fear the parents only, but the whole congregation.

The commonest occasion for elopement in the 1934–8 period was when marriage was delayed because the groom lacked the cattle to complete the number asked for before the wedding took place, because many christian fathers asked that all the cattle be given before the wedding.

Negotiations for betrothal and marriage followed much the same pattern in christian and pagan families. One detailed account (M. Wilson 1957a: 250–5) shows what prestige attached to generosity with food and what quantities were provided during negotiations for a wedding in 1934, even when the groom was a commoner. At the marriage of Chief Robert Mwakyusa II (172) in 1934, eleven bulls were killed for the feast at his home. At both feasts—that at the bride's home and that at the groom's—people delighted in some new dance, or style of dress, or other form of display. White duck suits for the groom and his men, and a long white dress and veil for the bride, were coming into fashion in 1934. The bride was carried under an umbrella 'to honour her' and became known throughout neighbouring villages.

Christian ministers or pastors who were registered as Marriage Officers in Tanganyika celebrated marriages between christians under the Marriage Ordinance of 1928. Seventy-one such christian marriages were registered in Tukuyu Boma during 1936. The Ordinance provided for the marriage of Africans who were professing christians, not other Africans, therefore the District Commissioner (who was also a Marriage Officer) was rarely called upon to celebrate a civil marriage for Africans. Whether the marriage took place in a church or at the Boma, both parties were required to be over 21 years or provide a written affidavit from father, mother, or guardian agreeing to the marriage, and neither might already be married to another under 'Native Law and Custom'.

Divorce was possible under an Ordinance of 1929, but in a case concerning Africans a decree *nisi* had to be declared absolute by the High Court, and few applications were in fact granted. In Tukuyu, between 1929 and 1937, there were four petitions for divorce of which one was granted. The grounds considered were adultery of the wife, adultery of the husband with desertion for two years, adultery with cruelty, bigamy with adultery, and unnatural crimes, but evidence had to be collected by the petitioner. If there was 'collusion' of husband and wife, or adultery had been condoned, no divorce was possible. If impotence were proved a marriage might be annulled. It was not illegal for a chief's court to allow the return of marriage cattle, though a divorce had not been granted by the High Court, but a man could not legally marry under Native Law and Custom so long as his christian marriage was still in existence.

The implications of this law were such that missionaries in Rungwe District were reluctant to marry any couple unless they were satisfied that the marriage was likely to be permanent. It was missionaries who had originally pressed their converts to be married in church, and inclusion of Africans in the Marriage Ordinance was the fruit of mission pressure on the Government, but in Rungwe District, with unstable marriage, church leaders were keenly aware of the difficulties that could arise if a husband went off to work at the coast and did not return, or if he took a second wife according to Nyakyusa custom, but illegally under the Ordinance. By 1937 it was therefore the rule in the Moravian Church that, only in cases where both parties were full members of the church, could the marriage be celebrated by the missionary who was a Marriage Officer. If one or other party were a catechumen or a pagan, then the marriage might be approved by the church, blessed by the elders, and 'written', i.e. entered in Church records, but not entered in the Marriage Officer's official register of which a copy was lodged in the Boma.

In Ngonde, christian marriages were celebrated in church and registered under the 'Native Marriage (Christian Rites) Registration Ordinance' of 1923 of Nyasaland. Applications for divorce by christians were considered by the kirk session, consisting of minister and elders, before they went to court, and if divorce were allowed the innocent party was not suspended from the church. But a legal divorce might be obtained from the chief's court, even though disallowed by the church. (Rev. Mr Marx, Rungwe Mission, Rev. Mr Faulds, Karonga, personal communications 1937. For continuing differences between Tanzania and Malawi in the marriage law affecting christians, see Hastings 1973: 93–6.)

The effectiveness of choice, the age of marriage, and the rejection of polygyny distinguished christian from pagan marriage, and also marked the difference between conservatives and radicals in Nyakyusa society during the period 1934–8. Among christians, 'making love' to a girl before approaching her father might imply no more than one conversation with her in the presence of others but it might also mean a long established friendship and correspondence. In 1937 Peter the Kyungu explained that in Ngonde, also, it had been customary to betroth girls as children, but both missions and government opposed this, and 'even pagan girls themselves began to say when they reached puberty: "I have not seen my husband, I was a child, I leave him . . ." So now we marry girls who have reached puberty and fathers ask them if they agree.' This did not necessarily mean that a girl's choice was free. The Kyungu himself had rejected three suitors favoured by one of his daughters, and she was anxiously discussing with her mother whether he could be persuaded to accept a fourth. An elder sister had not been allowed to marry a man with whom she had run off and by whom she had borne children, because he lacked cattle. But a determined girl who was a commoner's daughter might get her way, as the following story (told by a young man) shows.

CASE 52: MARRIAGE DESPITE PARENTAL OPPOSITION

When a girl has agreed with a man and they love one another and wish to marry, they sometimes succeed even though the girl's parents do not wish it. If the parents refuse the girl stays at home unmarried, thinking that they may later agree. If other men whom the parents like come as suitors, the girl turns her head aside. If they ask her why she refuses these fine men she replies: 'I love so and so, he will marry me.' Then her parents are defeated and she marries her lover. William, when he married a girl was in this situation. They made love, they agreed to marry, and they loved one another very much. However, the parents of the girl refused William, they wished another man to marry their daughter. But when he came to make love to her she refused him. Her parents said: 'Child why do you refuse that fine man whom we have chosen for you? It is said that there are witches in the lineages of William whom you love. Also he is bad.' The girl listened with closed ears and refused and said: 'William will marry me.' William heard that her parents refused and he could not go to betroth her, but he promised faithfully to marry her.

The girl had a grown up brother who also wished to marry. After five or six months he persuaded his parents that they should agree to her marriage with William, so that he himself could marry [with her cattle]. Then the parents told William to take his wife and when she was married her brother also married.

Two other cases were recorded in which parents had opposed the match, in one instance the bride's parents, in the other the groom's, but were finally persuaded to agree. In the younger generation of christians marriage for love was becoming the ideal: 'God gives love: no one can take it away.'

In 1937 girls approaching puberty were available in Ngonde but they were not in Nyakyusa, and there betrothal at eight or nine was common. The most acute difficulties arose when a well-to-do pagan father, generously concerned for his eldest son and anxious perhaps to cement a friendship with a neighbour, betrothed a girl for the son while he was still a school boy. Two published cases illustrate this (M. Wilson 1959:198–200).

The account given by another christian of his marriage negotiations showed what guile a young man might use to induce his father to accept his choice.

CASE 53: A FATHER PERSUADED

My father objected to my wife. He said 'I do not like the lineage because they are lazy at work.' I said 'Look father, we are poor. Her father is asking only two cows; others ask six.' But he refused and I made love to another girl, the daughter of a chief, and told my father. [Father:] 'But we have no cattle for a *chief's* daughter.' I replied: 'You did not like the commoner, and now you refuse the daughter of a chief.' 'All right. We will teach her to work.' Two years passed before father agreed.

By 1934 most christian parents thought it best for a son, at least, not to be betrothed young because he might later wish to choose for himself, but two cases were cited of old fashioned men in Selya, both christians, who had recently betrothed girls for sons who were 'just beginning to hoe', probably aged about fourteen. A christian elder from the same congregation gave two reasons for their action:

If I love my child saying he is my relative (*ukuti aje nkamu gwangu*) then I betroth a wife for him [*Aje nkamu gwangu* is the equivalent of *umwanangu naloli* (really my child) which is the opposite of the phrase *akaja unwanangu* (not my child) used when a father refuses to help a son with marriage cattle or refuses to receive cattle for a daughter.] And sometimes if the parents are close friends then they agree that they should be co-parents-in-law, for we choose a good person for our child's father-in-law so that if I die it may be as if I, the father, were there: his father-in-law cares for him on account of friendship for me.

Each local congregation took an active concern in marriages of members. A christian man might marry a pagan girl in the expectation that she herself would eventually become a christian, and in all the cases we knew of she entered the catechumen's class immediately; it was taken for granted that a ff156 FOR MEN AND ELDERS

wife would follow her husband's lead in this way. But it was not considered right that a christian girl should marry a pagan man. One case was cited in which a daughter of a christian elder had eloped with a pagan who was already married. Her father refused to agree to the marriage and she returned to him, the man paying a cow and a bull as damages. In another case the daughter of a pastor ran off with a pagan widower. Her father refused to agree to a marriage because he was 'a pagan, a man who would marry many wives'; he waived his right to damages on the ground that he did not wish to gain from his daughter's elopement and she was returned to him. Both cases came to court. A legal marriage was not possible without the father's consent, and in each case it was the father's refusal that blocked a marriage, rather than any action by the church, but both fathers had the support of their congregations. In a third case, the polygynist who wished to marry the daughter of a christian was a leading chief; the girl herself wished to marry him and, though her father refused to receive cattle for her, the marriage took place. A pagan kinsman accepted cattle for her.

Although christians agreed that a girl had the right of choice, most felt that she should be guided by her parents in exercising it, and remember her responsibilities to her family. In some circumstances it might be her duty to replace a dead sister. If the deceased were a young woman some, at least, of the marriage cattle would have to be returned if she were not replaced. Another responsibility that weighed heavily was the care of a dead sister's children. A christian friend, a young woman in her late teens, recently married, told us in 1937:

If my elder married sister dies and I am unmarried I do think of the children. Should they be orphans? And my father may say: 'Go and look after those children.' Sometimes a father compels a girl if she is young. If she has grown up she does not want to go, but if she loved her elder sister very much the children will bring her to that man. She thinks to herself: 'I must look after the children.' Both pagans and christians think like this. Sometimes a step-mother [unrelated to the children] is harsh and beats the children much when the husband is not there, but some are gentle like a mother.

CASE 54: CHRISTIAN GIRL REPLACES DEAD SISTER

[Another informant, Ndabili, cited two cases in which a wife who had died had been replaced by a younger sister, both families in each case being christian. In the second case:] A dying wife said to her husband: 'If you, my husband, have truly loved me, and if my work has pleased you, then marry my sister. Do not refuse to marry another sister.' So when she had died he feared, and honoured the oath he had given to his dying wife. The younger sister was told what her elder sister had said and accepted the marriage.

The issue was more complicated for christians if the widower were a polygynist, for then there was a conflict between obligation to the children and the church rule against a christian girl marrying a polygynist. A christian man living near Rungwe in 1937 raised the following problem with us:

CASE 55: CHURCH FORBIDS A PARTICULAR REPLACEMENT

I have an elder half-brother, son of the same father. He became a christian long ago.

He had a daughter who married a christian called Ulimbuka, but Ulimbuka left christianity and married a second wife. He loved the second wife very much, more than his senior wife, but he wished to return to christianity. He thought however: 'If I return the church will say, leave your second wife and come with your senior wife', and in his heart he constantly thought: 'If my senior wife left me I would be satisfied and return to christianity.' Then his senior wife died. But my elder brother had a daughter, the younger sister of the wife who died, and he wished to send her to replace Ulimbuka's wife. Ulimbuka liked the girl very much, saying he would take her to replace his senior wife. But the church refused saying to my brother: 'If you send your daughter to Ulimbuka you will be put out of the church.' It seemed that God judged Ulimbuka for leaving the church. He is very sad, he thinks: 'Perhaps I should leave my second wife and marry that girl.' But the church refuses saying: 'You have lived long with her, you cannot leave her.' Ulimbuka thinks: 'The girl is my senior wife' [i.e. she is identified with the sister who died].

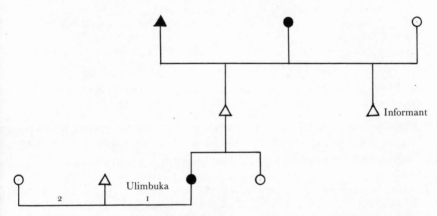

No, the girl does not want to go to Ulimbuka. She says: 'He always hated my elder sister.' What do you think of the case, Kagile [M.W.]? According to pagan custom she certainly ought to go, for if the dead sister had borne no child, and the younger sister did, her child would be senior to the children of the second wife. Formerly kinship (*ubukamu*) was very important, more important than marriage, but we now look to our wives more than to our other kinsmen. Now some christians even give a cow to buy clothes for a wife; christianity has created this, it did not exist formerly.

One other case reflects the attitude of a christian that a girl should accept the advice of her father and senior brother in the matter of marriage.

CASE 56: A GIRL SIDES WITH HER HUSBAND AGAINST HER FATHER

Angombwike's half-sister, a girl approaching puberty, was betrothed to Mwakanyamale, second senior son of the chief Mwaihojo, who had given her father three cows for the betrothal. The girl was a pagan but she had not been allowed to sleep with her 'husband' for two reasons: firstly, a 'coming out' was planned and she was to be one of the senior wives of Mwakanyamale, and secondly, her father followed the lead of his christian son, Angombwike, and refused to send his daughters to their husbands before they reached puberty. The girl disappeared. Her father called for her and then went to Mwakanyamale's house, who admitted taking her and sent her father two cows. Her father went home without her. Next day Mwakanyamale's friends came, spears in hand, and took back two cows. Nsusa, the senior village headman, pointed out that five cattle had been given and traditional custom followed, but Angombwike was very angry. A wife not yet grown up had been 'borrowed'. Mwakanyamale had acted outrageously in taking back two cows. Mwakanyamale returned two cows to the 'go-between' with apologies. The father, Mwaisyelage, refused them, and Angombwike laid a charge in court.Angombwike said: 'We wanted to make them ashamed. They insulted us. Does he not know I am a christian? I argued as a christian, but even if I had been a pagan I would have argued because he took the girl by force.' Mwakanyamale admitted in court to having had intercourse with the girl. Later Angombwike said: 'We want to take the girl home, we don't wish her to marry there.'

[Have you asked the girl?]

Angombwike: '*We* have the power to speak. Even if she loves Mwakanyamale and agrees to marry him *we* don't wish it. We will teach her childishness.'

The girl denied in court that Mwakanyamale had had full intercourse with her. She said: 'I loved him very much but I always slept on a separate bed.' When she was examined and found not to be a virgin she said she had been deflowered by a man to whom she had been betrothed previously. When it was pointed out that her senior classificatory mother had examined her and said she was a virgin until recently she said: 'Mother concealed it.' Angombwike was furious with her and said: 'She just supports Mwakanyamale, saying: "Indeed he is my husband, I love him, he is my husband. This man is my husband but father wants his cows."'

Everyone in her family said: 'A child of people!' [i.e. not our daughter!] And her father added: 'It's in the lineage, a runaway . . .' [Her mother is divorced from him. Her throwing over of the family was felt to be shocking.]

Christians were agreed that a widow could not be compelled to accept her husband's heir even if he were a bachelor; what was discussed was the return of marriage cattle. In the 1934–8 period the law applied in the courts was acknowledged, but earlier it had been argued that a christian should not claim for return of cattle. 'It is God who has killed the woman not her father, do not claim marriage cattle from your father-in-law.' Generally christians were ashamed to press for as quick a return of cattle as pagans might; they would demand the cattle if she married again but hesitated so long as she chose to remain 'in the hands of the mission'. A number of cases were recorded in which a widow had in fact agreed to go to a junior kinsman of her deceased husband, who was a bachelor.

CASE 57: A WILL STIPULATES FREEDOM OF WIDOW

[One case insuring freedom of choice for a widow was quoted with approval by a christian Nyakyusa, a shop-keeper:] A Safwa at Utengule mission (50 miles beyond Rungwe district) had made a will before he died in 1933. In it he stipulated that his wife should not be inherited. If she wished to marry again well and good but, he said: 'I worked myself for the cattle, you [my kinsmen] did not give them to me. She shall not be inherited.' [He had married in 1914.]

Polygyny was the chief stumbling block to a man becoming and remaining a member of a mission church. A man who already had several wives and divorced all but one in order to be baptised suffered loss of property, of prestige in the pagan community, and of labour. He was also thought to be sexually deprived for to live with one woman only was spoken of as being 'almost like a bachelor'. The wives suffered still more, being sent home to their fathers. Some remarried. Occasionally a wife nearing the menopause was built for by her husband, to live apart, but she, too, felt neglected. We watched two wealthy friends both anxious to be baptised, make different choices. One was baptised, built apart for his senior wife, kept a young wife, and sent the others to their fathers. Another concluded that he could not send away the women and dissipate the family property so he remained a pagan, a much loved husband and father. Various missionaries expressed great disquiet over the position of women divorced to allow for a man's baptism (Moravian and Scottish missionaries, personal communication, cf. Hastings 1973: 76–9). Many men baptised young lived for a number of years with one wife, but later broke the church rule either by accepting the inheritance of a widow, or by marrying some young woman who attracted them.

Women in BuNyakyusa had fewer difficulties for there all the wives of a polygynist might be baptised, though a christian could not marry a polygynist, but in Ngonde only the first wife of a polygynist could be baptised. In both areas the church status of a wife remained unchanged if her husband took a second wife. In Ngonde, where polygyny was already diminishing in 1937, a disproportion in marriageable men and women was beginning to be apparent. Not only was there a wide difference in the marriage age of men and women but many men were away as migrant labourers, and there was probably a difference in the survival rate. This disproportion only became apparent in BuNyakyusa about fifteen years later. In Ngonde in 1937 some Henga women were marrying in their twenties—one unmarried teacher was 28, and a junior wife of the Kyungu was married at 22—and two Ngonde girls were noted who were three years past puberty and had not yet gone to their husbands. One of them was not even betrothed. Nyakyusa men were shocked at this and spoke of the danger of premarital pregnancy and prostitution. In 1937 five cases were recorded in Ngonde of pre-marital pregnancy. The girls were strongly disapproved of both by seniors and contemporaries; they and their mothers were deeply ashamed, husbands even threatening to divorce their wives, mothers of the girls concerned, on this account. In Rungwe at that time husbands were plentiful. The rule of the Moravian church was that a christian girl should not go to her husband until a year after she reached puberty so that she 'might gain strength and wisdom'. Such girls, along with those approaching puberty, attended an elementary course in home economics run by the mission, but they were all restless in school, preoccupied with forthcoming marriages.

It was said that women who became prostitutes were mostly ex-christians who had left their husbands and refused to be married by polygynists 'because if a christian woman leaves her husband or her husband sends her away she is unable to marry a christian again, and she does not wish to be married to a pagan. She has become accustomed to eating good food, and become accustomed to European times. She cannot go back.' Indeed, of the ten prostitutes we knew on the Lupa gold-fields in 1937, six were ex-christians. Within BuNyakyusa a small number of pagan women lived at the court of one chief or another 'looking for their cows', i.e. they had left their husbands but not yet remarried. Most of them eventually found a man with cattle who was prepared to marry them.

In traditional law an heir was responsible for a widow whether she were young or old, but it seemed, in the 1934–8 period, that at the allocation of a large estate men tried to avoid the responsibility for elderly widows. As harems grew large and then women began to wear cloth which a chief was expected to provide, the obligations of an heir grew more onerous, and were resented (M. Wilson 1959: 209). A son more and more frequently built for his own mother, a little way apart in his homestead, instead of leaving her to go to the heir.

As trade goods increased, a wealthy man found many alternatives to polygyny in conspicuous consumption, building a brick house roofed with iron, furnishing it, providing clothes for wife and children, buying a plough or, later, even a jeep. Already in 1937 one Nyakyusa living on the Lupa gold-fields remarked that 'a man in town does not want more than one wife; he cannot afford it. It is better to have only one wife and go to prostitutes if he must,' but, up to 1938, land was still so plentiful in BuNyakyusa that the economic difficulties which have all but killed polygyny in South Africa (M. Wilson and Thompson 1969–71: II, 94) were not yet pressing in the country.

Men argued about forms of marriage and the proper age at which to marry but none ever mentioned celibacy as an ideal. One mission station staffed by White Fathers and Sisters, and another staffed by Benedictines existed in the district, but the ideal of celibacy which they represented was still totally foreign to Nyakyusa thought. Nigulela, a Moravian elder (a woman) remarked that if a man were unmarried he 'had nothing but leaves for the walls of his house' (for mudding was women's work), and if a woman were unmarried she had no house when her father died 'because we women cannot build,' and 'if she lived with her "mothers" she would be sworn at.' Marriage was therefore necessary. Mwaikambo knew *one* man who had not married but this was on account of poverty and thriftlessness, not from choice. A preacher was mentioned who had not married until he was about forty, but then he too had got a wife.

The relationship between husband and wife among christians differed from that among pagans in that the ideal was marriage for love, the intention was a monogamous marriage, and husband and wife prayed together to one God. Family prayers in the home, with both husband and wife praying aloud, was the accepted pattern in the christian community and contrasted with the pagan custom where a man prayed alone in the banana grove to his shades, and his wives shut the door because they should not even hear the name of their father-in-law mentioned. They had no part in prayer to a husband's shades. Among christians, also, the pattern of manners among Europeans was more familiar than it was among pagans, and in a few families it began to be copied. One man and his wife ate together regularly; others were said to do so sometimes, but many objected on the ground that 'it would make a woman proud and think herself the equal of a man.' Once we saw a man place a chair for his wife and sit on a mat himself, since it was she we had come to visit. Two men arranged for firewood to be bought, and in Karonga the firewood problem was often met by a woman arranging a work party and calling friends to help her bring in a large quantity at one time. This implied rewarding them with a feast which meant, in turn, drawing on food supplies with her husband's approval. There was an expectation of a more equal relationship than pagan wives aspired to: as one christian friend put it to us: 'I say *taa* [the humble assent] to my husband when others are present, not when we are alone together.' The criticism made by some christian men of christian girls was that they were not sufficiently submissive. 'Many people find that christian girls are foolish, they will not do the work which their husbands give them. A pagan girl is docile and does what she is told. . . .' 'The girl has been taught the gospel and thinks she knows everything. . . .' 'If you tell her things she will say to you: "Ha, you are not a pastor. . . ."' A missionary, himself a Nazi in 1938, felt so strongly about the iniquity of women asserting independence that he maintained the church should not baptise a woman unless her father (if she were unmarried) or her husband (if she were married) agreed. 'It is wrong', he said, 'that we baptise a woman or a girl without the consent of her husband or father. People think that the missionary does not require women to obey.'

The division of labour, and of property, between husband and wife was changing. As has been shown (p. 131), in 1938 women in Ngonde had begun to hoe and a very few Nyakyusa women were doing so, though it was still regarded as men's work. Christian women were not expected to carry heavy loads (other than firewood and water) as often as pagan women because the mission medical staff taught that it was bad for a woman's health to do so. Men, who were the first to learn western skills and the first to wear cloth, usually did their own washing and ironing, but christian wives wore cloth and were also learning to launder. A christian wife expected to be clothed by her husband and in case of divorce her clothes were treated as her personal property, not recoverable by her husband, though a pagan husband would claim cloths or bark-cloth belonging to a wife who left him.

The following case which occurred in September 1935 reflected the sort of quarrel between husband and wife over work that came before the leaders of a christian congregation. The woman's first husband had died earlier in the year and she had been inherited by his younger brother. The report came from a young man, a member of the same congregation.

CASE 58: MUST A WIFE CARRY THE TABLE?

The elders and deacons were sitting behind the elders' house among the bananas, arbitrating: a woman had come to the church and complained that her husband had beaten her. Her husband regularly borrowed a table to iron his clothes on: usually he sent some boys to take it back but one day when there were no boys about he told his wife to take it back. She refused saying: 'It is your clothes you have been ironing, take it back yourself. It is not the custom for us, children of Europeans, to carry.' Her husband replied: 'Very well, but I shall beat you when I return.' He carried back the table and on his return started to scold her: 'Why did you refuse to carry that table? And why do you show such pride towards me?' She refused to apologise and he beat her and beat her hard.

Late at night she ran to his elder brother to complain: 'Your younger brother has beaten me,' and she asked that he should summon his brother there and then and try the case. He refused because of the late hour. 'Why should I, a man, get up by night for you? Go home to your husband now and come early tomorrow.' But she went to her own people and from there brought a complaint before the church. The elders and deacons did not consider that the husband had done any wrong and remonstrated with her for her refusal to carry the table. They said women should help their husbands in this way. The husband complained also that when he prepared water to wash his feet she used to come and take it. She had drawn the water from the stream and he took it from the water-pot in the house.

The elders and deacons apportioned most of the blame to the woman. She was entirely wrong to refuse to carry the table considering that her husband normally made arrangements for it to be carried. To the husband they said: 'You know it is wrong to hit your wife. On this occasion we do not blame you but never do it again. What you should have done this time, and what you must always do in the future, is to bring your wife to us, the elders, or to some one of us whom you respect, and get him to judge the case and pray over the woman till she learns sense. You know that it is wrong to hit your wife with the hand or with a stick.'

[The comment from the young man who reported the case on the conventions of drawing water was as follows:] If a man wants to wash just a little his wife must carry water for him. My wife does so every day for me. But we, sensible men, do not make a wife draw water when she has a young child, because it makes too much work for her. At other times she draws. And we christians do not send our wives for water on Sunday. They are expected to draw a great deal of water on Saturday.

The expectations of christian women certainly were modified by what they saw of European ways. The following conversation took place in 1937 with a pagan chief's senior wife who herself was a christian. On coming to visit she found M.W. darning socks and enquired whether she were paid for darning her husband's socks.

[G.W. No! Are you paid for weeding your husband's fields even though he eats some of the food?]
No, but your wives are not slaves (*abatumwa*) as we are. I thought she might be paid. We are beaten.
[G.W. protested but she went on:] Yes, we are just slaves, we draw water, and fetch firewood, and cook. When my husband comes in from hoeing he just sits down but we have to work. He shouts at me 'Where is my food?' and sends me for water. And men eat the good food, but he may or may not give me meat or milk. If there are several wives he may give some meat to my friend and none to me. And he may say: 'Your friend knows her work but you don't know yours.'

Some men are greedy, some are harsh. Some are indeed harsh and are always beating you. Some wives run away when their husbands beat them but then they may be married to another who also beats them.
[G.W. Can't you tell if a man is harsh before you are married?]
How can we? Even if we know that a wife has run away from him we are told: 'But she did not know her work,' and we think: 'Perhaps we know our work,' and we are married to him. And then we find that it is all the man's fault, he beats his wife. When a man comes to woo us, if he is handsome we agree, and then we find he beats us. And sometimes, after a woman has had two or three harsh husbands she thinks: 'Well, I had better be married to an old man, perhaps he will be gentle' [said in a despairing voice]. Some run first to one husband then to another, some have as many as ten husbands.

But some stay, they think: 'Where shall I get another husband if I leave this one?' It is because of the cattle. If you [Europeans] don't give marriage cattle you can just run away. We think of the cattle, it is that which binds us.
[M.W. Don't women think of their children?]
No, a runaway just thinks: 'I will go, I will leave the child. I shall bear another.'

This woman never in fact left her husband, but she had told M.W. that the five wives who had run away from him had 'left on account of his stick'. There was no evidence that her queries were prompted by outside criticism of Nyakyusa marriage though she watched other manners closely.

Still in the 1934–8 period and in 1955, among christians a man was expected to enjoy the company of his fellow men rather than that of his wife. 'Yes, we christians also laugh at a man if he spends much time in the company of his wife. If by day he does not come to enjoy the company of us, his fellows, but stays in the house with his wife, we laugh at him. Or if he walks with her we laugh at him, we say he's a fool, because he has left us, his fellows. What should he hear from his wife? What will he remember? Such a man will not be a man of wisdom.'

A second difference among christians was that divorce carried a stigma as it did not among pagans and it was much less frequent. Of 275 marriages registered in the Rungwe book of the Moravian Church between 1928 and 1937 only 5 resulted in divorces granted by the Church (missionary in charge, personal communication, Rungwe 1937), though it is possible that some other couples separated without the consent of the church. Of the 275 marriages, 180 were celebrated by the pastor and were between full members of the church, 95 were blessed by elders. Every effort was made by the elders of a congregation and by the pastor, to reconcile quarrelling spouses but they might not succeed as the following cases show.

CASE 59: A CHRISTIAN DIVORCES HIS WIFE
BECAUSE SHE IS LAZY AND PROUD
A sent away his wife saying: 'She does not cook and she is very lazy.' He drove her away and she returned to her father. The elders discussed the case and told A: 'You cannot undo the marriage.' He said: 'If my wife were only lazy at work I would say "All right, what's work?" and would take her again, but she is *both* lazy and proud, I have left her, let her be married again. I want my cows.' The church objected very strongly to his leaving the woman at her father's and the husband said: 'If she is not married again let the cattle be, they are lost. I am determined to marry another woman.'

Another case was quoted of a christian who wished to divorce his wife caught in adultery, but who was persuaded by the elders and pastor to forgive her and receive her back. A third case described how a man slandered his neighbour's wife when she had rejected his advances, and the husband at first believed him, but later accepted his wife's account.

In six other cases a reconciliation was not effected though husband and wife were taken to the arbitrators of the congregation. The partners were divorced and remarried.

Christians like pagans, sometimes beat a harsh son-in-law.

CASE 60 CHRISTIAN FATHER AND BROTHERS BEAT A HARSH HUSBAND

H, in Selya, who had been trained as a carpenter at Kondowe, married a daughter of J. He used to beat her when he was drunk for nothing at all. Once when very drunk he beat her shockingly so that her clothes came off. She ran home, borrowing a cloth on the way. Her father sent to enquire. Neighbours said: 'He comes from beer and beats her without cause.' H came to her father to fetch her, very blustering and rude. J and his sons beat him thoroughly so that his eye was closed up. He went home and later sent a friend to fetch his wife. J said: 'You must pay us because you are always beating our child.' H refused, and then he went to the church and complained: 'They refuse to give me my wife and also they beat me.' The church called J who said: 'He has beaten my daughter. Let him bring a cow, let him pay, he shall not beat our child.' [H.] 'Let me think first about paying.' Then his friends said to him: 'Will you pay? You have also been beaten!' They swore at him. H said to J: 'Then your daughter will leave me.'

[J.] 'Yes we are glad.' [H.] 'I want my cows, I want another wife'. [J.] 'We have only one daughter, God has chosen to give us sons, shall we kill her?' Some of the marriage cattle had gone to engage a wife for a brother who was working in Dar-es-Salaam, but they got them back saying: 'We will return them all in anger, quickly.'

The Church agreed because they feared that blood would be spilt. They said 'We reject the husband, he will beat the girl exceedingly badly.' The girl stayed four years at home. Her husband came to make love to her in secret but she refused him. Other men thought: 'The fathers are harsh, they will refuse.' Finally she ran off with a man, and her fathers agreed to cattle being brought one by one.

CASE 61: WOMAN IN LABOUR ADMITS ADULTERY

N was married to a christian who was working as a tailor. She was constantly beaten by her husband, and then ran home to her father who repeatedly sent her back to her husband. One day when she had been beaten and run home and her 'fathers' were angry, her husband followed her immediately. Her father and brother swore at him saying: 'Perhaps you think us fools, since we constantly send our child back when you have beaten her?' And they proceeded to beat him calling him a slave, and a good-for-nothing, and telling him that if he wanted to drive away his wife he should take his cattle. He admitted that he was in the wrong. They said: 'If we hear of trouble again we will take back our child. See! We shall kill one another!' The girl returned to her husband but later they separated. The original cause of trouble was that when she was in labour she had admitted to the midwives that she had committed adultery with so-and-so and the midwives had told her husband. Later her husband caught her with a man and beat her.

Another notorious case was that of K who lived on mission land, until suspended from the church.

CASE 62: YOUNGER BROTHER SEDUCES WIFE OF ELDER BROTHER

K's father was a village headman in a neighbouring chiefdom. K lay with a wife of his elder brother and got her with child, and when his brother died it was said that K had killed him. K refused to inherit from his brother and his father said: 'I know that it is you who have killed your elder brother. Why do you refuse the inheritance? I am astonished at your christianity. If you were of another house your case would be heard, but as you are of one mother you ought to inherit.' Then K's father died, and again he refused to inherit, saying he was a christian, but one of his father's wives who had not yet borne a child conceived. The other widows beat her saying: 'You have soiled us, people will say it is we who have killed our husband.' When they beat her she admitted that K was the father of her child.

When K refused the inheritance one of his elder brother's widows lived for a time in a house near him. She was offered a young boy as husband and agreed, but his friends mocked him and said: 'How can you inherit a middle-aged woman?' And he was so ashamed that he ran away to the Lupa and from there went with a European employer to Dar-es-Salaam. The widow had two children by K illegitimately and brought them up and is now living with a son who built for her. A younger brother of K came back from Dar-es-Salaam and inherited his father's wives. He could not come immediately but said: 'Wait a little, my European [employer] is going to Europe, wait.'

Acute difficulties occurred when men, married according to church law, went off to work and disappeared, not communicating with home for perhaps five years or more.

CASE 63: A DESERTED WIFE REMARRIES
A girl L, of Kabembe was married to a man of Manow, T. When they had been married two years she had a child which died. Then he went to work in Dar-es-Salaam and left is wife L behind. She remained five years. Then she went to the pastor to say: 'I am tired of being at home. I am in much trouble over clothes and with being single for such a long time.' After some delay the pastor agreed to her remarriage. The second husband gave six cows and the bull of puberty [not usually returned] to restore to T. After a long time we were startled by T's arrival; he came saying: 'I've come for my wife.' He went to the pastor who told him to go to the government. T feared to do so and he received his cows.

Sometimes, also, a man betrothed a girl and went off to work, but found on his return that she did not really want to marry him.

CASE 64: BRIDE REFUSES MIGRANT WORKER
TO WHOM SHE WAS BETROTHED
When M had betrothed the daughter of A he went to Dar-es-Salaam to work. While he was there young men made love to the girl saying to her: 'Leave your husband because at the coast he has become a Swahili [implying that he had been circumcised which is not customary among the Nyakyusa]. So, on account of what they said, their sister agreed. Then M came for the wedding with his wife. When he entered the house she refused to sleep with him saying he was a Swahili. . . . She fled and hid in the grave yard; sometimes she ran and threw herself in the water where they found her shivering; or she smeared herself with mud, as if she were mad. The marriage was celebrated by the pastor and registered by the government, but both agreed to a divorce [annulment?] and M's cattle were returned. The girl is still a christian and is now married [1937].

CASE 65: WIFE RUNS AWAY FROM HUSBAND
WHO HAS NOT SENT HER CLOTHS
Another girl, Afwilile, was betrothed to a young man called Luke. He went off to work leaving his wife who was still a child, for four years. His wife reached puberty when he was away: he returned for the wedding when he heard that she had grown up. However, from the time she grew up, his wife began to make love with others. When the wedding day came they were married, but to those who knew her well the girl said: 'My parents are compelling me. The young man left me for a long time and did not

send me cloths.' Later she ran off. Luke's cattle have all been returned. The girl has not been married again, and is not in the church.

These cases indicate that common grounds of friction between husband and wife were over the changing division of work, over the sharing of food and other property, and over adultery. One contradiction stands out in the accounts of both pagan and christian marriage. Again and again it was said that it was cattle that bound a marriage: 'with us love is small'; but in fact in eight cases a man and a woman went off together because they were attracted to one another, disregarding the loss in cattle to the new husband or the woman's father, or both, in four of the eight they ran off more than once and in three other cases a wife refused to leave (or ran back to her husband) when her marriage cattle had been seized for a debt. In theory property overshadowed personal affection; in practice there were many cases in which property was subordinated to personal choice. Divorce cases of course highlight this and are not to be taken as a true sample of marriages, for where considerations of property were dominant there was neither seduction nor elopement.

In analysing the changes which took place in the colonial period it is not possible to separate the effects of religious, economic, and political influences. Education and christianity went hand in hand; the best educated were likely to get posts in government service, and those trained in handicrafts (such as carpentry) often became migrant workers and stayed away longer than unskilled men, for if they had found skilled jobs they were loath to relinquish them (cf. M. Wilson 1951a: 193). The German missions first established coffee before 1914. Planting and marketing was developed after 1925 by a dedicated British agricultural officer, and later a coffee co-operative was established, again by an inspired ex-patriate paid by the British administration, but during the 1934-8 period educated Nyakyusa men who had grown up on or near mission stations were conspicuous in developing coffee gardens, as they were after 1955 in developing peasant tea gardens.

By 1938 three categories of people were distinguished: conservative pagans who observed the traditional ritual cycle, and who valued cattle and polygyny as the proper form of wealth; christians who celebrated new rituals at birth, marriage, and death, who worshipped together week by week, who had accepted monogamy, and who sought new forms of wealth; and sceptics who neglected at least some of the traditional rituals and did not observe new ones, who still valued polygyny, but welcomed economic change. Lines of division were not clear cut, and each category merged into the next.

NOTES

[1] Godfrey Wilson did not include Ndali among Nyakyusa in his 'Introduction to Nyakyusa Society', 1936. Relying on evidence collected in 1955 from Rev. Amon Mtawa, himself an Ndali, I have included Ndali among the Nyakyusa, though recognizing that they did not have the distinctive age-villages. They are much closer in language and custom to Nyakyusa than they are to Lambya and Safwa, as a visit (in 1955) to Lambya country where many Ndali had settled showed.

Chapter 8

BEGINNERS AND THE RESISTANCE

R ADICAL change continued among the Nyakyusa–Ngonde people over five centuries, much of it initiated by outsiders: it speeded up greatly during the past century. This chapter takes note of the outsiders but is primarily concerned with identifying the insiders who accepted change—*the beginners*—and the conservatives who opposed it. The evidence is thin but some has been assembled: more will doubtless emerge from the study of government and mission records, and oral tradition, not yet tapped.

Outsider innovators

In Nyakyusa tradition, as related during the 1934–8 period, the great innovators who had brought fire, cattle, iron, and the institution of chieftainship itself were the chiefs. They had also brought a power of growth in their own bodies. Their coming, and their benefactions were celebrated, by chiefs and commoners alike, each generation, at the 'coming out'. Then there was talk of doctors who had brought new crops and new medicines, one of whom had been installed as priest at the cave of the hero, Kyala (M. Wilson 1959:47). Such tales of chiefs or priests who had come as strangers and benefactors were not confined to the Nyakyusa–Ngonde people, but were widely believed in the Corridor area (M. Wilson 1958: 21–2, 33–4, 38). Among the Nyakyusa–Ngonde, as elsewhere, the most powerful medicines were traded from afar, and certain outstanding families of doctors were known to be of foreign descent; for example the family of Mwaisyelage in Selya were Sangu, and that of Mwanjesi in Rungwe were 'from Nyasaland'.

Before whites arrived, Arab and Swahili traders had come and gone in Ngonde and at Utengule, the capital of the Sangu chief, Merere, fifty miles north of the Nyakyusa boundary, but they were not spoken of as benefactors: to the Nyakyusa they were raiders like the Ngoni, and in Ngonde, even before the war with Mlozi in which many Ngonde people were killed, the attitude towards traders from the coast had been ambivalent. Towards whites attitudes were also ambivalent: the harshness of the German administration was spoken of; the horrors of the 1914–18 war when whites were fighting one another and Nyakyusa were impressed as carriers by both sides; the suffering of Nyakyusa converts on former German mission stations under the British military administration. An underlying fear of loss of land to settlers was also evident, though little had in fact been alienated within the Nyakyusa–Ngonde area. Nyakyusa commoners spoke bitterly of the increasing power of chiefs bolstered by white authority.

At the same time, whites were fitted into the category of chiefs who had brought benefactions, and such views were not expressed merely out of politeness. Fibombe, living near Rungwe mission, who himself had been captured as a slave by Merere's raiders, and his family, spoke repeatedly of the relief of escape from slavery; in Ngonde it was generally recognized that whites had been allies against Mlozi and saved Ngonde from devastation. Chief Mwaipopo (116) and Kasitile (86) in Selya spoke of 'peace and cloth' as the fruits of white administration. An increase in the number of cattle in the country was generally acknowledged in the 1934–8 period, and this was judged to be good; christian teaching, schools, and literacy were welcomed by many. It was taken for granted that whites had powerful medicines and not only mission and government hospitals and clinics were patronized, but any white, however ignorant of medicine, was expected to provide treatment for fever, wounds, boils, and other ills.

Outsider innovators of whom people spoke included the heroes, founders of royal lineages; the Arabs; Swahili; and whites (among whom missionaries, soldiers, administrators, traders, and planters could be distinguished) and the other Africans with whom Nyakyusa–Ngonde came into close contact through missions, government, and employment. The first missions and traders in Ngonde, and the German missionaries north of the Songwe, were accompanied by Africans from further south, and on Kabembe station of the Berlin mission rescued slaves were settled. Migrant workers on the Lupa gold-fields, the coast, the Copperbelt, and the gold mines of South Africa met many different peoples. In the later colonial period clerks, teachers, and administrators from other areas served in Tukuyu and North Nyasa districts—the first African District Officer appointed in Tukuyu came from the coast—and by 1954 representatives of TANU from outside were recruiting members in Tukuyu district. The independent churches that started in Ngonde were influenced from South Africa (M. Wilson 1959: 171–3, 190–7).

The outsider innovators were conceived of as operating both through gifts and force, precept and example. The heroes had brought fire to people who ate their food raw; iron to those who used wooden hoes; cattle to cultivators; the institution of chieftainship to those who lived unorganized, in scattered villages. There was no word of conquest except at Mbande where the first Kyungu had beaten his drum and caused the previous occupant, Simbobwe, a Fipa, to flee. The whites brought cloth, literacy, medicines, the gospel. The English as opposed to the Germans were praised for teaching their own language: the Germans had pressed Swahili whereas, before independence, Nyakyusa and Ngonde were much more interested in learning English than another African language which they considered no more useful than their own. One Scottish mission doctor, John Brown, was celebrated as the man who had first taught Nyakyusa boys to read music. This was a skill from Europe which was greatly sought after. Knitting socks was another much prized skill, learnt by one Nyakyusa woman from Mrs. MacKenzie. These examples underline what has long been recognized that, in the interaction between peoples, what is offered by those of different cultural traditions is highly selective. Borrowing is partly determined by what is offered (Fortes 1936: 53).

The line between example willingly followed and economic pressure of some sort is ill defined. From the first, missionaries were employers of labour, a source of much sought after cloth and, though by 1934 their economic function was relatively small, there were situations in which it was significant. For example, a Swiss missionary of the Pentecostal church living near Rungwe was a large employer of labour in coffee production. A number of young men had left the Moravian church to join the Pentecostalists, and some observers connected conformity to Pentecostal doctrine with the desire for employment. Jobs were scarce. When this missionary assured us that he knew a number of Nyakyusa men who 'ate with their wives' we, living in villages, remained sceptical that this was a regular practice, even in his congregation, though approval in principle might have been expressed by men he employed.

Force was never used by whites against the people of Ngonde; they together with certain Nyakyusa chiefdoms of the plain, were allies in the war against Mlozi (Fotheringham 1891: *passim*; Lugard 1893: I, 108–67); but in Tanganyika force was repeatedly used by German military rulers to subdue Nyakyusa chiefs who resisted their authority (Wright 1971: 51–61). Throughout the colonial period, on both sides of the Songwe, pressure was exercised through courts, and a certain system of law was ultimately enforced through police backed by military. Reference was repeatedly made to the fact that 'Europeans do not allow spearing'; '*mwafi* (the poison ordeal) is no longer allowed'; 'the courts say that a girl should not go to her husband before puberty.' The pressure of the British administrative authorities towards stopping 'child marriage' and 'forced marriage' was, in fact, effective.

Precept and example were perhaps as important as gifts and force in compelling change. The missionaries believed the gospel they preached and succeeded in communicating it. Some of them were men and women of outstanding personality and devotion. One of the achievements of the first generation was a good translation of the Bible into the Selya dialect of KiNyakyusa, and a translation of the *Pilgrim's Progress* into KyaNgonde. Nyakyusa of the 1930s contrasted the second generation of missionaries with those of the first generation who, they said, went about the villages and enjoyed the company of men (*ukwangala*). They felt that the second generation remained aloof in the mission stations, teaching and preaching from a distance. To a people who set so much store by 'good company' the general aloofness of whites was a cardinal sin. Other criticisms concerned the inconsistency of whites and their quarrelling among themselves. Germans and British had fought twice, involving Nyakyusa and Ngonde in the wars, and policies had changed even within the period of British administration. There were indeed profound differences in attitude and policy even within one national administration or mission. The gap between Bishop Gemeseus of the Moravian church and others of the same mission who were convinced Nazis and reflected Nazi doctrine in their own family relationships, was enormous (Wright 1971: 184–99, 215–9). The discrepancy between christian doctrine and the pursuit of wealth among whites was noted and lampooned in the song 'To Whom Do They Pray', in which the crucial lines were:

'The Europeans, the Europeans to whom do they pray?
To money, to money! (M. Wilson 1957a: epigraph)

In the 1934–8 period, and still in 1955, the Nyakyusa–Ngonde thought well
of themselves. They insisted on their skill as cattle-owners, their diligence and
skill in cultivation, their prowess as warriors in the defeat of the Ngoni, the
fame of their lineages of chiefs, their democratic institutions as contrasted with
the subservience of the Bemba and other peoples; the 'good company'
enjoyed in their villages; the order and cleanliness of their homesteads and
persons, as compared with neighbouring Kinga, Safwa, Nyiha. All their
neighbours, said the Nyakyusa, were learning their language. They often
spoke disparagingly of Swahili, particularly of Swahili women, as dirty and
immoral; they were equally disparaging about the manner of life of some
Europeans on the Lupa gold-fields, and about certain South Africans who
had trekked north to Kenya. The Henga presented a challenge to Ngonde
because Kondowe was in Tumbuka country, and the Henga section of
the Tumbuka had accepted education early, some also travelling far as
labour migrants. Ngonde women had copied from Henga women in
beginning to hoe. The Kyungu's most sophisticated wife was a Henga, and so
was Nyasuru (her mother's brother) who was leader of the African National
Church (M. Wilson 1959:190–7). But the Henga had taken refuge in the
Kyungu's kingdom, and had been regarded as disloyal subjects (Fotheringham 1891:47, 112–5), so relationships were ambivalent. Attitudes toward
Sangu who had been slavers were also inconsistent, but they were regarded
with some respect. The Ngoni were spoken of as equals who, without
question, could be joking partners of Nyakyusa at labour centres (M. Wilson
1957b). English was the acceptable second language both because of its
practical use when men travelled for work, and because it obviated invidious
comparisons with other African languages. Despite criticisms, whites were
recognized as knowledgeable and skilled, people from whom men could learn
and profit. Their material possessions outshone all others. We treasured the
remark of a small boy, heir to a chiefdom and the epitomy of elegance in a
patterned cloth, who said to us two exceedingly shabby anthropologists: 'I
think you are the best-dressed people I have ever seen.'

The example of outsiders was repeatedly spoken of as something that
influenced family relationships: 'You do not know what being a woman is
like, you eat with your husband.' 'We saw Europeans eat with their children
and also Swahili, and it seemed as if we hated our children.' 'Henga women
brought the custom that women should hoe.' 'A Safwa man made a will. That
was a good thing to do.' By and large Nyakyusa and Ngonde people accepted
change as something good; in this they contrasted sharply with the
conservative section of Xhosa-speakers among whom I had worked
previously (Hunter 1936). But in certain situations the occurrence of change
was scarcely admitted, even by Nyakyusa and Ngonde. In marriage
contracts, when cash was substituted for labour service or for cattle, the
substitution was often not mentioned in later discussion: what was important
was 'hoeing' for in-laws and handing over a specified number of 'cattle'.

The beginners within

Who were these insiders who were innovators? The sons of the heroes were insiders because their fathers married commoner women. In contrast to Rwanda, the incoming chiefs did not form a separate caste: they married girls of the country, giving cows to commoner fathers-in-law and, so the tradition goes, they did this from the time they arrived. Moreover commoners, as village headmen, were integrated into the new system of administration with a certain power over chiefs. Even if daughters of other chiefs were preferred as senior wives (p. 64), every chief married many commoner women and his kinship connections and distribution of cattle ramified. Chiefs, then, were beginners, in the sense the term is used in this book, and the myth that they had created all things new was celebrated at each coronation.

The first christian converts were beginners, and many of them came from among the dispossessed. The first Nyakyusa to be baptised was a woman on Rungwe station. Among those who followed were ex-slaves such as Fibombe at Rungwe, and refugees at Kabembe. In Ngonde it was otherwise: Robert Laws, the Scottish missionary at Kondowe, persuaded the Kyungu and subordinate chiefs to send some of their sons to school and from among them came the first Ngonde converts. At least until 1955, schools were an important recruiting ground for christians, many boys who attended school seeking baptism. Young men were those who first accepted employment with whites and this experience also engendered new ideas. Women were more often converted through kinsfolk: a mother followed her son in seeking baptism, or a girl the man she was to marry. It was taken for granted in the 1934–55 period that if a christian man became betrothed to a pagan girl she would enter the catechumen's class and become a christian, but difficulties arose if the wife of a pagan sought baptism. Even if she were the sole wife her husband might oppose it on the ground that she might then make difficulties over brewing ritual beer, and in Ngonde, in the Presbyterian Church, she could not be baptised and remain the wife of a polygynist unless she were the first wife married. In the Moravian and Berlin communions junior wives could be baptised. The impediments to a man becoming and remaining a christian were felt to be greater than for a woman. A man might be heir to family property and agree to inheriting a widow, although he was already married; he might marry a second wife and indeed be under pressure from his family to do so if it were wealthy; he was more tempted than a woman to become a heavy drinker. Whether for these or other reasons, women outnumbered men by 3:1 in Ngonde congregations of the Presbyterian Church, and by 3:2 in the Moravian congregations of the Rungwe valley in 1937 (M. Wilson 1959: 168).

Boys who went to school commonly sought and obtained paid employment: they became teachers, evangelists, and medical aids; clerks and storemen; craftsmen, house-servants, and policemen. Kondowe school supplied clerks for five territories: Nyasaland, Tanganyika, Northern Rhodesia, Southern Rhodesia, and the Belgian Congo, because the education in Nyasaland was in advance of that elsewhere. Asked how he had learnt

enough French to become a postmaster in a Congo post office a man of
Ngonde explained that he had first taken a job in the Congo as a house-
servant and, after two years, when he spoke some French, he had applied for
and obtained the post office job, for 'None of the people there are educated'.
The 'old boy' links that attendance at a famous school had created were
particularly important at the time of discussions preceding the Federation of
Northern and Southern Rhodesia and Nyasaland. Africans knew at first hand
the differences in the position of educated men in the various territories, and
spoke of it publicly to the Bledislow Commission, as well as talking of it
privately to us in Livingstone. They opposed Federation knowing that in
Southern Rhodesia skilled jobs were monopolized by whites.

The wives of a few teachers, clerks, policemen, and soldiers travelled with
their husbands, and those who did returned with new ideas. A daughter of the
chief Mwaihojo (147), married to a man from Selya who was in the police at
Zanzibar, had lived there with him for many years. Coming home to visit, she
wore a cotton frock and sandals, unusually sophisticated dress for Selya, in
1935; she remarked that in Zanzibar women did not work in the fields, and
bought their firewood and water. They earned the cash to do so by weaving
mats for sale. She and her husband were 'in the class': this meant literally
under instruction as christians, but it also implied adherence to a church as
distinct from full membership. Mwaihojo's daughter is cited to show how
some Nyakyusa women did travel and return home to visit, even in 1935; at
that time the majority of wives, even of educated men, remained at home with
their children leaving the men to travel to work; but by 1955 far more women
were accompanying their husbands.

The example of insiders was more powerful even than that of outsiders.
Again and again it was remarked that, in some regard, the pagan community
was changing 'because they see the custom of the christians'. The girls'
initiation ritual and the twin ritual had been widely dropped in Ngonde in
1937, and this was the reason given; these rituals were still celebrated by most
pagans in BuKukwe at that date, but some living near Rungwe mission had
dropped them and the same reason, the example of christians, was given, with
the added argument: 'Formerly, men said if they did not celebrate the rituals
the child would go mad, but now they say it does not matter.' Though in 1937
the chief, Porokoto, was not yet a christian, and his second lady was not one
either, her twin daughters were not initiated, nor was the pagan daughter of
his full-brother. The twins had not been baptised but were 'in the class'.

The women who changed their way of life and ideas fast were of three
categories in the 1934–8 period. One category consisted of the handful in
Ngonde who continued in school for perhaps eight years (to Standard VI)
and became teachers, and some married women in the Moravian
congregations who were literate, though not highly educated, and who were
appointed as elders, responsible for the women of the congregation. In 1935
Maria (M. Wilson 1959: Pl. 13) was already an elder of Rungwe mission
congregation and the most independent-minded Nyakyusa woman I knew;
by 1955 she was travelling to church meetings outside the Rungwe valley and
her interests and sympathies were extending.

The second category of women who changed fast were the unhappily married and widowed or deserted wives who ran away and became, at least for some time, paid prostitutes on the Lupa gold-fields. In 1937 most of the ten such women we knew had travelled—some as far as Dar-es-Salaam—at a period at which few Nyakyusa women left the Rungwe valley. One reason for going to the Lupa was that diggers, both black and white, had money, and a prostitute could earn 3s to 25s a night from a white and perhaps 10s a month from a fellow African. Another reason, repeatedly mentioned, was that a woman who had left her husband and whose father then refused to receive marriage cattle for her from anyone else 'dies of shame'. On the Lupa there was no shame.

The third category of women 'beginners' were widows who refused to be inherited, and those whose husbands were away for long periods, who began to hoe for themselves. This was a very important innovation for it implied that a woman could maintain herself by her own efforts, and therefore live alone, independent of a man. No such category of women existed in most of the Rungwe valley in 1934-8 but three christian widows living near Rungwe mission, who did not wish to be inherited, had begun to hoe for themselves. They had 'learned from Ngonde' where the practice of women hoeing was general. Ngonde women 'had seen Henga women hoeing'. By 1955, women throughout the Rungwe valley, pagan as well as christian, were beginning to hoe. This revolutionary change in the division of labour between men and women illustrates how necessity compels change. Women only began to hoe when they were in need, and in many aspects of society it can be shown that radical conflict compelled change.

Nyakyusa legal procedures were largely concerned with resolving conflict (G. Wilson 1937: 16–36) and in the changing society law was modified to obviate conflict. Arbitrators, court assessors, chiefs, and later a professional bench thus played a part as 'beginners'. Case 66 illustrates this.

CASE 66: CHANGE IN THE LAW OF INHERITANCE

[G.W. made the following report of a discussion at which he was present:] In Mwaipopo's country the inheritance in Mwaisalwa's lineage was discussed over a pot of beer, the ritual beer brewed for the inheritance in another lineage. No member of Mwaisalwa's lineage was present but Kakuju, the headman of the village in which Mwaisalwa II, who had just died, had lived, was there. Three men had died in succession: Mwamenembanga, Mwaisalwa I and Mwaisalwa II. Mwaisalwa I had inherited from his senior half-brother Mwamenembanga some time previously, when Mwamenembanga's son was still young: Mwaisalwa I inherited both cattle and a widow, but four of the widows refused Mwaisalwa I and went to other half-brothers. Mwaisalwa II inherited from Mwaisalwa I. Now Mwaisalwa II had died, but Mwaijumba, son of Mwamenembanga, had grown up. The question at issue was: should Mwaisalwa III take all the inheritance or only that part of it attaching to his mother's house, leaving the property that had come from Mwamenembanga to Mwamenembanga's son, Mwaijumba.

The traditional law was clear. Nsyani, who was already married when Europeans first settled in Selya in 1891, formulated it thus: 'Formerly, if there were two sons of one man, each with his own mother, then if one died, even though his children were grown

174

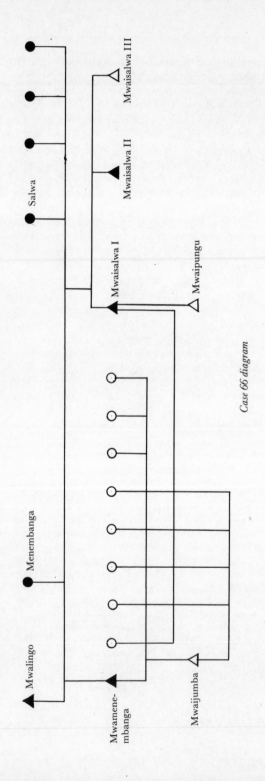

Case 66 diagram

up they said: "Father is there: he ought to inherit the mothers." This continued until all the brothers had died. But now the sons grudge handing over property; if the sons of a man are grown up they inherit, even though their "father in the lineage" is alive. He now says: "Let my children [sons of the dead man] inherit." The wisdom of old, and that of today differ. Formerly their fathers divded the property and they all kept on good terms, but now they quarrel, even the sons of one mother quarrel now. Each one consumes his own property; he milks the cows which come from his daughters alone, and his brother keeps his property separate.'

Opinion was divided as to what should be done. It was argued that Mwaisalwa III, being the son of Mwalingo, should take all the property, and Mwaijumba should wait until he died. On the other hand, and this argument found general favour, it was insisted that if Mwaisalwa III were to take all disputes would follow 'for Mwaijumba is grown up, and if Mwaisalwa III takes all now, when he dies Mwaijumba will claim all saying: "Now the property returns to me. You Ba-Mwaisalwa inherited from my father so I, as the senior of the family, inherit from you." Then Mwaipungu, son of Mwaisalwa I, will be very angry and claim his share.'

Kakuju, with general but not universal support, finally said: 'Well I, the village headman, told them: "Let Mwaisalwa III take the inheritance of his elder brother, Mwaisalwa II, his own property, and let Mwaijumba take that of Mwamenembanga now, then when Mwaisalwa III dies, Mwaipungu will inherit from him and there will be no dispute. If Mwaisalwa III takes the whole estate now there will be war."'

A latecomer, when the case was explained to him, said: 'Yes, now in European times I agree Kakuju is quite right, they should divide the property or else there will be war. But the old custom would have been for Mwaisalwa to take it all now. Mwaipungu would not have inherited at all in the old days, but now in European times, Kakuju is right.'

[There was a precedent for a judgement such as Kakuju's if, in a wealthy family, the rightful heir voluntarily relinquished the inheritance (p. 39), but in this case judgement was given that Mwaisalwa III should *not* inherit everything.]

The law was modified because of conflict in the family. It may be asked why such conflict had not been obvious earlier. One reason was that argument over inheritance increased as cattle increased. Secondly, once men could earn cattle for themselves they were less willing that property inherited from them should go to anyone other than their own son: what they had earned was felt to be personal rather than family property.

It seems that during the colonial period women grew increasingly dissatisfied with the traditional form of marriage for four reasons: harems became larger and more numerous; old men retained control of wealth longer and young wives of old men grew restless; women saw an alternative way of life; the sanction against divorce was no longer spearing. It is suggested that not only was the form of marriage harsher in 1935 than in 1875, since harems had grown and old men clung to power, but the form of marriage tolerated in 1875 was no longer felt tolerable by many women because they had conceived the idea that change was possible. The notion that things-as-they-are need not be endured, that another way of life, glimpsed in the manner of life of strangers, might be achieved is the root of revolution. Missionaries in particular, but whites generally and often unwittingly, created a 'divine discontent'.

Causation is not single but complex. Cloth spread first because it carried

great prestige: the Kyungu distributed headcloths to his *amakambara* and later
to others he favoured; the first whites paid wages in cloth because that was
what was sought (Thomson 1881: I, 274; Ballantyne and Shepherd 1968:
250); missions pressed converts, both men and women, to cover themselves;
European, Asian, and African traders displayed their goods and attracted
buyers; returning soldiers insisted on their women-folk wearing cloth. The
status of men, pagan as well as christian, was quickly reflected in wearing a
loin cloth, shorts, a khansu, a toga, a suit—there were many variations in
style, but cloth was essential. In the 1934–8 period, pagan women north of the
Songwe took pride in showing their bodies: 'It is only Swahili women with
dirty diseases who must cover themselves' was a common comment. And a
woman who possessed a cloth might slip it off to dance, and wear it folded over
her shoulder, or wave it as a flag. Cloths were then displayed rather than used
as a covering: only after about 1945 was the absence of covering felt in any
way improper in the Rungwe valley. What was improper in 1935 was any
blurring of sex differences in dress, and M.W. was hotly criticized for this.

'Eccentricities of genius'

In an attempt to analyse the process of change we follow Mr. Pickwick
(Dickens 1838) in considering some of those individuals who had the courage
and imagination to be eccentric. Certain dramatic occasions on which radical
change took place were remembered: for example, in 1909, the chief
Mwaikambo brought a cow to the funeral of the wife of Mwasulama, his
father-in-law, and the cow was refused, since christians held that to slaughter
cattle to 'accompany the dead' was incompatible with their faith.
Mwasulama's action was the culmination of long discussion and argument on
the matter, but his particular initiative was public and symbolic, and refusal
of funeral cattle became the norm among christians.

Changes which required continued adjustment in behaviour, rather than
one dramatic action were more difficult. Sekela (M. Wilson 1951a: 84–5) was
a christian girl who had worked as a nursemaid for German missionaries in
the most conservative part of the Rungwe valley. Then she married a
christian younger son of the chief Mwaipopo (116) and was pressed by the
mission not to observe the strict rules of avoidance required by a daughter-in-
law. A missionary nurse, 'Margaret', had taken her formally to the chief who
had killed a bull to free her from the rules of avoidance, and she had told me of
this with some pride. Sekela was the most sophisticated woman I knew in
Selya, spotlessly clean, well dressed, accustomed to decorate her table with
flowers, she was very much the model of the 'new woman' for that area. She
was visiting me one day along with a christian woman friend when the chief,
her father-in-law, unexpectedly came to call. Before he was visible Sekela
leapt up, gasped 'father-in-law!' and hid herself in the corner of the room
behind the door. Then she sat down on the floor murmuring: 'I won't avoid
him, I *won't* avoid him.' Her friend also slipped off her chair and sat on the
floor. Godfrey Wilson warned the chief as he came in: 'There is a daughter-in-
law here,' but he replied with perfect self-possession and courtesy: 'It's all
right,' and later he added: 'She does not avoid me because Margaret brought

her to me one day and I killed a bull for them.' Sekela, crouching on the floor
with head averted, had gone grey, and sweat was pouring down her face.
When tea came in Mwaipopo rose, murmuring politely to G.W.: 'Let us stay
outside for they would be ashamed to eat.' As soon as they had drunk their tea
the women hurried off, crouching down with their backs towards the men as
they answered their farewell greetings.

That happened in 1935. Twenty years later, in the same area, I found
young men leaving their wives in their fathers' homesteads 'in the bananas',
while they went off to work. The danger of a wife being seduced if left
unsupervised was held to be greater than the danger of living in the same
homestead as a father-in-law, and Sekela's divergence from custom was no
longer so eccentric. Already in 1935, Sekela had been aware that the Selya
custom of avoidance was more rigid than it was among the Kukwe, and
Kukwe more rigid than Ndali; moreover that the Nyakyusa were laughed at
by other Africans for the rigidity of avoidance practised. By 1965 the shortage
of land made the seclusion of daughter-in-law in separate villages impossible
in many families.

A third eccentric of genius was Maria, the elder of the church at Rungwe
mission mentioned above. She was a woman of position in the traditional
system since she was a sister of the chief Porokoto. She was devout and self-
sacrificing, leading groups of women on preaching tours among the
neighbouring Safwa whom the Nyakyusa regarded as very dirty and
uncivilized. As she explained to me, she found the dirt trying and, when they
visited overnight, always washed out the cooking pot they were to use, if she
got a chance to do so. She was deeply concerned with changing family
relationships since the women of the congregation, and their family disputes,
were her special care. One day she remarked to me: 'I lost my keys and
hunted and hunted for them and did not find them. Then I said to my
husband: "See, Martin, why don't you help me look for my keys? When you
lose something I hunt and hunt for you."' In terms of traditional family
relationships that was revolutionary.

Maria's niece, a daughter of the chief, was one of the women unhappily
married who had run away from her husband and gone to the Lupa, where,
according to local gossip, she lived as a prostitute. But she was very strict
about the upbringing of her daughter and sent her to live with Maria.
Furthermore, out of her earnings, she was returning to her father a sum
equivalent to the marriage cattle he had forfeited. She came to visit Maria
while we were living nearby in Ilolo village.

A taste for western cooking was growing among Nyakyusa–Ngonde men,
during the 1934–8 period. At least one chief employed as cook a man who had
been in domestic service with whites. Another chief married a woman who
had spent four years as a maid to a Scots missionary; she cooked for him and
was ordered to teach a wife married after her. She also did the chief's laundry
and mending, having learnt these skills which, like western cooking, were
unknown to the senior wives of the chief. A similar case occurred in Sotho
history (Mokgatle 1971: 39–41).

Segelile, a christian living near Rungwe, and his wife were also innovators.

In 1938 he kept a store at which produce was bought, some of it from Safwa in the hills, and cloth, paraffin, cooking oil, salt, sugar, rice, soap, bangles, beads, dye for mat-making, and enamel dishes were sold. Segelile also had a sewing machine for making up shorts and shirts for customers, and he had a large coffee garden. His wife was a daughter of Porokoto, the chief, by a christian wife. She spent the greater part of her day serving in the shop, and she bought firewood which was cut and carried by a woman neighbour. Her husband hired a Safwa youth to hoe in his fields, and assist in drawing water. On one of my visits home-grown coffee was served and this was becoming fashionable as a means of hospitality among the more sophisticated. It also involved much less time in preparation than brewing beer. Segelile was one of the handful of men who chose to employ help in cultivation and for fetching wood and water, rather than marry additional wives. The view of such men was, 'Yes, it is very difficult for a rich man with only one wife to entertain guests, but it is much better for a man to hire help for his wife as you Europeans do, than to marry many wives.' It was conspicuous that some men chose monogamy when, with ample land available, the most profitable investment of cattle was in additional wives which gave command of their labour and of that of their children. By 1965–8, when labour commanded by polygynists was still an asset, Jan Konter noted that 90% of the men in two villages considered it better to hire labour than to marry additional wives, and the percentage of polygynists was falling (Konter 1974b:166; on innovators cf. Richards, Sturrock and Fortt 1973: 294–305).

The growth of the christian church among the Nyakyusa and Ngonde people turned on the character of church elders, who were the village leaders in a new way of life. Often they were men with six or eight years' education in Ngonde, usually less north of the Songwe. It was they who celebrated morning and evening worship in remote villages, who began the instruction of catechumens, who taught reading and writing in innumerable 'bush schools'. These filled an essential function before the spread of government-aided primary schools in Rungwe district in the 1950s. The life of one remarkable elder, our friend Fibombe (as he was known in Ilolo village in 1934–8) has been published (Gemeseus and Busse 1950). We missed getting to know his contemporary, Sakalija Mwakasungula, who was later ordained as a pastor, since he worked at Utengule (Gemeseus 1953). There were other such men and women to be numbered among the foremost 'beginners'. Most of them remained faithful members of the church into which they were baptised: three others of our acquaintance established independent churches which have been described elsewhere (M. Wilson 1959: 171–2, 190–7, 213).

A 'beginner' of very great influence was Peter the Kyungu. He was a teacher, then became a storeman for the African Lakes Corporation, and eventually set up as a trader on on his own, and established a number of shops. His elder brother, Mwangalaba, had been chosen as Kyungu in 1904. He began to fail in 1912 and Peter became his assistant. Since a failing Kyungu was no longer killed, Mwangalaba lingered on. In 1927 Peter was appointed regent, and in 1932 he succeeded as Kyungu. Godfrey Wilson wrote in 1939:

Both before and after his succession he has used his private fortune without stint to maintain his public position; and the historical accident of his personal ability and wealth has played a very large part in shaping the course of the political and social revolution through which Ngonde is passing.

It is Peter who has completed the emergence of the Kyungus from their religious seclusion at Mbande. He has, in the first place, abandoned all claims to divinity and, with them, all interest in the traditional prayers and sacrifices to his ancestors which the nobles of Ngonde still occasionally undertake. And in the second place, he has built his capital, not at Mbande with the nobles of Ngonde, but at Bwiba, half way between Mbande and the Government Boma at Karonga—symbolic of the new age (G. Wilson 1939: 68–9).

In 1933 the Kyungu was recognized by the Nyasaland government as 'Paramount Chief' of Ngonde, and except for a short break he continued in office until his death in 1966. Peter did not remain a church member—he married many wives as his traditional position required but he was sympathetic to christians and strongly favoured education.

The resisters

Change during the century of revolution did not proceed unobstructed. Many of those who were secure in positions of dominance in Nyakyusa–Ngonde society resisted it bitterly. North of the Songwe resistance came from chiefs, village headmen, priests, wealthy polygynists, fathers of families and, in a later generation, elders of the church. South of the Songwe, where whites had been allies of the Ngonde against slavers, the Kyungu and chiefs were much more receptive to change than were their contemporaries north of the river. It is true that Nyakyusa chiefs from the plain had joined in the war against Mlozi and joined the Kukwe in driving off Merere's raiders, but Nyukyusa chiefdoms had never been in so precarious a position as those of Ngonde and they fought against the German administration.

In the first generation of christians, the elders of the church were all 'beginners', but in the second many were more conservative than the foreign missionaries. As one young German missionary naïvely remarked in 1935: 'It is more difficult for us than for the early missionaries for customs have been established in the church and people want to stick to them. When the first missionaries began they had a clean slate.' Typical of the 'conservative' elders was Nsangalufu of Kabembe, a man of perhaps 60 years old in 1935. He had been employed in building the mission station as a very young man, and had settled there. He strongly disapproved of education for girls: 'If they learn to write they will just write letters to lovers'; he insisted upon the traditional authority of a father over his sons, and the subservience of a wife.

One important innovation that failed to catch on was the abolition of *ukukwa*—the giving of marriage cattle—among christians. Fibombe's action (p. 148) was followed thirty years later in Ngonde by a minister of the church, but not by the christian community as a whole. A second innovation, the establishment of christian villages, survived north of the Songwe for a generation and then began to disappear. The German missionaries bought land from chiefs and established their converts on it. Christians were at first pressed to live in these villages, and most early converts did so, but by 1934 many preferred to move off mission land and settle elsewhere, sometimes with a group of fellow christians, but rarely in a village of christians only. This was most apparent in coffee-growing areas where the better educated were aware of the advantage of acquiring rights over a coffee plantation. Christian boys often built their own 'village section' or quarter, and adherents of the Watch Tower and the Church of Christ, were establishing quarters for fellow believers. South of the Songwe, there had at no time been christian villages: converts were pressed by Scottish missionaries to remain in their own home villages. There was a long history behind this policy, formulated in 1865 by Tiyo Soga, the first Xhosa to be ordained (M. Wilson and Thompson 1969–71: I, 266). The Lovedale and Livingstonia (Kondowe) missions were closely linked through James Stewart, William Koyi and, later, James Henderson. Exclusive christian villages or quarters were disappearing by 1955 as pressure on land increased, though still in the 1965–9 period many Nyakyusa christians preferred to build beside fellow believers.

The resistance to changes in the relationship of men and women, particularly in regard to the right of choice in marriage, is reflected in a number of the court cases quoted (pp. 44, 49, 111, 150); and changes in the division of labour between men and women were bitterly contested. The question of whether or not polygynists might be baptised was repeatedly discussed within the mission congregations (Wright 1971:99, 106, 132), and some missionaries refused to recommend to a potential convert that he divorce his additional wives.

Neither 'beginners' nor 'resisters' were wholly consistent: there was a 'compartmentalized rebelliousness' and conformity. Mwaipopo (116) had been a chief before whites came and he appeared the epitomy of conservatism; he administered traditional law; he attended and provided cattle for traditional rituals, whether kinship or communal celebrations; he hoed, he danced, he feared 'the breath of men'. He was generous, urbane, shrewd in court judgements. But when one looks closely at the evidence his manner of life was not wholly traditional. He had 41 wives and large harems were something new; his heir (son of Mwaipopo's deceased elder brother) had come out but Mwaipopo remained in power drawing a government salary; he refused to marry for sons in their late twenties because, he said, they were still 'boys' who should hoe for him, but even a conservative opinion thought he refused too long. He set new fashions in wearing a splendid white toga, and a fringed black alpaca shawl; he carefully planted an exotic tree to add to the dignity of his homestead; and he agreed to killing a bull to release Sekela from a daughter-in-law's obligation of avoidance.

Chapter 9

THE CENTURY OF REVOLUTION: A SUMMARY

Changes in wealth and power

There is no reason to doubt the tradition that stranger lineages came into the Rungwe valley and Ngonde plain bringing cattle, iron, and the institution of chieftainship itself. Iron and salt brought to the sacred groves of heroes were controlled by priests and chiefs and the first Kyungu was spoken of as beginning a tiny export of ivory, exchanged for cloth. The Nyakyusa chiefs, as they spread through the Rungwe valley, are believed to have established order, each within his own country, but without securing any rule of law between chiefdoms. To maintain order was one of the prime functions of a chief whose authority was carefully nourished with medicines and symbolized by fire. The Kyungu gradually established a kingdom through which some measure of order was secured over an area wider than one tiny chiefdom but, before colonial rule was established, fighting was endemic between chiefdoms north of the Songwe: they raided each other for cattle, and men whose wives had fled to another chiefdom with a seducer avenged themselves with the help of their kinsmen. From the mid-nineteenth century there was war against raiders who came from outside the Nyakyusa–Ngonde area seeking cattle or slaves.[1] All this was vividly remembered by old men in the 1934–8 period. In the genealogies collected a dozen cases were noted of wives or children taken by Ngoni or other raiders (*tuta*) in the grandfather's generation to that of men who were young adults in 1934. Still in 1934–8, pagan men normally carried spears and, at a funeral dance, fighting easily began if a man from one chiefdom bumped into a man from another, or splashed him with mud. It has been questioned whether, in the pre-colonial period men indeed resorted to self-help in cases of adultery and theft, and feared to travel in distant chiefdoms; those of our friends who had lived during that time had no doubt that they did and cases 8, 9, 10, 11, 29, 30, 31 and 36 support this view. In 1936 the old myth was being refurbished: Europeans brought 'peace and cloth' as chiefs had brought cattle, iron, and authority. In fact Europeans did establish a much wider area of security than had previously existed and employment for wages and trade (with cloth as the first commodity in general demand) developed fast.

Chiefs led the resistance to invaders in the nineteenth century: Ngoni, Bemba, Arab, Sangu, German, and some chiefs increased their power considerably during the period of colonial rule, but other sorts of power were emerging. The basis of wealth gradually changed from control of cattle, and in Ngonde ivory, and in a lesser degree everywhere iron and salt, to access to education and skilled employment, or control of the best land and export crops. It is possible to trace a shift, both in the basis of wealth and power, and in its balance between men and women, and between generations.

Ownership of cattle was never confined to chiefs, but lineages differed in wealth, and those disposing of cattle increased more rapidly since their sons married many wives. Marriage with cattle and marriage by service existed side by side within the memory of men still living in 1934, i.e. in the 1870s and 1880s, but the one form ousted the other. Whether marriage was with cattle or by service it was virilocal, the husband taking his wife to his age-village. Where no cattle were given the children belonged to the wife's father: only if the wife bore several daughters might the husband persuade his father-in-law to allow him to keep the cattle when their third or fourth daughter married. Marriage with cattle did not abolish service by a son-in-law but it shortened the period of service and gave a husband greater control over his wife: this was clearly recognized. Therefore it is likely that as marriage with cattle spread among the Nyakyusa the freedom of women diminished. Very few Nyakyusa women acquired cattle and inheritance was normally through men. Legally a woman was subject, throughout her life, either to her father (or his heir) or to her husband (or his heir), one or other controlling her procreative power and her labour, until the new marriage law of 1971. The woman who established greatest independence between 1934 and 1938 were runaway wives who lived on the Lupa gold-fields as prostitutes, and two of these had secured acceptance by their fathers through paying back to their fathers, from their own earnings, the marriage cattle (or part thereof) originally given for them.

By 1934 there were three main sources of wealth: inherited cattle, money earned in employment, and money gained by selling crops and stock. Men controlled all three sources. Few women were in paid employment; those that were earned less than men; and the vegetables and chickens marketed by women were of much less value than crops and cattle sold by men. By 1955 education leading to skilled employment or professional posts, and land suitable for growing rice or coffee were the most important resources and, with the exception of a small acreage of rice land, these again were controlled by men.

There was a radical change in the division of labour when women began hoeing and the ability to grow her own food gave a widow or deserted woman greater independence than when she relied on a man to hoe for her, and the practice of growing millet and brewing beer for sale (begun when men returned from the army), provided women with a means of earning a little cash which was not previously available to them. But women's access to land was limited. Since they did not hoe for themselves traditionally but were allocated hoed strips by their husbands, women had a lesser claim than they had among Xhosa, Mpondo, or Tonga, where cultivation was once primarily women's work, and a woman's claim to a field cleared for her was once unassailable. As land grew scarce among these peoples men claimed it, and women's rights diminished (Elton-Mills and Wilson 1952:18, 24, 34–5, 51–4, 73, 80–1, 124, 133–4, 147–8). It is not surprising, therefore, that as scarcity of land increased in BuNyakyusa, the only land rights of a woman recognized were those of a wife living with her husband, or of a widow who remained single or accepted a kinsman of her husband in leviratic union. Such a woman was permitted to cultivate her field until her death, then it passed to her son. Women who had obtained rice fields before land became very scarce retained them and had their own food and income, but new allocations were not made to women, and in monogamous families women's fields were not distinguished from the fields of their husbands. Only in a polygynous family were a woman's fields or strips specifically defined so, as elsewhere, monogamy tended to *diminish* a woman's rights (Krige 1964: 172–5).

Nyakyusa and Ngonde women were slow to take to education and employment. In 1967, 86·7% of females in rural Tanzania were illiterate as against 69% of males. In the 50–54 age group 97·30% of the women were illiterate and 75·16% of the men (Mbilinyi 1972). In Ngonde in 1966, 48% of the males of 5 years and over had never been to school and 64% of the females (*Malawi Population Census* 1966). Though the figures are not strictly comparable, this suggests a continuing lead in education among Ngonde over Nyakyusa, but the proportion of women to men who had been to school on both sides of the Songwe was in marked contrast to the proportions in South Africa (M. Wilson and Thompson 1969–71: I, 262; M. Wilson 1974: 7). In the competition for school places and school fees girls came off badly in Nyakyusa, and only a little better in Ngonde (Mbilinyi 1972: 67). Nyakyusa–Ngonde women did not participate in the new types of political power during the colonial period: only within the church itself was there clear evidence of independent choice and leadership among women. The basis of power shifted but the new types of wealth—education, skilled employment, and cash crops—were controlled primarily by men. A woman's economic opportunity was confined to the few professional jobs open to those who achieved education, prostitution, and beer-brewing. Women played no part in the traditional political hierarchy but potentially they were not excluded from the new: possibility of leadership in TANU was open to them as was some measure of leadership in the church.

Before the colonial period, the power of young men turned on their strength as warriors and in hoeing. Their fathers depended upon them both to defend the herds and to hoe, and a dutiful son received recompense in a marriage cow (or cattle) and at least a calf with which to start a herd. Mystical sanctions reinforced the obligations of fathers and sons to each other. Employment for wages made a young man partially independent of his father; he could earn some and, if driven to it, all of his marriage cattle himself, but he still feared lest he fall ill if he neglected his duty to his father.

Nyakyusa and Ngonde men worked as migrant labourers in large numbers from 1925 when the Lupa gold-fields began to develop, until (for Nyakyusa) 1963 when movement of men to Rhodesia and South Africa was prohibited by the Tanzanian government. The peak of employment opportunity was during the 1950s. From 1934, a young man without wives and children could earn more even as an unskilled labourer on the Lupa than he could by cultivating at home, though an older man, commanding the labour of wives and children and owning a herd of cattle, could make a comparable income by growing rice or coffee for sale, along with food crops. A man with sufficient education to become a government clerk or certificated teacher could earn more by his profession than as a peasant cultivator. In Rungwe district, by 1955, profits of £150 (3,000s) a year, made by the most successful coffee growers, compared with the salary of a clerk, and many growers made £30 (600s) to £60 (1200s), as much as an unskilled labourer, but by 1965–9 profits on ordinary holdings were down again to 150s a year. Profits from coffee were largely dependent upon the effectiveness of co-operative organisation in grading and marketing, and to a lesser extent in production. The Rungwe coffee co-operative, under an enthusiastic organizer, led the way for cash crops. But disease began to spread and, by 1965, expectations turned on production of peasant tea in the hills and cocoa on the plain.

Since 1963, older men owning land have wanted the labour of their sons, as they always have done, but with loss of cattle and a fall in the price of cash crops they have little to offer them in return. Where money is given as a substitute for cattle, the wealth coming in for a daughter is more likely to be dissipated than cattle are; it may be spent on immediate needs rather than given or invested for a son's marriage. Peoples in Africa who guarded breeding stock, saving for the future and never killing a cow unless for ritual purposes, have repeatedly proved less thrifty when they exchanged stock for money. Saving against future need depends on attitudes towards capital which must be symbolized in a familiar way (M. Wilson and Thompson 1969–71: I, 71–2; II, 57). Moreover, among pagans, competition between fathers and sons for wives, such as has long existed still continues (Konter 1971: 32–3). The shift in inheritance from fraternal to filial means that if men live only as long as in the pre-colonial period sons will tend to inherit younger than before but, with medical services, the expectation of life is likely to be rising, so the change in the average age of inheritance may not be great. Access by young men to land held in their own right, in a village of their own, turned on a redistribution of land in each generation which has not survived the planting of long term crops like coffee, and increasing scarcity of land. By 1965–9 almost all cultivated land was inherited; old men no longer moved aside to make room for the young men's villages but retained until death the greater part of the best land. What they lacked was labour. Young men despaired of getting ahead through agriculture and sought jobs, for wage-earning paid better than cultivation.

There was a direct conflict between the traditional values of the age-village and economic achievement for individuals. In the 1934–8 period men talked a great deal about the value of *ukwangala*, of enjoying the company of their fellows and sharing food and beer with them. The surly, aloof, or unneighbourly man was likely to be accused of practising witchcraft or to fear the witchcraft of others. Clerks were criticized for being 'proud', and for 'eating alone'. Great stress was laid on keeping in step in cultivation, no man starting to burn his rubbish in a millet field ahead of his neighbours, no woman planting before her neighbours or lagging behind them. Prestige turned on hospitality and generosity with food, and it has been shown how men and women boasted about the quantities of food provided at their weddings. Co-operation was maintained by a mixture of the carrot and the stick: urbanity and generosity won friends and prestige; meanness and aloofness were believed to bring ill health and death upon the wrongdoer and his immediate family, and a man who proved intolerable was driven from the village as a witch. 'Shame' (*isoni*) was also repeatedly mentioned as something feared. With a shift to a money economy, there has been a radical conflict between getting on in the new trading world, and being generous to neighbours and kinsfolk (Turner 1968: 23; Long 1968: *passim*). Many men in Africa have been caught by the incompatibility of buying tools to develop their land, or stock for a shop, or a lorry for transport, or saving for education, and fulfilling traditional obligations to distribute wealth to dependents and neighbours through hospitality, gifts, or loans. In BuNyakyusa, by 1965–9 'only those who are wage-earners in a regular job and not living in a village but are far from members of their families could dream of becoming rich' (Konter 1975b (early draft): 356). The Nyakyusa–Ngonde people have been conspicuous for the enthusiasm with which they have pursued new forms of wealth: since migrant labour began they have had a reputation for being diligent and pushing workers who stood on their rights, complained about rations and, particularly on the Copperbelt, were accused by others of being 'quarrelsome'. Gradually prestige attached to consumption in trade goods— clothes, iron roofing for a house, a bicycle or even a car, meat bought on the market—rather than to hospitality. Potential consumption far outstripped income, though in the subsistence economy most wants had been satisfied. Intense competition for the new forms of wealth made co-operation in the village, as well as between father and son, husband and wife, more and more difficult, and competition for land increased the tension. Services came to be reckoned in terms of money. Already in 1935, a boy herding cattle for a Nyakyusa man in paid employment was asking for a monthly wage instead of the traditional fee of a calf after perhaps three years' herding, and by 1965–9, men and women working in the fields preferred a cash wage to participating in the traditional work parties (Konter 1971: 35).

The decline in hospitality was one facet of a decline in the relative abundance of food. Early travellers all spoke of the enormous quantities of food available among Nyakyusa and Ngonde; they had no difficulty in obtaining supplies such as they had had elsewhere (Thomson 1881: I, 267–74; Fotheringham 1891: 21–5). This was still so in 1934–8 when, except for short periods in particular localities, there was an abundance of plantains and bananas, maize, rice, groundnuts, sweet potatoes, beans, milk, and chickens; all these were readily obtainable for cash and many families had ample supplies. Only millet and fresh fish were scarce on the markets. By 1955, the situation had changed. A great deal of time, energy, and land was being devoted to cultivating coffee and rice for the market; pastures were shrinking and deteriorating; and milk, vegetables, and even bananas were scarce. Many people complained of shortages. At the same time, more beer was being drunk, particularly by young men. It seems that in BuNyakyusa, as in so many other areas in Africa, local food supplies and probably nutrition of ordinary families has declined as more labour and land is used for cash crops, and the return expended on a variety of goods other than food, and at the same time a greater share of resources in grain, as well as in cash, is devoted to beer (Read 1938; M. Wilson and Thompson 1969–71 : II, 55–9). Konter noted that by 1965–9 participation in village life was a 'drain on income' and recognized as such by christians who tended to associate with fellow christians rather than with pagan neighbours since, by the rules of their church, Moravians were 'excluded from the centre of village life, namely the beer-club'. Up to 1955 there were no village beer-clubs: hospitality was provided in a man's own home and curds, chicken with rice, or baked plantain and a groundnut sauce were fine food (*ifisisya*) fit to set before a guest, and frequently offered rather than beer. Before wage-earning began unmarried men had no access to beer and even married men were expected to bring their millet (from which beer was brewed) to their fathers to divide. The son got only a portion. Individual women were invited by men to taste the beer they had brewed and modestly a wife would enter the hut in which men alone were gathered and kneeling, suck a moutful through a straw from the pot she had provided. So in the 1934–8 period almost all the beer was reserved for men and elders: young men who earned wages were just beginning to buy beer and still women did not drink with them. By 1955 young men regularly bought beer, and by 1965–9 young men and women were drinking together in beer-clubs. Decline in hospitality and feasting, and increasing consumption of alcohol in clubs has coincided with the shift in relationships of generations and of men and women.

The age-village was incompatible not only with the cultivation of long term crops and shortage of land, but with migrant labour. The physical separation of fathers-in-law and daughters-in-law was first breached when young married men going out to work chose to leave their wives in the care of their mothers, rather than alone or with small children in the young men's village. Husbands insisted that their wives move to live under the supervision of the wife's father or, preferably, the husband's mother 'because others will make love to them'. A temporary house was built for a migrant's wife on the edge of his father's homestead, screened perhaps by bananas but near enough to his mother for the migrant to feel that his wife was under proper supervision. She might continue to weed and reap fields or strips already allocated to her, and pick her husband's coffee, and her father-in-law or brother-in-law hoed her strips. Only a mature wife with three or four children growing up might be left in her own home. All this I saw in 1955 in conservative Selya, where the separation had been most rigid, and heard it defended in a slightly embarrassed manner on the ground that a young wife could not be left alone in a young men's village. By the time land became so scarce that a son was often forced to live close to his father, the principle had already been established, even in Selya, that in a case of necessity a daughter-in-law might live on the fringe of her father-in-law's homestead, avoiding meeting him so far as was possible. Still, conventions were observed. If the father-in-law should shake hands with his daughter-in-law or enter the same house it was suspected that he was making love to her: 'We [Nyakyusa] make love to one another much.'

'The beginners' identified included a wide range of men and women, both those of high status in the traditional society, and outsider refugees; women elders of the church and prostitutes. Among beginners the young, the poor, and women probably predominated, but the Kungu, Peter, who held highest office in traditional terms was himself a beginner, and those who were innovators in one respect might be conservative in others. To be a 'beginner' itself implied an increase in status for the eccentric, once followed, gained power.

Political development in Ngonde and Nyakyusa has been markedly different since 1961. Nevertheless, on both sides of the Songwe boundary membership of the ruling party probably now outweighs birth, wealth, and education as a factor in political power (van Hekken and van Velzen 1970: I, 22–3). In Buloma village in the Rungwe valley most people in the 1965–9 period were glad that traditional chiefs and village headmen were losing their authority (Konter 1974b: 246). Konter concluded that 'The new *ujamaa* villages are not a replica of the old traditional villages in which the elders had the supreme economic power. In the new socialist villages all inhabitants have a vote in the organization and functioning of their villages' (Konter 1974b (early draft): 357). It has been argued that, so long as the 'coming out' was celebrated, young men did acquire power and wealth, but they no longer did so as land became scarce and old men remained in office. The *ujamaa* village offered an alternative access to power for young men and theoretically, but not in practice, in 1965–9 for women (van Hekken 1970: 27). If deductions drawn from oral tradition and radiocarbon dating are correct, the institution of chieftainship spread and developed over five hundred years, while colonial rule lasted barely seventy among Nyakyusa and Ngonde, a very short period in historical perspective. The experiment in 'African socialism' is only just beginning.

Demography and marriage

Rapid population increase since 1931 is amply documented and in 1969 large families were still desired by most women and men. A preponderance of women has been noted since 1931, and this, combined with the difference in marriage age of men and women, means that there are many more wives, or would-be wives, than husbands. The marriage age of men and women is known to have changed somewhat over time, though precise records do not exist. According to our men informants who had themselves grown up before 1890, they and their contemporaries were occupied as warriors, and did not marry until nearing thirty. Girls were betrothed before puberty but commonly, it seems, not long before, and the puberty and marriage rituals were fused. Girls' houses in which girls approaching puberty slept and entertained young men existed in each village. With the increase in wealth in the district, and the opportunity of earning cattle through paid employment, coinciding with peace, the marriage age of men began to fall. This was particularly marked in christian families where a cattle-owner, not wishing to marry a second wife himself, might marry for a son still in his early twenties. Large harems, which had probably not existed in the pre-colonial period, also appeared, and by 1934 among the Nyakyusa (as opposed to Ngonde) there was a shortage of marriageable girls. So the marriage age of women fell, very few pagan girls approaching puberty were not betrothed, and many were betrothed before they were ten years old and visited their husbands from that time. Under pressure from the missions, christian girls married later and gradually the courts limited early betrothal by refusing to take cognisance of claims for any cattle other than a single betrothal cow, which might be passed before a girl reached puberty. By 1955 the marriage age of girls was rising both because many girls had become interested in opportunities of education, and because the feeling was spreading among men that to marry a girl eight or ten years old was foolish, since she might reject her husband when she reached puberty and be supported by the courts, and he would lose his cattle. Marriage before puberty had become exceptional (M. Wilson 1959: 208). During the prosperity of the 1950s it is likely that the gap in the marriage age of men and women diminished, for even unskilled men at that time could earn marriage cattle with two years' work on the Copperbelt or South African mines, and marriage of men still in their early twenties was common. But after 1963, when opportunity for employment was more restricted and the price of coffee fell, but the cost of cattle and the number asked in marriage remained high, the average marriage age of men again approached thirty (28·2 years) whereas girls married at 16·9 years, a difference in 1967 of eleven years (de Jonge and Sterkenburg 1971: 104). Minimum ages for marriage of girls and men respectively, laid down in the 1971 law, are 15 years and 18 years. One aim of the TANU recommendations on marriage (Tanzania Government 1969: para. 14) was to make it easier for young men to marry by allowing for payment of marriage cattle in instalments (something which was traditional in BuNyakyusa), and asserting that non-payment of bride price should not make the marriage void. Table 4 (pp. 80–1) indicates changes in the number of cattle given in marriage over time, their cash value, and their cost in terms of current wages. What does not appear, because evidence is lacking, is the average size in holding of cattle per family. In 1934 all but the poorest families expected to be able to help a son with marriage cattle, at least when a sister married, and in 1967 in Kapugi, a village investigated in detail, 67% of the married men had received at least part of their marriage cattle (45% of the cows) from their fathers, but Dr. Konter concluded that help on this scale was no longer available. 'Boys intending to marry are expected to pay the bride wealth themselves and can expect little or no help from their father' (Konter 1974a: 12, 24).

In 1955 older men were strongly in favour of the demand that ten cattle be the accepted standard for a commoner's daughter, and more might be asked for an educated girl; they held that so large a number would 'bind the marriage', however, the administration, aware of the difficulties of young men, was pressing that the number be limited to five. In 1965–9 a bye-law of the Rungwe District Council limited it to six cows but the average number given in 86 marriages was 6·8 (Konter 1974a:5).

Before 1935, if a wife died she was either replaced or the cattle given returned. Progeny might also be claimed though, in fact, the whole number was seldom returned. In 1935 the courts agreed that no progeny be returned, but the original cattle were still claimed if a woman died young, even though she had borne children. By 1955 the District Council had agreed that no cattle could be reclaimed when a wife died. This was important to younger sisters in that it meant much less pressure on them to replace an elder sister who had died instead of accepting a suitor of their own choice. Likewise the law requiring cattle to be returned if a widow refused the heir of her deceased husband was abrogated. 'Formerly, if a woman refused to be inherited, her husband's people said: "Where are our cattle then? We gave cattle for you." And the woman's father said to her "Go back! Where am I to get the cattle to return?"' After 1955 cattle were only returnable if the widow herself chose to remarry, and women very much approved this change which freed them from any compulsion to accept a deceased husband's heir. Thus the freedom of choice of women was enlarged by abandonment of compulsory replacement of a husband or wife who had died.

In spite of eleven years difference in the marriage age in 1967, the proportion of polygynists in Rungwe district had fallen markedly since 1934, when almost 44% of married men were polygynists. By 1957 the figure had fallen to 38% and by 1967, to 26·1% (de Jonge and Sterkenburg 1971: 103–4). What were the relative importance of religious and ideological, as opposed to economic factors, in this decline, we do not know. In 1934–8 polygyny was the most profitable investment for a wealthy Nyakyusa man, but christians chose to remain monogamous, and economic pressures were certainly not the sole determinant of choice either for men or for women, though fear of poverty as the wife of a polygynist was one factor in the preference expressed by most women for monogamy.

In South Africa decline in polygyny has been linked to shortage of land (M. Wilson and Thompson 1969–71: II, 94), and with increasing pressure of land in BuNyakyusa a further fall seems likely, though control of labour through polygyny is profitable to a farmer, particularly where employment for wages is not approved (Luning, Mwangoka and Tempelman 1969: 10). Hiring labour had begun as an alternative to polygyny by 1938. A second factor reducing polygyny is the growing attraction of alternative goods such as brick houses, furniture and motor cars: indeed it was during the period when wealth increased—particularly the wealth of chiefs in receipt of government salaries—and these new goods were not yet readily available or attractive, that large harems developed. The strongest force supporting polygyny (or its alternative, concubinage) is the gap in the marriage age of men and women which, combined with emigration of men, creates a surplus of wives. In 1967 there were 1·37 married women to one married man in Rungwe district (de Jonge and Sterkenburg 1971: 104). By then harems which had flourished between 1914 and 1938 had disappeared, and plural wives were more evenly distributed; the proportion of married men who were polygynists had nearly halved and the proportion of women married in polygynous households had fallen still faster. The average number of wives shown in genealogies collected in 1934–38 was 4 for commoners and 11·5 for chiefs (not including widows inherited), whereas by 1967 the average number of wives per polygynist was 2·35 (de Jonge and Sterkenburg 1971: 104). The growth of large harems in the early colonial period, followed by a sharp decline in polygyny, is not peculiar to the Nyakyusa. In 1881, the Bishop of St. John's (Pondoland) stated that 'polygamy has become more extended since the settlement of the white man in the country' (Cape of Good Hope Government 1883: II, 72), but, at least from 1921, there has been a steady fall in the Transkei and Ciskei (M. Wilson and Thompson 1969–71: II, 94–5).

Since 1916 there have been statements by missionaries and administrators that marriage among the Nyakyusa was very unstable. In 1934–8, elderly Nyakyusa insisted that though adultery and elopement occurred before whites came their frequency had greatly increased. The meagre statistical evidence suggests a divorce rate of under 10% of all marriages before 1934 but many divorce suits were then coming to court; by 1955 the number of divorce cases coming to the courts had risen sharply, and the general opinion was that divorce had greatly increased (M. Wilson 1959: 207). In 1967 the divorce rate in Rungwe district was 29% of all marriages except those ended by death (de Jonge and Sterkenburg 1971: 105; van Hekken and de Jonge 1970: 26), but only 1,724 cases came before the courts as opposed to 2,689 in 1954. This fall was believed to be linked to the fall in migrant labour. It might also be linked to diminishing opportunity for a divorcee to remarry, as polygyny declined. Though the statistical evidence over time is so inadequate, there is no reason to doubt the Nyakyusa view that divorce increased from early in the colonial period at least until 1963. The reasons for this are more debatable.

In 1934–8 the view of older men, repeatedly expressed, was that the increase in divorce, which they were sure had taken place, was due to the abrogation of the right of a husband to kill and spear an adulterer. It was also true, as some older men pointed out, that young men were no longer preoccupied with war as once they had been. To anthropologists, something equally significant was the presence of many bachelors and no unmarried girls with whom they could flirt and dance, though previously there had been girls' houses where young men met unmarried girls. Moreover, there were large harems in which many wives were bored and neglected, and readily accepted lovers. Nevertheless, cases occurred in which *married* men ran off with women, and one case has been quoted in which a young woman returned to an elderly polygynist, Mwakelebeja, after eloping with a lover and bearing him a child, so the discontent of bachelors and wives in harems was not the sole cause of divorce. Stability of marriage was valued and an increase in adultery fines in 1935 was accepted as a means of stabilizing marriage, but an unforeseen effect was a chain reaction in divorces. When a man was heavily fined he might divorce his wife to obtain the cattle due, and his wife's brother might in turn be compelled to divorce his wife.

In 1955 divorce was still on the increase. One reason given by conservatives was loss of parental authority. As one village headman put it: 'Formerly a father beat his daughter with a stick if she ran home, and sent her back to her husband who also beat her.' A teacher's wife, herself an educated woman, put it differently. She said: 'Wives leave their husbands because they are beaten with a stick. They are beaten because their husbands say they are proud and don't answer submissively.' A christian man who in 1934–8 had been notorious for beating his wife gave as one of the causes of increasing divorce in 1955 the fact that wife beating was now illegal and 'a man might be fined for it.' There was a radical conflict of ideas about proper behaviour between husband and wife, stemming from mission teaching and from the support given by the courts to an adolescent girl who refused a man betrothed to her when she was a child, to a widow who refused her husband's heir, and to a wife beaten by her husband. Women were rejecting the old pattern of subservience which was expressed in crouching to greet a husband and addressing him in a very deferential fashion, and questioning the assumption that to be beaten was the common lot of women, a thing to be endured. Some men copied the manners of Europeans towards their wives, but neither husband nor wife was quite sure what the change in manners implied, and both were often inconsistent. In 1955 an educated Nyakyusa man commented: 'They do not know what to expect from each other.'

De Jonge and Sterkenburg saw as the primary reason for frequent divorce the difference of eleven years in the average age of first marriage of men and women, a difference which was almost certainly smaller on the average than in 1934, when most girls married before puberty, but probably larger than it was in 1955, when the marriage age of girls had risen and that of men had dropped (since they could earn cattle for themselves) and divorce was at its peak.

Factors which are relevant over the whole period include the following. Women did not wholly accept the low position in society allocated to them, even in the period 1934–8. Property in cattle was not allocated to houses during a man's lifetime, and there was bitter competition between co-wives for a husband's favours, since the sons of a favourite wife were likely to benefit by obtaining cattle to marry, as well as the wife herself being given choice food and ornaments, and enjoying the love and favour of her husband. Some women moved from one husband to another hoping to find one who would favour them and not constantly beat them. Women moved most often before the birth of a child, or after the birth of only one child 'within the first three years' (de Jonge and Sterkenburg 1971: 95). Wives of monogamists escaped the problems of competition with co-wives but often complained of being overworked. Women had no identification with an age-village; their sons were always in other villages and daughters commonly married in other villages also. A woman's closest bonds were with a younger sister who became a co-wife; if she had no sister, she hoped at least for a 'friend' in the polygynous household. Beyond the village her ties were with her mother, her sisters, her father or brother who had received cattle for her and was responsible for looking after her interests and, as they grew up, her sons and daughters.

Young men did not accept the monopoly in wives which old men tried to establish. Fathers and sons were in competition for marriage cattle and wives in the 1934–8 period and still were in 1965–9 (Konter 1971: 32). When employment for wages was readily available during the 1950s young men could marry more easily, but as this opportunity diminished they found themselves in conflict with fathers of daughters demanding ten or, by 1965–9, six marriage cattle, which they had no hope of acquiring. Konter (1974a: 11) noted the acute frustration of sons unable to marry.

Administrators and others repeatedly asked anthropologists why divorce should be much more frequent among the Nyakyusa than among neighbouring people in Tanzania. It is perhaps worth discussing some points of contrast between the Nyakyusa and another group of patrilineal cattle-owners, the Xhosa, living mingled with Mfengu, in the Keiskammahoek District of South Africa. Wider comparisons are beyond the scope of this book (cf. Gluckman 1950; Mitchell 1963; Fallers 1957). Among the Xhosa most property was allocated to houses during a man's lifetime, only a portion was divided at his death, and this system made for less competition between wives than that in which they lived until their husband's death as rivals for property for their sons.[2] Though ideally a Nyakyusa man was expected to treat his wives alike none did so. Where marriage is initially patrilocal, a man taking his wife to his father's homestead, a bride lives under the supervision of her mother-in-law. That is often a source of friction but it also cushions conflicts between husband and wife and provides a scapegoat. It is the mother-in-law (and when she is dead the senior wife) who organizes the work of the wives of the homestead, and admonishes those who are lazy. She is also there in the homestead to protect a wife beaten by a drunken or angry husband, and she may indeed exercise her authority to do so. Though conflicts between women of Xhosa homesteads develop and are expressed in accusations of witchcraft, the women have much closer ties than the wives in a Nyakyusa village, and divorce implies more of an upheaval. Thirdly, the ability to maintain the peace among his following is a quality greatly admired in a Xhosa man, whether the following be his own wives and children or some wider group, and to one who is hot tempered the proverb is quoted: 'A stick has no house' (*intonga ayinendlu*). There seemed much less stress among the Nyakyusa on the prestige attaching to skill in maintaining a happy household. Fourthly, a Xhosa wife gained in prestige and authority as she grew older. If she were the senior wife or the mother of the head of the homestead she was the mistress (*inkosikazi*) and occupied the great hut facing the cattle-byre, whereas a Nyakyusa widow who was 'built for' by her son lived at one side, on the periphery of the homestead. The difference in the position of their huts reflected a real difference in social status; the expectation of becoming 'the mistress' offered far greater inducement to a Xhosa woman to remain in the homestead in which she first married (moving only with a son if he moved) than was offered a Nyakyusa woman, who might count herself fortunate if her husband's heir or her own son hoed her field and kept her hut in repair, as she grew old. An elderly Xhosa woman was cared for by daughters-in-law; an elderly Nyakyusa woman fetched her own wood and water. Similarly, a Xhosa man when he grew old could count on being looked after in the homestead by wives of married sons, but a Nyakyusa man was dependent upon an able-bodied wife of his own. Marriage has remained very stable among the Xhosa though migrant labour has been accompanied by a growing illegitimacy rate and concubinage tends to replace polygyny (M. Wilson, Kaplan et al. 1952: 91–106).

The work load of Nyakyusa–Ngonde women increased very considerably when they began to hoe; they continued to perform their traditional part in cultivation, weeding and reaping; and if the husband were growing cash crops they had additional work in weeding and reaping rice, or picking coffee and tea. The Rungwe team noted that women alone weeded rice and they could not cope with the work required though the family might have done so had the men weeded also. A woman still had to fetch firewood and water, cook, brew, and clean for her household, and repair the mud walls and floor of her house. The only women's work that diminished was cleaning the byre and cutting and carrying thatching grass, as cattle became fewer and the more well-to-do roofed their houses with tiles or corrugated iron in place of thatch. But as polygyny diminishes and land grows scarce the rights of a woman over what she produces grow less in spite of the explicit aim of TANU 'to see that the Government gives equal opportunity to all men and women' (Nyerere 1967: part I). David Feldman (1969: 107) quotes J. Brain to the effect that, in various farming schemes 'there has been no attempt to give the wives an independent status in terms of rights on the schemes such as they had in the more traditional homesteads. They have thus been unwilling to contribute to the new schemes.' Adult sons may eventually become group members but not wives.

The President's remark that 'village women work harder than anyone else' (Nyerere 1967: part II) applied in BuNyakyusa as elsewhere: it was revolutionary that this should be noted, and the Tanzania Government proposals (1969) for a new marriage law make it plain that the premise of inequality between men and women was being questioned.

Paragraph 4. Most of the existing marriage laws do not allow a woman to decide anything in respect of her marriage. . . .
18. . . . in order to remove the injustices inflicted upon a wife, the Government proposes that in any kind of marriage neither the husband nor the wife would be allowed to inflict corporal punishment on his spouse. If either party has a complaint he or she may go to the appropriate authority.
19. The Government proposes that the new law should provide expressly that it is the duty of either spouse to take care of each other. It is the duty of a husband to maintain his wife or wives but where the husband is impecunious and the wife is capable of maintaining him, then she will be under a duty to maintain her husband. Moreover, the proposed law should provide expressly that either spouse may own his or her own separate property which he or she owned before marriage or acquires after marriage.
20. At the moment a husband has a right of action for damages against a man who commits adultery with his wife. On the other hand the wife has no right of action for damages against a woman who commits adultery with her husband. There is no valid reason why a woman should not have the same rights as a man. Hence the Government proposes that the new law should allow the woman a right of action for damages against a woman with whom her husband has committed adultery.

Rungwe district is remote from the capital, but the new marriage law of 1971 (Tanzania Government 1971) applies throughout Tanzania and new attitudes percolate. The law allows a girl of eighteen to marry without the consent of her parents and transfer of cattle is not a condition of legal marriage. Free consent to the marriage is required of both partners. Custody of children, in case of divorce, is left to the discretion of the court.

Complexity

What stands out when one considers change in kinship over 96 years, is the complexity in social trends, even in a society as small scale as that of the Nyakyusa–Ngonde during the past century. We have traced an increase in stock population in proportion to human population and then its decrease; a lowering of the marriage age of both girls and men, then a raising of the age particularly for girls; an increase of polygyny during the first third of this century and the growth of large harems, then a decline in polygyny; an increase in the power of chiefs in relation to commoners and then a decrease. There are indications of a fall in the status of wives in relation to husbands with the increase in the number of marriage cattle given; a growing independence of women as the courts protected the right of a girl to refuse a husband to whom she had been betrothed as a child, or of a widow to refuse her husband's heir; but diminishing control of land by women.

Three trends have been constant over the 96 years: first, an increase in population leading to pressure on land, magnified by the shift from subsistence cultivation to producing both for subsistence and for a market; second, a lessening of isolation, with the increase in trade, employment at a distance, communication through the written word and radio which makes villagers aware of events distant in space and distant in time, membership of a state, and of churches with world-wide connections; third, an increase in diversity, a questioning of traditional patterns, an uncertainty as to what was right, what was true, what was good. This diversity was already marked in 1934–8, and eccentricity, diverging from custom, is identified as the point of growth, the point of change.

The identity and history of 'beginners' discussed in the last chapter reflect both the zigzag pattern of change and increasing diversity. Among the Nyakyusa–Ngonde there was no section which consistently opposed all change, no deep cleavage between innovators and resisters such as was created elsewhere in Africa by particular historical circumstances (M. Wilson and Thompson 1969–71: I, 265–8; II, 74–5). In the Rungwe valley and in Ngonde there was diversity within families and in the attitudes of the same individuals towards change.

Changes in kinship turn on the relations between generations and between men and women. A struggle for power between fathers and sons was something explicitly recognized and institutionalized in the system of age-villages and the ritual of 'coming out'. In 1934–8, the power of the older men turned on the possession of cattle, the control of the labour of wives and children, and of the marriages of daughters, and mystical support for their authority. The power of the young men depended upon their earning capacity as labour migrants, their access to education, and through that to posts in the administration. This partly replaced their loss of power as warriors, but it seemed in 1934–8 that the balance had tipped in favour of the old men since they, like the chiefs, had behind them the power of the colonial government maintaining peace. In the pagan, as opposed to the christian community, old men, particularly chiefs, tended to monopolize cattle and women. With increasing scarcity of land, the older men controlled the best land, and after 1963 opportunities for young men to earn independently diminished, but their opportunities to gain political power increased. A constant trend, linked to the opportunity of accumulating wealth by individual effort, has been the shift in inheritance from fraternal to filial, and the rejection by a young man of authority exercised by his father's heir, whether that heir was his father's brother or his own senior brother. By 1969 there was no 'milking-one-another's-cows', i.e. giving one of the cows received from a daughter to a brother or half-brother in the expectation of a return when a daughter of his married (Konter 1971 : 33–4).

In the relations of men and women, the most radical change has been the acceptance by a section of the population of the value of monogamy, reflected in a halving of the percentage of married men who were polygynists between 1934 and 1967, though it is likely that polygyny increased in the previous generation, 1901–34. The other crucial changes have been the rise in the average marriage age of girls (following a generation during which the age fell) and the establishment of the right of a girl to reject a betrothal arranged by her father when she was a child, and of a widow to reject her husband's heir. Property rights and the conventional division of labour have also been modified, sometimes to the detriment of women, and sometimes in their favour, but the Tanzanian Government's proposals on the unitary marriage law in 1969, and the new code itself, adopted in 1971, clearly raise the legal status of a wife, giving her control of her person and property. What maintains polygyny is the difference in the marriage age of men and women owing to the difficulty of young men in accumulating the cattle (or money) with which to marry.

A contradiction in the ideas of Nyakyusa informants about their system of marriage has already been noted. We were told 'kinship is cattle', 'with us love is small, it comes from cattle, we look very much to property. . . .', but in practice, both men and women showed a very great desire to live with a particular partner of their choice, and they were prepared to sacrifice wealth in cattle, the approval of their families, and being beaten to achieve it. One girl even committed suicide after twice being separated from her lover and sent back to her husband by her father.

Change in family relationships is epitomized first in establishing the right of a woman to dispose of her own person and control her own reproductive capacity, which implies a right of control over her children equal to that of the father who begot them, as opposed to the right of the man who gave cattle for her or, failing such a husband, her father or brother; secondly in acceptance of the principle of majority, whereby sons and daughters become legally free from control of parents on reaching a certain age; thirdly in the erosion of the rigid separation between generations and sexes that once existed.

The analysis has been made in terms of one African people but the sort of changes described are similar in general trend (though not in detail) from the Cape to the Sahara (Little 1973: *passim*). The unanswered question is what will be the pattern of relationships in different parts of Africa between men and women and between generations. In what relationships will deference be shown, and how will it be expressed? From the Nyakyusa evidence it is plain that traditional patterns will not remain unaltered: already radical changes have been embodied in the Tanzania marriage code of 1971. It seems equally improbable that the adjustment will be that of Europe or North America in 1971: what is sought is a new creation springing from diverse traditions.

NOTES

[1] It is not possible to be certain how frequent raids or wars were in any one chiefdom, but oral tradition suggests turbulence.

[2] This was the traditional Xhosa pattern. By 1950 polygyny had disappeared in Keiskammahoek District but I saw it in operation in Pondoland in 1931–3.

BIBLIOGRAPHY

ABRAHAMS, R. G. 1967 *The Political Organization of Unyamwezi*, Cambridge University Press.

ARIÈS, PHILIPPE 1960 *L'enfant et la vie familiale sous l'ancien régime*, Librairie Plon (transl. as *Centuries of Childhood*, Jonathan Cape, 1962).

BALLANTYNE, M. S. & SHEPHERD, R. H. W. 1968 *Forerunners of Modern Malawi*, Lovedale Press.

BARNES, J. A. 1954 *Politics in a Changing Society*, Oxford University Press.

BLAKE, WILLIAM 1804 *Jerusalem*

BROCK, B. 1966 'The Nyiha of Mbozi', *Tanzania Notes and Records*, 65.

BROCK, P. W. G. & BROCK, B. 1965 'Iron Working among the Nyiha of South Western Tanganyika', *South African Archaeological Bulletin*, XX, 78.

BRODY, H. 1973 *Inishkillane*, Allen Lane.

BURTON, R. 1859 'The Lake Regions of Central Equatorial Africa', *Journal of the Royal Geographical Society*.

CAPE OF GOOD HOPE GOVERNMENT 1883 *Report of the Government Commission on Native Laws and Customs*, Cape Town (G.4-'83).

CARLYLE, T. 1833 *Sartor Resartus*.

CHARSLEY, S. R. 1969 *The Princes of Nyakyusa*, East African Publishing House.

—— 1974 Letter, *Africa*, XLIV.

CLARK, J. D. 1974 *Kalambo Falls Prehistoric Site*, vol. II, Cambridge University Press.

COLSON, E. 1958 *Marriage and the Family among the Plateau Tonga*, Manchester University Press.

—— 1971 *The Social Consequences of Resettlement*, Manchester University Press.

—— & SCUDDER, T. 1972 *The Social Effects of Removal*, Manchester University Press.

COTTERILL, H. G. 1878 'On the Nyasa and a Journey from the North End to Zanzibar', *Proceedings of the Royal Geographical Society*, XXII.

CROSSE-UPCOTT, A. R. W. 1956 *The Social Structure of the KiNgindo-Speaking Peoples*, University of Cape Town PhD. thesis, unpublished.

DE JONGE, K. & STERKENBURG, J. J. 1971 *Evaluation of the 1967 Population Census in Rungwe (Tanzania)*, Afrika-Studiecentrum, Leiden.

DICKENS, CHARLES 1838 *Pickwick Papers*.

DOUGLAS, MARY 1969 'Is Matriliny Doomed in Africa?', in Douglas, M. and Kaberry, P. M. (eds) *Man in Africa*, Tavistock.

ELTON, J. F. 1879 *The Lakes and Mountains of Eastern and Central Africa*, John Murray.

ELTON-MILLS, M. E. & WILSON, M. 1952 *Land Tenure*, Keiskammahoek Rural Survey IV, Shuter and Shooter, Pietermaritzburg.

FAGAN, B. 1969 'Radiocarbon Dates for Sub-Saharan Africa', *Journal of African History*, 10.

—— & YELLEN, J. E. 1968 'Ivuna: Ancient Salt-working in Southern Tanzania', *Azania*, III.

FALLERS, L. A. 1957 'Some Determinants of Marriage Stability in BuSoga', *Africa*, XXVII.

FELDMAN, D. 1969 'Rural Socialism in Tanzania', in C. Leys (ed.), *Politics and Change in Developing Countries*, Cambridge University Press.

FORTES, M. 1936 'Culture Contact as a Dynamic Process', *Africa*, IX.

—— 1970 *Kinship and the Social Order*, Routledge and Kegan Paul.

FOTHERINGHAM, L. M. 1891 *Adventures in Nyasaland*, Sampson Low.

FÜLLEBORN, F. 1906 *Das Deutsche Njassa- und Ruwuma-Gebiet, Band IX, Atlas*, Dietrich Reimer.

GEMESEUS, O. 1953 *Sakalija Mwakasungula*, Appel, Hamburg.

—— & BUSSE, J. 1950 *Ein Gebundener Jesu Christi, Fiwombe Malakilindu*, Appel, Hamburg.

GIRAUD, V. 1890 *Aux lacs de l'Afrique Equatoriale*, Hachette.

GLUCKMAN, M. 1950 'Kinship and Marriage among the Lozi of Northern Rhodesia and the Zulu of Natal', in Radcliffe-Brown, A. R. and Forde, Daryll (eds.), *African Systems of Kinship and Marriage*, Oxford University Press.

GOODE, W. J. 1963 *World Revolution and Family Patterns*, Collier MacMillan.

GOODY, JACK 1969 *Comparative Studies in Kinship*, Routledge and Kegan Paul.

GOULDSBURY, G. & SHEANE, H. 1911 *The Great Plateau of Northern Rhodesia*, Edward Arnold.

GULLIVER, P. H. 1957 'Nyakyusa Labour Migration', *Rhodes-Livingstone Journal*, XXI.

—— 1958 *Land Tenure and Social Change among the Nyakyusa*, East African Institute of Social Research, Kampala.

—— 1963 *Social Control in an African Society*, Routledge and Kegan Paul.

—— 1964 'The House Property System', in Gray, R. F. and Gulliver, P. H. (eds.), *The Family Estate in Africa*, Routledge and Kegan Paul.

HALL, R. DE Z. 1945 'Local Migration in Tanganyika', *African Studies*, 4.

HARWOOD, A. 1970 *Witchcraft, Sorcery and Social Categories among the Safwa*, Oxford University Press.

HASTINGS, A. 1973 *Christian Marriage in Africa*, S.P.C.K., London.

HAUTVAST, J. & DE JONGE, K. 1972 'Family Limitation in Rural Tanzania', *Tropical Geographical Medicine*, 24.

HINTON, WILLIAM 1966 *Fanshen*, Monthly Review Press.

HOUGHTON, D. H. & WALTON, E. M. 1952 *The Economy of a Native Reserve*, Keiskammahoek Rural Survey II, Shuter and Shooter, Pietermaritzburg.

HUNTER, [WILSON], MONICA 1933 'The Effects of Contact with Europeans on the Status of Pondo Women', *Africa*, VI.

—— 1934 'Methods of Study of Culture Contact', *Africa*, VII.

—— 1936 *Reaction to Conquest*, Oxford University Press.

—— 1937 'An African Christian Morality', *Africa*, X.

KERR-CROSS, D. 1890 'Geographical Notes on the Country between Lakes Nyassa, Rukwa, and Tanganyika', *The Scottish Geographical Magazine*, VI.

—— 1895 'Crater Lakes North of Lake Nyasa', *Geographical Journal*, V.

KINGDON, Z. E. 1951 'The Initiation of a System of Local Government', *Journal of African Administration*, III.

KONTER, J. H. 1971 *The Developments in the Land Resources of the Nyakyusa*, Afrika-Studiecentrum, Leiden.

—— 1972 *The Implications of Family Planning in the Changing Socio-Economic Structure of the Nyakyusa*, Afrika-Studiecentrum, Leiden.

—— 1974a *Changing Marital Relations among the Nyakyusa*, Afrika-Studiecentrum, Leiden.

—— 1974b *Facts and Factors in the Rural Economy of the Nyakyusa*, University of Leiden PhD. thesis, unpublished.

KRIGE, E. J. 1964 'Property, Cross-Cousin Marriage and the Family Cycle among the Lobedu', in Gray, R. F. and Gulliver, P. H. (eds.), *The Family Estate in Africa*, Routledge and Kegan Paul.

LASLETT, P. & WALL, R. (eds) 1972 *Household and Family in Past Time*, Cambridge University Press.

LEVINE, R. A. 1962 'Witchcraft and Co-Wife Proximity in Southwestern Kenya', *Ethnology*, I.

LEYS, COLIN (ed) 1969 *Politics and Change in Developing Countries*, Cambridge University Press.

LITTLE, KENNETH 1973 *African Women in Towns*, Cambridge University Press.

LONG, NORMAN 1968 *Social Change and the Individual*, Manchester University Press.

LUGARD, F. D. 1893 *The Rise of our East African Empire*, 2 vols, Blackwood.

LUNING, H. A., MWANGOKA, N. K. & TEMPELMAN, A. 1969 *A Farm Economic Survey in Rungwe District*, Afrika-Studiecentrum, Leyden.

—— & STERKENBURG, J. J. 1970 *A Planning Survey of Rungwe District*, Afrika-Studiecentrum, Leyden.

McCRACKEN, K. J. 1969 *Livingstonia Mission and the Evolution of Malawi, 1875–1939*, University of Cambridge Ph.D. thesis, unpublished.

MacKENZIE, D. R. 1925 *The Spirit-Ridden Konde*, Seeley, Service.

MACMILLAN, H. M. 1972 'Notes on the Origins of the Arab War', in Pachai, B. (ed), *The Early History of Malawi*, Longman.

MAGUBANE, B. 1973 'The Xhosa in Town', *American Anthropologist*, 75 (5).

Malawi Population Census 1966 *Final Report*, Government Printer, Zomba.

MARWICK, M. G. 1965 *Sorcery in its Social Setting*, Manchester University Press.

MBILINYI, M. J. 1972 'The New Woman and Traditional Norms in Tanzania', *Journal of Modern African Studies*, 10.

MITCHELL, J. C. 1956 *The Yao Village*, Manchester University Press.

—— 1963 'Marriage Stability and Social Structure in Bantu Africa', in *International Population Conference Proceedings, New York, 1961*, Tome II, London.

MOIR, F. L. M. 1923 *After Livingstone*, Hodder and Stoughton.

MOKGATLE, NABOTH 1971 *The Autobiography of an Unknown South African*, Hurst.

MOORE SMITH, G. C. 1928 *The Letters of Dorothy Osborne to William Temple*, Clarendon Press.

MPHAHLELE, E. 1962 *The African Image*, Faber.

—— 1971 *The Wanderers*, Macmillan.

NYASALAND PROTECTORATE 1936 *Report of the Committee appointed by His Excellency the Governor to enquire into Emigrant Labour, 1935* ('Lacey Report'), Zomba.

NYERERE, PRESIDENT JULIUS 1967 *The Arusha Declaration*, Dar es Salaam.

OHADIKE, P. O. 1969 *Development of and Factors in the Employment of African Migrants on the Copper Mines of Zambia, 1940–66*, University of Zambia, Institute for Social Research, Zambian Papers 4.

PARK, G. 1966 'King or Priests: the Politics of Pestilence', in Swartz, M. J., Turner, V. W., and Tuden, A. (eds), *Political Anthropology*, Aldine.

PARSONS, TALCOT 1952 *The Social System*, Tavistock.

PERLMAN, M. J. 1966 'The Changing Status and Role of Women in Toro', *Cahiers d'Etudes Africaines*, VI.

—— 1969 'Law and Status of Women in Uganda', *Tropical Man* (Royal Tropical Institute, Amsterdam), 2.

READ, M. 1936 'Tradition and Prestige among the Ngoni', *Africa*, IX.

—— 1938 'Native Standards of Living and African Culture Change', *Africa*, XI, Supplement.

—— 1942 'Migrant Labour in Africa and its Effects on Tribal Life', *International Labour Review*, XLV.

RICHARDS, A. I. 1935 'Tribal Government in Transition', Supplement to *The Journal of the Royal African Society*, XXXIV.

—— 1939 *Land, Labour and Diet in Northern Rhodesia*, Oxford University Press.

—— 1940 *Bemba Marriage and Present Economic Conditions*, Rhodes-Livingstone Institute (reprinted 1968, Manchester University Press).

—— 1966 *The Changing Structure of a Ganda Village*, East African Institute Press, Nairobi.

—— STURROCK, F. & FORTT, J. M. 1973 *Subsistence to Commercial Farming in Present-day BuGanda*, Cambridge University Press.

RIGBY, PETER 1969 *Cattle and Kinship among the Gogo*, Cornell University Press.

ROBERTS, A. 1973 *A History of the Bemba*, Longman.

ROBINSON, K. R. & SANDELOWSKY, B. 1968 'The Iron Age of North Malawi', *Azania*, III.

St John, C. 1970 'Kazembe and the Tanganyika–Nyasa Corridor', in Gray, R. and Birmingham, D. (eds), *Pre-Colonial African Trade*, Oxford University Press.

Simons, H. J. 1968 *African Women: their Legal Status in South Africa*, Hurst.

Sonnabend, H. 1934 'Demographic Samples . . .', *South African Journal of Economics*, 2.

Southall, A. W. 1953 *Alur Society*, Heffer.

Steiner, G. 1971 *In Bluebeard's Castle*, Faber.

Stewart, J. 1879 'The Second Circumnavigation of Lake Nyassa'. *Journal of the Royal Geographical Society*.

Tanzania Government 1969 *Mapendekezo ya Serikali juu ya Sheria ya Ndoa*, Kimepigwachapa na Mpigachapa Mkuu wa Serikali, Dar es Salaam.

—— 1971 *The Law of Marriage Act*, Dar es Salaam.

Thomson, Joseph 1881 *To the Central African Lakes and Back*, 2 vols, Sampson Low.

Thwaites, D. H. 1944 'Wanyakyusa Agriculture', *The East African Agricultural Journal*.

Trevelyan, G. M. 1942 *English Social History*, Longman.

Turner, V. W. 1968 *The Drums of Affliction*, Clarendon Press.

van der Horst, S. T. 1942 *Native Labour in South Africa*, Oxford University Press.

van Hekken, P. M. 1970 *The Ten House Group in Ngamanga* (translated by V. A. February), Afrika-Studiecentrum, Leiden.

—— & de Jonge, K. 1970 *Echtscheiding bij de Nyakyusa*, Afrika-Studiecentrum, Leiden.

—— & van Velzen, H. U. E. Thoden 1970 *Relative Land Scarcity and Rural Inequality*, 2 parts, Afrika-Studiecentrum, Leyden.

Wangemann, Th. 1957 *Maléo en Sekoekoeni* (edited by G. P. J. Trümpelmann), van Riebeeck Society, Cape Town.

Willis, R. G. 1966 *The Fipa and Related Peoples*, International African Institute.

Wilson, Francis 1972 *Labour in the South African Gold Mines, 1911–1969*, Cambridge University Press.

Wilson, Godfrey 1936 'An Introduction to Nyakyusa Society', *Bantu Studies*, X.

—— 1937 'Introduction to Nyakyusa Law', *Africa*, X.

—— 1938 *The Land Rights of Individuals among the Nyakyusa*, Rhodes-Livingstone Institute (reprinted 1968, Manchester University Press).

——— 1939 *The Constitution of Ngonde*, Rhodes-Livingstone Institute (reprinted 1968, Manchester University Press).

——— 1941–2 *The Economics of Detribalization in Northern Rhodesia*, 2 vols, Rhodes-Livingstone Institute (reprinted 1968, Manchester University Press).

——— & WILSON, MONICA 1945 *The Analysis of Social Change*, Cambridge University Press.

WILSON, MONICA, 1950 'Nyakyusa Kinship', in Radcliffe-Brown, A. R. and Forde, Daryll (eds), *African Systems of Kinship and Marriage*, Oxford University Press.

——— 1951a, *Good Company*, Oxford University Press.

——— 1951b 'Witch Beliefs and Social Structure', *American Journal of Sociology*, LVI.

——— 1957a *Rituals of Kinship among the Nyakyusa*, Oxford University Press.

——— 1957b 'Joking Relationships in Central Africa', *Man*, LVII.

——— 1958, *Peoples of the Nyasa-Tanganyika Corridor*, University of Cape Town.

——— 1959 *Communal Rituals of the Nyakyusa*, Oxford University Press.

——— 1964 'Traditional Art among the Nyakyusa', *South African Archaeological Bulletin*, XIX, 75

——— 1969, 'Changes in Social Structure: the Relevance of Kinship Studies to the Historian', in Thompson, L. (ed), *African Societies in Southern Africa*, Heinemann.

——— 1971a 'Problems for Research in Tswana History', *Botswana Notes and Records*, 3.

——— 1971b *Religion and the Transformation of Society*, Cambridge University Press.

——— 1972a 'Reflections on the Early History of North Malawi,' in Pachai, B. (ed.), *The Early History of Malawi*, Longman.

——— 1972b 'The Wedding Cakes', in La Fontaine, J. S. (ed), *The Interpretation of Ritual*, Tavistock.

——— 1974 *The Changing Status of African Women*, Bertha Solomon Lecture, National Council of Women of South Africa.

——— 1975 Letter, *Africa*, XLV.

——— 1976 'Zig-Zag Change', *Africa*, XLVI.

——— KAPLAN, S., MAKI, T. & WALTON, E. M. 1952 *Social Structure*, Keiskammahoek Rural Survey III, Shuter and Shooter, Pietermaritzburg.

——— & MAFEJE, A. 1963 *Langa*, Oxford University Press.

——— & THOMPSON, L. (eds) 1969–71 *The Oxford History of South Africa*, 2 vols., Clarendon Press.

WOOLF, VIRGINIA 1938 *Three Guineas*, Hogarth Press.

WRIGHT, MARCIA 1971 *German Missions in Tanzania*, Clarendon Press.

——— 1972 'Nyakyusa Cults and Politics in the Later Nineteenth Century', in Ranger, T. O. and Kimambo, I. (eds), *The Historical Study of African Religion*, Heinemann.

YANG, C. K. 1965 *The Chinese Family in the Communist Revolution*, Massachusetts Institute of Technology Press.

YOUNG, E. D. 1877 'On a Recent Sojourn at Lake Nyassa', *Proceedings of the Royal Geographical Society*, XXL.

APPENDICES

1235 ± 110	Cattle bones at Ivuna, near Lake Rukwa
1410 ± 80	Pottery like Kisi ware on Mbande Hill, Ngonde
1800 ±	Change in direction of ivory trade: first crossed lake in time of Kyungu Mwangonde, whose son Mpeta fought Ngoni
1835	Ngoni crossed Zambezi on day of solar eclipse
1840 ±	First Ngoni raids of Ngonde
1875	First circumnavigation of lake by E. D. Young. Party from Livingstonia mission landed at Kambwe lagoon in Ngonde
1876	Elton and party transported by Stewart and Laws in mission steamer to Mbaka mouth. Travelled through Rungwe valley to Utengule (Sangu chief's stronghold)
1879	Joseph Thomson travelled from Pupangandu pot-market across Nyakyusa plain and through Kukwe to Malila
1879–80	John Moir at Mbashi mouth building African Lakes Corporation house. Fred Moir hunting elephant between Mbaka and Mbashi
1881	Stevenson road begun
1882	African Lakes Corporation trading at Karonga
1883	Giraud travelled through Rungwe valley to Karonga
1884	Mlozi at Mpata near Karonga. A.L.C. Store built at Karonga
1887	Fighting with Arabs at Karonga began
1888	Kerr-Cross travelled through Rungwe valley and over Ndali hills. He and Bain opened mission station at Kararamuka (near present Kyimbila)
1889	Sangu raid on Kukwe. British Protectorate over Shiré Hills. (British Central Africa Protectorate)
1891	Protectorate included Ngonde. German missionaries settled at Rungwe and Wangemanshoe
1892	Merere raided Kukwe, Rinderpest, lakeshore plain
1893	German administration established at Langenburg on Lake. Rinderpest in Selya
1894	Kondowe (Overtoun) school established. Robert Laws in charge
1895	Mlozi defeated and executed at Karonga by Ngonde and British
1897	Rising of Nyakyusa chiefs against German Administration
1899	Tax first collected by German administration. New Langenburg Boma built at Tukuyu
1907	O. Gemeseus arrived in Moravian mission, Rungwe
1914–18	World War I
1916	Fighting between British and Germans through Rungwe valley
1916–22	Major Wells in charge in Tukuyu
1920–25	D. R. MacKenzie from Livingstonia Mission, Karonga, in charge of former German mission stations throughout Rungwe valley
1925	Establishment of Indirect Rule under British Mandated Territory of Tanganyika in Rungwe Valley. Lupa gold-fields attracting diggers
1926	Courts established, Rungwe district
1934–8	Anthropological field studies (G. & M. Wilson)
1935	Change in marriage law: calves of marriage cattle no longer returnable; increase in fines for adultery and divorce. 'Coming out' of Mwangoka's heirs

1939–45	World War II
1939	All German missionaries required to leave Rungwe district
1945	Return of soldiers
1946	Lake steamer, Vipya, sank
1949	Five Rural Councils established, Rungwe District. New divisions and names. Gordon Mwansasu elected President of Rungwe District Council
1953	'Coming out' of Mwanyilu (177) in Selya
1954	Death of Kasitile (86) in Selya. TANU established
1955	Floods. Landslide on Mbaka
1954–5	Anthropological field studies (P. H. Gulliver)
1955	Anthropological field studies (Monica Wilson)
1955	Air-lift from Chitipa to Orange Free State gold mines operating
1961	Independence of Tanganyika
1962	Independence of Malawi
1963	Chiefs and village headman dismissed in Tanganyika. Migrant labour to South Africa from Tanganyika prohibited
1964	Tanzania created (Tanganyika united with Zanzibar)
1966	Death of Peter the Kyungu in Ngonde. Succession by Rev. Amon Mwakasungula
1965–9	Field studies in Rungwe District (Leiden team)
1967	Arusha Declaration. Village Development Committees abolished, Rungwe District. Functions taken over by TANU leaders of Ten House Cells
1969	Government's proposals on Uniform Law of Marriage, Tanzania
1971	Tanzania: The Law of Marriage Act

[1] A detailed chronology for the Rungwe valley appears in de Jonge and Sterkenburg 1971: 116–9. Certain of the dates may be questioned but the chronology as a whole is very useful.